THE MACARTHUR NEW TESTAMENT COMMENTARY

TITUS

John MacArthur, Jr.

MOODY PRESS/CHICAGO

ISBN: 0-8024-0758-7

9 10 8

Printed in the United States of America

With love and gratitude to Kelly and Erika,
my two daughters-in-law,
who are "loving wives and mothers."
Each is devoted to being "sensible and kind,
as well as a good homemaker,
who puts her own husband first."
(Titus 2:4–5 CEV)

Contents

Preface

It continues to be a rewarding divine communion for me to preach expositionally through the New Testament. My goal is always to have deep fellowship with the Lord in the understanding of His Word and out of that experience to explain to His people what a passage means. In the words of Nehemiah 8:8, I strive "to give the sense" of it so they may truly hear God speak and, in so doing, may respond to Him.

Obviously, God's people need to understand Him, which demands knowing His Word of truth (2 Tim. 2:15) and allowing that Word to dwell in us richly (Col. 3:16). The dominant thrust of my ministry, therefore, is to help make God's living Word alive to His people. It is a refreshing adventure.

This New Testament commentary series reflects this objective of explaining and applying Scripture. Some commentaries are primarily linguistic, others are mostly theological, and some are mainly homiletical. This one is basically explanatory, or expository. It is not linguistically technical but deals with linguistics when this seems helpful to proper interpretation. It is not theologically expansive but focuses on the major doctrines in each text and on how they relate to the whole of Scripture. It is not primarily homiletical, though each unit of thought is generally treated as one chapter, with a clear outline and logical flow of thought.

Most truths are illustrated and applied with other Scripture. After establishing the context of a passage, I have tried to follow closely the writer's development and reasoning.

My prayer is that each reader will fully understand what the Holy Spirit is saying through this part of His Word, so that His revelation may lodge in the minds of believers and bring greater obedience and faithfulness—to the glory of our great God.

Introduction

Paul's authorship of this letter has never been seriously questioned, nor has the identity of Titus. Because the two men had been longtime associates, Paul's introducing himself as an "apostle of Jesus Christ" (1:1) was solely for the sake of believers in the churches of Crete who did not know him. This was the next to last letter that Paul wrote.

RECIPIENT

It seems probable that Titus came into Paul's life during the apostle's second missionary journey, although, for some reason, Luke makes no mention of him in the book of Acts. We do not know where or how he was converted or precisely when or how he met and became associated with this great apostle. Paul's calling him "my true child in a common faith" (1:4) suggests that Titus, like Timothy (1 Tim. 1:2), was led to saving faith by Paul. After Paul's first imprisonment, he took Titus with him to Crete, where the two ministered together for some time. When the apostle departed, he left Titus behind to carry on the ministry (1:5).

Titus had traveled and served with Paul extensively. He was with the apostle in Corinth and is mentioned nine times in Paul's second letter to the church there. Paul lamented that "when I came to Troas for the gospel of Christ and when a door was opened for me in the Lord, I had no rest for my spirit, not finding Titus my brother" (2 Cor. 2:12–13). On the other hand, he rejoiced "for the joy of Titus, because his spirit has been refreshed by you all" (7:13). Titus was not simply Paul's understudy but was his beloved brother and his "partner and fellow worker" (8:23).

Titus accompanied Paul and Barnabas to Jerusalem to attend the Council of Jerusalem, during which the issue of Judaizing was settled once and for all (Acts 15; Gal. 2:1–3). Titus, in fact, was Paul's model of a born-again, Spirit-filled Gentile convert, who had no need to identify himself in any way with religious Judaism, either through circumcision or obedience to the Law of Moses (Gal. 2:3–5). This young Gentile elder was therefore well acquainted with the arguments of the Judaizers that he later had to deal with on Crete (Titus 1:10, 14) and well understood the church's official position on and arguments against their false gospel.

Because Titus had been associated with Paul for many years before beginning his ministry on Crete, it is unlikely that any of the doctrines and standards mentioned in this epistle were new to him. As noted above, he had spent a year or so with Paul ministering to the church at Corinth, the prototypical problem church of New Testament times. He was twice in charge of gathering a collection from that church for poverty-stricken believers in Jerusalem (2 Cor. 8:6, 22–24). He later returned to continue the ministry there at Paul's request, delivering the apostle's second letter to them (2 Cor. 8:16–19). He knew firsthand the trials and disappointments of leading a group of believers who were immature, selfish, factional, and worldly. The very fact that he was entrusted with such assignments indicates Paul's great confidence in his doctrine, his spiritual maturity, his leadership, his dependability, and his genuine love for those he shepherded. This duty to build churches in Crete that could effectively evangelize the island demonstrates Titus's commitment to reach the unconverted with the gospel.

MESSAGE

The letter to Titus is much like Paul's two letters to Timothy and was written for much the same purpose—to encourage and strengthen a young pastor whom he had discipled, in whom he had great confidence, and for whom he had great love as a spiritual father. He was passing the baton, as it were, to those young pastors who were ministering in difficult situations—Timothy in the church at Ephesus and Titus in the numerous churches on the island of Crete. Both men had been carefully trained by this great apostle, both were highly gifted by the Holy Spirit, and both had proven their unflagging devotion to Paul and to the Lord's work. Both men also faced formidable opposition, from within and from without the church.

This letter was designed to instruct Titus, to instruct the other elders on Crete who ministered under his leadership, and to instruct members in the various congregations. It also served to back up Titus's leadership with Paul's authority. Chapter 1 focuses on the qualifications of the church leadership, specifically, their theology and their personal character and conduct. Chapter 2 focuses on the character and conduct of church members among themselves and chapter 3 on the character and conduct of both leaders and members before the unbelieving world in which they lived and to which they witnessed. All three of those areas of concern are essential to the real purpose of the letter, which was to build strong churches that would be effective in evangelism.

Although the book of Titus is not as doctrinal as some of Paul's other letters, such as Romans, it nevertheless contains many doctrinal treasures, including some of the cardinal doctrines of the faith, such as salvation by God's grace alone working through the believer's faith (3:5-7). Although the letter recounts many magnificent realities of salvation, it is preeminently practical, setting forth the obligations and responsibilities we have as God's children and fellow heirs with our Lord Jesus Christ (3:7). The letter presents a compact guide to the kind of Christian ministry and personal Christian living that leads the unconverted to salvation.

Titus is an evangelistic letter whose ultimate purpose was to prepare the church for more effective witness to unbelievers on Crete. Paul speaks repeatedly of both the heavenly Father (1:3; 2:10; 3:4) and of Jesus Christ (1:4; 2:13; 3:6) as Savior. One of the purposes for silencing false teachers was to remove the poison of their corrupt ideas and corrupt living, which threatened not only the spiritual life of believers themselves but also the very salvation of those to whom they witnessed. Paul knew that the saving truth of the gospel message falls on deaf ears when those proclaiming it live ungodly lives that show no evidence of redemption. When Christians live in open sin, they can hardly expect unbelievers to heed a message that purports to save men from sin. One of the most compelling testimonies a Christian can give is that of a righteous, holy, self-giving life. It was for that same reason that Paul reminded Christians on Crete that our Lord "gave Himself for us, that He might redeem us from every lawless deed and purify for Himself a people for His own possession, zealous for good deeds" (2:14). And it was for that reason that the Lord Himself commanded, "Let your light shine before men in such a way that they may see your good works, and glorify your Father who is in heaven" (Matt. 5:16).

God is a saving God, who saves people that they might live godly lives in order that others might also be saved through the proclamation of gospel truth supported by the testimony of transformed lives. God demonstrates His saving power through saved people. Although Paul was speaking in Titus 2:10 specifically of bondslaves, the life of *every* Christian should "adorn the doctrine of God our Savior in every respect. For the grace of God has appeared," he continues, *"bringing salvation to all men"* (v. 11, emphasis added).

THE CHURCHES ON CRETE

Crete was located in the Mediterranean Sea, southeast of Greece, southwest of Asia Minor, and north of Africa. The island is some 160 miles long and varies in width from 7 to 35 miles. Because of its strategic location, Crete had long been exposed to Greek and Roman civilization, despite its citizens' reputation for being "liars, evil beasts, [and] lazy gluttons" (Titus 1:12). Some of the Jews in Jerusalem at Pentecost were from Crete and heard the gospel preached in their own tongue (Acts 2:11). It seems safe to assume that at least some of those who heard were converted, carried the gospel back to Crete, and established fledgling churches in their hometowns. If that is true, there may have been a significant number of Christians on Crete by the time Paul first arrived there.

The churches on Crete were new, immature in the faith, and doubtless small, although their total membership may have been sizable. In order to supervise so many congregations spread across such a large area, Titus obviously would need help, and Paul's first instruction to this chief elder was to appoint and ordain other elders in each church (1:5). The letter not only was a guide for Titus himself but was a written document that attested his delegated apostolic authority. When Titus faithfully implemented the admonitions of the letter, he did so with apostolic, and therefore divine, authority. His written commission from Paul made clear that any leader or member of the churches who opposed Titus would be opposing Paul and therefore opposing the Lord who commissioned the apostle.

The Cretan churches had attracted "many rebellious men, empty talkers and deceivers, especially those of the circumcision" (1:10), false teachers who not only taught ungodly doctrines but lived ungodly lives. Some of those men may have been among the Jews from Crete who heard the gospel at Pentecost but did *not* believe. And because this was still a formative time for many, if not most, of the churches on Crete, believers there were especially vulnerable. Even after having the immense privilege of Paul's personal teaching and example, they continued to need faithful, competent leaders to ground them further in God's truth and to be models of godly living.

Commitments of a Faithful Leader

1

Paul, a bond-servant of God, and an apostle of Jesus Christ, for the faith of those chosen of God and the knowledge of the truth which is according to godliness, in the hope of eternal life, which God, who cannot lie, promised long ages ago, but at the proper time manifested, even His word, in the proclamation with which I was entrusted according to the commandment of God our Savior; to Titus, my true child in a common faith: grace and peace from God the Father and Christ Jesus our Savior. (1:1–4)

The first four verses of this letter, which form the salutation, comprise one long, involved, and poignant sentence. The greeting is somewhat more formal than those in either letter to Timothy, but the purpose of all three letters was much the same—to encourage and strengthen a young pastor who had succeeded the apostle in a difficult ministry. As will become apparent throughout this epistle, the emphasis is on God's saving work (both God and Christ are repeatedly called Savior: 1:3, 4; 2:10, 13; 3:4, 6). The opening greeting sets this theme by centering on the nature of gospel ministry.

Because Paul had spent much less time himself in founding and establishing the churches on the island of Crete than he had spent with the single congregation in Ephesus (where Timothy now pastored), it was particularly important that believers in the Cretan churches understood that Titus was not operating on his own but ministered with the designated authority of Paul. Titus was the direct legate, envoy, or ambassador of the apostle, sent to Crete to strengthen the churches for the purpose of effective evangelism in that pagan culture. Anyone, therefore, who attacked the authority and teaching of Titus would be attacking the divinely delegated authority and teaching of Paul himself.

But Paul's opening statement about himself (one of the clearest representations of his ministry anywhere in the New Testament) is much more than a dogmatic declaration of apostolic authority. Although he had deep personal feelings and even certain personal objectives in ministry—such as his desire to bring the gospel to Bithynia (Acts 16:7) and to Spain (Rom. 15:24)—he did not write under the impetus of emotion or personal desire, much less of impulse, but under the compulsion of divinely revealed absolutes from the Lord in the power of the Spirit. God, who desires to save sinners, wanted to prepare Titus for the building of congregations able to reach the lost.

In this rich salutation to Titus, Paul reveals five core features that guided his living and his service to the Lord, foundational principles on which the service of every dedicated leader in Christ's church must be built.

COMMITTED TO GOD'S MASTERY

Paul, a bond-servant of God, and an apostle of Jesus Christ, (1:1a)

The first feature is that of commitment to God's mastery. Above all else, the apostle saw himself as a man totally under divine authority, as expressed in the phrase **a bond-servant of God.**

As mentioned in the Introduction to this volume, the apostle's Hebrew name was Saul, after the first king of Israel. Soon after his miraculous conversion and calling by Christ, however, he came to be known exclusively by his Greek name, *Paulos* (**Paul**).

With full truthfulness, **Paul** could have identified himself as a brilliant scholar, a highly educated Jewish leader who also was learned in Greek literature and philosophy. He could have flaunted his inherited Roman citizenship, an extremely valuable advantage in that day. He could have boasted of his unique calling as apostle to the Gentiles, who was granted full privilege and authority alongside the Twelve. He could have boasted of being "caught up to the third heaven, . . . into Paradise" (2 Cor. 12:2, 4), of his gift of miracles, and of being chosen as the human author of a great part of the Scriptures of the new covenant. He chose, rather, to identify himself foremost as **a bond-servant of God.**

Doulos (**bond-servant**) refers to the most servile person in the culture of Paul's day and is often translated "slave." Paul was in complete, but willing, bondage to **God.** He had no life that he called his own, no will of his own, purpose of his own, or plan of his own. All was subject to his Lord. In every thought, every breath, and every effort he was under the mastery of **God.**

Because Paul refers to himself as **a bond-servant of God** only here—at all other times referring to himself as a bond-servant of *Christ* (see, e.g., Rom. 1:1; Gal. 1:10; Phil. 1:1)—he may have intended to place himself alongside Old Testament men of God. John calls Moses "the bond-servant of God" (Rev. 15:3), and the Lord Himself spoke of "Moses My servant" (Josh. 1:2). His successor, Joshua, is called "the servant of the Lord" (Josh. 24:29). Amos declared, "Surely the Lord God does nothing unless He reveals His secret counsel to His servants the prophets" (Amos 3:7). Through Jeremiah, God said, "Since the day that your fathers came out of the land of Egypt until this day, I have sent you all My servants the prophets" (Jer. 7:25).

Because many of the false teachers in the churches on Crete were Judaizers, "those of the circumcision" (Titus 1:10; cf. v. 14), Paul may have desired to affirm his authority as the **bond-servant of** Yahweh (Jehovah), the covenant name of the **God** of Israel.

There is a general sense in which every believer in the Lord Jesus Christ has "been freed from sin and enslaved to God," a bondage that results "in sanctification, and the outcome, eternal life" (Rom. 6:22). To be a Christian is to be **a bond-servant of God.** We are not our own but "have been bought with a price" (1 Cor. 6:20), being "redeemed [not] with perishable things like silver or gold, . . . but with precious blood, as of a lamb unblemished and spotless, the blood of Christ" (1 Pet. 1:18–19). And because we no longer belong to ourselves, we "should no longer live for [ourselves], but for Him who died and rose again on [our] behalf" (2 Cor. 5:15).

Paul's specific duty to God was to fulfill his servanthood by being **an apostle of Jesus Christ** (cf., e.g., Rom. 1:1; 1 Cor. 1:1; 2 Cor. 1:1; Eph. 1:1). Even as he neared the end of an extraordinarily blessed and fruitful life, he was still driven by the desire to be an obedient bondservant. His apostleship, in fact, had brought increased duties of servanthood, demanding greater faithfulness, greater submission, and often greater sacrifice.

Nevertheless, Paul counted his bondage to God and his escalating suffering to be a blessing. He testified to believers at Philippi that "even if I am being poured out as a drink offering upon the sacrifice and service of your faith, I rejoice and share my joy with you all" (Phil. 2:17).

He reminded the elders from Ephesus, "I do not consider my life of any account as dear to myself, in order that I may finish my course, and the ministry which I received from the Lord Jesus, to testify solemnly of the gospel of the grace of God" (Acts 20:24).

Apostolos (**apostle**) carries the basic meaning of "messenger" and was sometimes used of even the lowliest person who carried a message on behalf of someone else. But the term was used most often of a special messenger, a type of ambassador, who was sent with a specific message and spoke with the authority of the one who sent him. The authority of the message, therefore, did not derive from the messenger but from the sender.

Above all things, Paul was an ambassador of his divine Lord and Savior, **Jesus Christ** (cf. Acts 9:15–16; 22:14–15; 26:15–18). Just as calling himself **a bond-servant of God** may have been meant to establish his authority with Jews in the churches on Crete, his referring to himself as **an apostle of Jesus Christ** may have been meant to establish his authority with Gentiles in the churches there.

All effective, fruitful, and genuinely spiritual leaders in Christ's church have a deep awareness that they are under divine authority. That awareness becomes the controlling reality of their lives. They do not seek to fulfill personal agendas, create personal fame, or build personal empires. They are content and feel honored for the privilege of being wholly subject to the Master who has chosen and sent them.

COMMITTED TO GOD'S MISSION

for the faith of those chosen of God and the knowledge of the truth which is according to godliness, in the hope of eternal life, (1:1b–2a)

Because of Paul's devotion to God's mastery, he had unswerving commitment to God's mission. It is the same mission that binds every preacher and teacher and, in a more general sense, every church leader and even every believer. As seen in this text, that mission includes evangelization, edification, and encouragement.

EVANGELIZATION

for the faith of those chosen of God (1:1b)

Paul first recognized his responsibility to help bring God's elect, **those** who are **chosen of God,** to saving **faith** in Jesus Christ. About a year after he wrote this letter, the apostle told Timothy, "I endure all things for the sake of those who are chosen, that they also may obtain the salvation which is in Christ Jesus and with it eternal glory" (2 Tim. 2:10). Paul was called as a divine bond-servant and apostle to proclaim the message of the gospel in order that the elect might be brought by the Holy Spirit to **faith,** which is required to activate, as it were, their election by **God.** As he explained to believers in Rome, "Faith comes from hearing, and hearing by the word of Christ" (Rom. 10:17).

Faith actuates justification, God's gracious act by which He considers and declares as righteous those who have placed their trust in His Son, Jesus Christ. "To the one who does not work, but believes in Him who justifies the ungodly, his faith is reckoned as righteousness" (Rom. 4:5). Yet even "faith in Jesus Christ for all those who believe . . . [is] a gift by His grace through the redemption which is in Christ Jesus" (Rom. 3:22, 24). "By grace you have been saved through faith," the apostle explains in his letter to the Ephesian church; "and [even] that [faith is] not of yourselves, it is the gift of God" (Eph. 2:8).

Paul himself rejoiced in his own reception of this grace when he wrote that he was found in Christ "not having a righteousness of my own derived from the Law, but that which is through faith in Christ, the righteousness which comes from God on the basis of faith" (Phil. 3:9). All the other aspects of salvation attend this justification by faith—including regeneration and conversion, by which the believer not only is declared righteous but is transformed into a new creature (2 Cor. 5:17).

We sometimes hear even evangelical preachers and teachers say that the simple biblical gospel is not "relevant" to modern man and needs to be bolstered and adorned by various cultural adaptations to make it more attractive and acceptable. But how presumptuous it is to think that an imperfect, sinful human instrument could improve on God's own message for bringing men to Himself! When the gospel is clearly preached to those who have been chosen, at some point the Holy Spirit will awaken them and they will believe and enter into the full benefit of their election.

Even as an apostle, Paul knew that the saving **faith** that he was called to preach could not be produced or enhanced by his own wisdom, cleverness, persuasiveness, or style. In his first letter to the immature and worldly church in Corinth, he reminded them that "we preach Christ crucified, to Jews a stumbling block, and to Gentiles foolishness, but to those who are the called, both Jews and Greeks, Christ the power of God and the wisdom of God. Because the foolishness of God is wiser than men, and the weakness of God is stronger than men" (1 Cor. 1:23–25). "When I came to you, brethren," he added a few verses later, "I did not come with superiority of speech or of wisdom, proclaiming to you the testimony of God. For I determined to know nothing among you except Jesus Christ, and Him crucified" (1 Cor. 2:1–2). The simple but infinitely powerful truth of the gospel of "Jesus Christ, and Him crucified" will never fail to elicit saving **faith** at the appropriate time in **those chosen by God.** The reality of divine election is all through the New Testament. It is the foundation of the whole building of the redeemed.

Jesus told the Twelve, "You did not choose Me, but I chose you, and appointed you" (John 15:16). Because Jews were the original chosen people of God to evangelize the nations under the old covenant, "It was necessary that the word of God should be spoken to you first," Paul and Barnabas told unbelieving Jews in Pisidian Antioch. But "since you repudiate" the gospel, they continued, "and judge yourselves unworthy of eternal life, behold, we are turning to the Gentiles. For thus the Lord has commanded us, 'I have placed You as a light for the Gentiles, that You should bring salvation to the end of the earth.' And when the Gentiles heard this, they began rejoicing and glorifying the word of the Lord; and as many as had been appointed to eternal life believed" (Acts 13:46–48). The church, taken from all nations (not excluding individual Jews), has replaced Israel as God's chosen people until "the fulness of the Gentiles" has been completed and Israel is restored (Rom. 11:25–27). God has chosen sinners from all nations to save and to bring to Himself eternally, a vast gathering of elect individuals.

As divine sovereign of the universe He created, God is able to say with perfect justice and righteousness, "I will have mercy on whom I have mercy, and I will have compassion on whom I have compassion" (Rom. 9:15; cf. v. 18). To those who ask, "Why does He still find fault? For who resists His will?" the apostle replies, "Who are you, O man, who answers back to God? The thing molded will not say to the molder, 'Why did you make me like this,' will it? Or does not the potter have a right over the clay, to make from the same lump one vessel for honorable use, and another for common use?" (Rom. 9:19–21).

Paul reminded believers in Ephesus that God "chose us in [Christ] before the foundation of the world, that we should be holy and blameless before Him. In love He predestined us to adoption as sons through Jesus Christ to Himself, according to the kind intention of His will" (Eph. 1:4–5). To believers in Thessalonica he said, "God has chosen you from the beginning for salvation through sanctification by the Spirit and faith in the truth" (2 Thess. 2:13). He told Timothy, "Join with me in suffering for the gospel according to the power of God, who has saved us, and called us with a holy calling, not according to our works, but according to His own purpose and grace which was granted us in Christ Jesus from all eternity" (2 Tim. 1:8–9).

Peter addressed his first letter "to those who reside as aliens, scattered throughout Pontus, Galatia, Cappadocia, Asia, and Bithynia, who are chosen according to the foreknowledge of God the Father, by the sanctifying work of the Spirit" (1 Pet. 1:1–2). Later in that letter he refers to them as "a chosen race, a royal priesthood, a holy nation, a people for God's own possession" (1 Pet. 2:9). From eternity past, every believer's name has been "written in the Lamb's book of life" (Rev. 21:27).

The duty of evangelization can be summarized as preaching the gospel clearly, because of which the Holy Spirit will sovereignly and miraculously cause the elect to believe and be saved. That is the priority ministry of all who are servants of God and messengers of Jesus Christ.

EDIFICATION

and the knowledge of the truth which is according to godliness, (1:1c)

Paul's second responsibility in fulfilling his commitment to God's mission was to edify those who believed by teaching them the full counsel of God's Word so that they might be sactified by **the knowledge of the truth.**

Knowledge translates *epignōsis*, which refers to the clear perception of a **truth.** Paul has in mind saving **truth,** the truth of the gospel that leads to salvation. It is that aspect of the truth that he mentions in his first letter to Timothy, in which he assures us that "God our Savior . . . desires all men to be saved and to come to the knowledge of the truth" (1 Tim. 2:3–4; 2 Tim. 2:25). By contrast, a person who does not genuinely seek God or His way of salvation is "always learning [but] never able to come to the knowledge of the truth" that saves (2 Tim. 3:7).

Upon salvation, the believer is given an appetite for this **truth,** which causes him to desire to know more and to grow and mature **according to godliness.** Saving **truth** leads through salvation to sanctification as it produces increasing **godliness,** without which salvation cannot be considered genuine. **Godliness** is the manifestation of the Spirit's work of sanctification. "For the grace of God has appeared, bringing salvation to all men," Paul later explains, "instructing us to deny ungodliness and worldly desires and to live sensibly, righteously and godly in the present age" (Titus 2:11–12; 1 Tim. 4:7–8). Divine **truth** and **godliness** are inextricably related. No matter how sincere our intentions might be, we cannot obey God's will if we do not know what it is. We cannot be godly if we do not know what God is like and what He expects of those who belong to Him.

Paul told the Ephesian elders that it was the Word that would build them up (Acts 20:32). Jesus summed up the relation between the truth and sanctification when He said to His Father, "Sanctify them in the truth; Thy word is truth" (John 17:17).

There is therefore no way to exaggerate the importance of sound doctrine. "If anyone advocates a different doctrine and does not agree with sound words, those of our Lord Jesus Christ, and with the doctrine conforming to godliness, he is conceited and understands nothing" (1 Tim. 6:3–4). "God has not called us for the purpose of impurity, but in sanctification," Paul declares (1 Thess. 4:7). As always, God's grace provides that which His righteousness demands. "His divine power has granted to us everything pertaining to life and godliness, through the *true knowledge* of Him who called us by His own glory and excellence" (2 Pet. 1:3, emphasis added).

D. Edmond Hiebert writes, "There is an intimate connection between truth and godliness. A vital possession of truth is inconsistent with irreverence. . . . Real truth never deviates from the path of piety. A profession of the truth which allows an individual to live in ungodliness is a spurious profession" (*Titus and Philemon* [Chicago: Moody, 1957], p. 21).

In his first letter, Peter admonishes: "Therefore, putting aside all malice and all guile and hypocrisy and envy and all slander, like newborn babes, long for the pure milk of the word, that by it you may grow in respect to salvation, if you have tasted the kindness of the Lord" (1 Pet. 2:1–3). In his second letter, he calls us to "grow in the grace and knowledge of our Lord and Savior Jesus Christ" (2 Pet. 3:18). Every pastor and teacher has divine responsibility "for the equipping of the saints for the work of service, to the building up of the body of Christ; until we all attain to the unity of the faith, and of the knowledge of the Son of God, to a mature man, to the measure of the stature which belongs to the fulness of Christ" (Eph. 4:11–13).

Like 1 and 2 Timothy, the epistle of Titus contains numerous warnings against false teachers and false teaching. In addition to being proved wrong when held against the truths of Scripture, false teaching also is exposed by the ungodliness that inevitably follows in its wake. "Beware of the false prophets, who come to you in sheep's clothing," Jesus warned, "but inwardly are ravenous wolves. You will know them by their fruits. Grapes are not gathered from thorn bushes, nor figs from thistles, are they? Even so, every good tree bears good fruit; but the bad tree bears bad fruit" (Matt. 7:15–17). Both truth and falsehood can be discerned by what they produce. God's **truth** produces **godliness.** The transformation wrought through saving faith is visibly manifest in holy conduct.

As noted above, God "chose us in [Christ] before the foundation of the world, that we should be holy and blameless before Him" (Eph. 1:4). God's very purpose for choosing and saving us is to make us like Himself—holy, pure, blameless, righteous, and perfect. The evidence of our election is found in our justification. The evidence of our justification is found in our sanctification. And one day the evidence of our sanctification will be manifested in our glorification.

The spiritual leader and messenger of Christ is devoted to proclaiming the Word, which by the Spirit edifies the believer and trains him in godliness.

ENCOURAGEMENT

in the hope of eternal life, (1:2a)

Paul's third responsibility in fulfilling his commitment to God's mission was to bring biblical encouragement to believers, based on their divinely guaranteed **hope of eternal life,** of one day being glorified, wholly perfected in Christ's own righteousness. That is the marvelous encouragement of **hope** about which every minister of God can assure God's people and, in fact, all of God's people can assure one another. Later in this letter he speaks of our "blessed hope and the appearing of the glory of our great God and Savior, Christ Jesus" (2:13) and still later of our "being justified by His grace [that] we might be made heirs according to the hope of eternal life" (3:7).

Paul is not speaking of a wistful desire for something that is possible but uncertain. **The hope of eternal life** is the believer's deepest longing for that which is affirmed and unalterably guaranteed by God's own Word. Jesus will raise up His own on the last day, and no one who belongs to God will fall short of that promise (see John 6:37–40). The "Holy Spirit of promise" not only seals us in Jesus Christ but also is "given as *a pledge of our inheritance,* with a view to the redemption of God's own possession, to the praise of His glory" (Eph. 1:13–14, emphasis added; cf. 2 Cor. 1:22). "For indeed while we are in this tent, we groan," Paul reminded Corinthian believers, "being burdened, because we do not want to be unclothed, but to be clothed, in order that what is mortal may be swallowed up by [eternal] life. Now He who prepared us for this very purpose is God, who gave to us *the Spirit as a pledge*" (2 Cor. 5:4–5, emphasis added).

Eternal life is the pervading reality of salvation, and the **hope** of that **life** gives believers encouragement in a multitude of ways. It is an encouragement to holiness. "Beloved, now we are children of God," John says, "and it has not appeared as yet what we shall be. We know that, when He appears, we shall be like Him, because we shall see Him just as He is. And everyone who has this hope fixed on Him purifies himself, just as He is pure" (1 John 3:2–3).

The hope of eternal life gives encouragement for service. We are assured that "if any man builds upon the foundation [Jesus Christ] with gold, silver, precious stones, . . . he shall receive a reward" (1 Cor. 3:12, 14). By far the greatest reward will be to hear our Master say, "Well done, good and faithful slave" (Matt. 25:21). Every believer should be able to say with Paul, "I press on in order that I may lay hold of that for which also I was laid hold of by Christ Jesus. . . . I press on toward the goal for the prize of the upward call of God in Christ Jesus" (Phil. 3:12, 14). The "prize" when we are called up is Christlikeness (1 John 3:2–3), and while we are on the earth it is the "goal" that we strive for (1 John 2:6).

The hope of eternal life also gives encouragement to endure whatever suffering we may experience for the sake of Christ. Again, every believer should be able to sincerely say with Paul, "I count all things to be loss in view of the surpassing value of knowing Christ Jesus my Lord, for whom I have suffered the loss of all things, . . . that I may know Him, and the power of His resurrection and the fellowship of His sufferings, being conformed to His death; in order that I may attain to the resurrection from the dead" (Phil. 3:8, 10–11). We know "that the sufferings of this present time are not worthy to be compared with the glory that is to be revealed to us. . . . And not only this, but also we ourselves, having the first fruits of the Spirit, even we ourselves groan within ourselves, *waiting eagerly* for our adoption as sons, the redemption of our body" (Rom. 8:18, 23, emphasis added). Whomever God has chosen He will justify, and whomever He justifies He will glorify and make into the image of His Son (vv. 29–30). This glorious, eternal hope transcends all temporary pain.

COMMITTED TO GOD'S MESSAGE

which God, who cannot lie, promised long ages ago, but at the proper time manifested, even His word, (1:2b–3a)

That contemplation of the content of gospel ministry leads Paul to a third foundational principle of ministry, namely, uncompromising commitment to God's message, to divinely revealed Scripture. That commitment is an obvious corollary of the first two. Understanding of God's sovereign mastery and mission comes exclusively through Scripture. We know about His chosen people, about His requirement of faith for salvation, about knowledge of the truth that leads to godliness, and about the hope of eternal life only through His gracious revelation. And we know certain profound realities regarding the eternal plan of redemption of sinners because God inspired men to write down those realities.

That **God . . . cannot lie** is self-evident as well as scripturally attested. The prophet Samuel reminded the disobedient King Saul that God, "the Glory of Israel, will not lie" (1 Sam. 15:29). Because God is the source and measure of all truth, it is, by definition, "impossible for God to lie" (Heb. 6:18). Just as "whenever [the devil] speaks a lie, he speaks from his own nature; for he is a liar, and the father of lies" (John 8:44), so it is that, whenever God speaks the truth, He speaks from His own nature, because He is the Father of truth.

The **God** of truth **promised long ages ago** that those whom He has chosen, those who come to faith in Him through His truth that leads to godliness, have the certain hope of eternal life. **Long ages ago** does not refer to ancient human history. It actually means "before time began." God reiterated His plan of salvation and eternal life to such godly men as Abraham, Moses, David, and the prophets, but the original promise was made and ratified in eternity past. Our gracious God "called us with a holy calling . . . in Christ Jesus from all eternity" (2 Tim. 1:9). "He chose us in Him [Christ] before the foundation of the world, that we should be holy and blameless before Him. In love He predestined us to adoption as sons through Jesus Christ to Himself, according to the kind intention of His [eternal] will" (Eph. 1:4–5). His eternal will was manifested in His "eternal covenant [through] Jesus our Lord" (Heb. 13:20).

The plan of redemption for sinners did not come after men fell but before man was even created. The Father showed His perfect love to the Son (cf. John 17:23–24, 26) by promising Him a redeemed humanity who would serve and glorify Him forever. The Son's role was to be the sacrifice for the sins of the elect so that they could be redeemed and brought to glory. Before God provided the marvelous promise of forgiveness and heaven to sinful mankind, He had given a promise to His beloved Son. That is the promise of which Jesus reminded the Father in His prayer on our behalf: "Father, I desire that they also, whom Thou hast given Me, be with Me where I am, in order that they may behold My glory, which Thou hast given Me; for Thou didst love Me before the foundation of the world" (John 17:24). A year or so earlier, Jesus affirmed that promise of the gift of redeemed souls when He publicly proclaimed: "All that the Father gives Me shall come to Me, and the one who comes to Me I will certainly not cast out. . . . For this is the will of My Father, that everyone who beholds the Son and believes in Him, may have eternal life; and I Myself will raise him up on the last day" (John 6:37, 40). One glorious day in eternity future, when our Lord Jesus has received the full promise of the Father to Him and all the saved are glorified and made like Jesus to serve and praise Him forever, the Son, in a gesture of divine love, will give everything back to the Father. Paul records that future moment: "When all things are subjected to Him, then the Son Himself also will be subjected to the One who subjected all things to Him, that God may be all in all" (1 Cor. 15:28).

It is astonishing to consider that those who are redeemed are caught up in this magnificent eternal covenant that two members of the Godhead have made with each other in order to demonstrate the infinite scope of their love for each other. **At the proper time,** that is, when the Bible was being written, that eternal covenant, together with its related truths, was **manifested, even His Word.** The only source of this monumental truth, the one true message about God, the only effective way of finding Him, the only way of pleasing Him, and the only hope of being forever with Him are **manifested** in **His Word.**

One wonders, therefore, how a preacher or teacher who names the name of Christ can proclaim anything other than God's own **Word.** Whatever truth we need for evangelism is found in **His Word.** That **Word** is the only seed that gives eternal life (1 Pet. 1:23). Whatever truth we need to edify believers is found in **His Word** (cf. 1 Pet. 2:1–2). All of the truth we are to teach is found in **His Word** (John 17:17; Acts 20:32). Those absolute truths and all others related to spiritual life are found there and nowhere else.

COMMITTED TO GOD'S MEANS

in the proclamation with which I was entrusted according to the commandment of God our Savior; (1:3b)

A fourth basic principle of Paul's life and ministry was his commitment to God's own means for fulfilling the ministry to which he was called—**the proclamation** of His complete and inerrant Word.

Proclamation translates *kērugma*, which was used of the message that a herald would give on behalf of the ruler or town council under whom he served. In the New Testament, this term (often rendered "preaching") is always used of the public **proclamation** of God's Word, which, as the apostle has just pointed out, brings men to saving faith, builds them up in divine truth, and strengthens them for godly living.

It is for that reason that expository preaching—preaching that systematically and thoroughly explains the meaning of Scripture—is the only legitimate way to preach. The preacher's responsibility is not to create messages from his own wisdom or cleverness or to manipulate or sway his listeners by means of his own persuasiveness or charisma but to interpret, explain, and apply God's Word as clearly and completely as possible.

In his excellent book *Toward an Exegetical Theology*, Walter C. Kaiser writes,

> It is no secret that Christ's Church is not at all in good health in many places of the world. She has been languishing because she has been fed, as the current line has it, "junk food"; all kinds of artificial preservatives and all sorts of unnatural substitutes have been served up to her. As a result, theological and Biblical malnutrition has afflicted the very generation that has taken such giant steps to make sure its physical health is not damaged by using foods or products that are carcinogenic or otherwise harmful to their physical bodies. Simultaneously, a worldwide spiritual famine resulting from the absence of any genuine publication of the Word of God (Amos 8:11) continues to run wild and almost unabated in most quarters of the Church. ([Grand Rapids: Baker, 1981], p. 7)

Although the full gospel truth had not yet been revealed in Jonah's day, Jesus said that it was through "the preaching" (*kērugma*) of that ancient prophet that "the men of Nineveh . . . repented" (Matt. 12:41). Throughout his first imprisonment and trial in Rome, "The Lord stood with me, and strengthened me," Paul testified, "in order that through me the proclamation [*kērugma*] might be fully accomplished, and that all the Gentiles might hear" (2 Tim. 4:17). He reminded believers in Corinth that "since in the wisdom of God the world through its wisdom did not come to know God, God was well-pleased through the foolishness of the message preached to save those who believe" (1 Cor. 1:21; "message preached" translates the single Greek word *kērugma*). Later in that epistle Paul again reminded readers that his "message and [his] preaching [*kērugma*] were not in persuasive words of wisdom, but in demonstration of the Spirit and of power" (2:4).

Jesus Himself began His public ministry by preaching (Matt. 4:17), exactly as the prophet Isaiah had predicted (see Luke 4:17–21). The Lord called His earliest followers to "proclaim everywhere the kingdom of God" (Luke 9:60). After Pentecost, the apostles "kept right on teaching and preaching Jesus as the Christ" (Acts 5:42), just as the Lord had instructed (10:42). Paul told Timothy to "preach the Word" (2 Tim. 4:2).

Paul **was entrusted** with a unique apostolic commission to proclaim God's Word according to **the commandment of God our Savior.** God "set me apart, even from my mother's womb, and called me through His grace," he testified, and "was pleased to reveal His Son in me, that I might preach Him among the Gentiles" (Gal. 1:15–16). Both as "a bond-servant of God [the Father] and as an apostle of Jesus Christ [the Son]" (Titus 1:1), Paul was under **the commandment of God** to preach the gospel of salvation. "I was made a minister according to the stewardship from God bestowed on me for your benefit," he told believers at Colossae, "that I might fully carry out the preaching of the word of God" (Col. 1:25; cf. 1 Tim. 2:7). "I am under compulsion," he said in his first letter to the church at Corinth, "for woe is me if I do not preach the gospel. . . . I have a stewardship entrusted to me" (1 Cor. 9:16–17).

Paul here speaks of **God** as **our Savior** rather than as **God** the Father, as in the following verse. He refers to **God** as **Savior** five other times in the pastoral epistles—in 1 Timothy 1:1; 2:3; 4:10; and two other times in the present letter (2:10; 3:4). God is not reluctant to save, as are some imaginary deities who must be appeased by their devotees and begged to be merciful. Jesus declared that "God [the Father] so loved the world, that He gave His only begotten Son, that whoever believes in Him should not perish, but have eternal life. For God did not send the Son into the world to judge the world, but that the world should be saved through Him" (John 3:16–17; cf. 1 John 4:14). Jesus also declared that "unless one is born of water and the Spirit, he cannot enter into the kingdom of God" (John 3:5). The unfolding saga of salvation is the plan and the work of the entire Trinity. It is the joy of God to save sinners (see Luke 15:7, 10, 20–24) and the sorrow of God when they are lost (see Luke 19:21–24).

COMMITTED TO GOD'S PEOPLE

to Titus, my true child in a common faith: grace and peace from God the Father and Christ Jesus our Savior. (1:4)

A fifth foundational principle of Paul's life that is illustrated here was his commitment to God's people. He had loyal devotion to those such as **Titus,** his **true child in a common faith.** He used almost identical words of Timothy (1 Tim. 1:1; cf. 2 Tim. 1:2).

True translates *gnēsios*, which has the basic meaning of "being lawfully begotten." **Child** translates *teknon*, which was used of a legitimate child, in contrast to one born out of wedlock. The two words together, therefore, intensify Paul's statement of his close relationship to Titus, his spiritual son in the fullest sense. The apostle was likely the human agent used to bring Titus to salvation, and he clearly had the major responsibility for nurturing him in spiritual growth and for training him for spiritual service.

The phrase **common faith** can be interpreted subjectively or objectively. Subjectively it would refer to saving faith, which Titus shared in **common** with Paul and all other believers. Objectively it would refer to the truths of the Christian **faith,** which Titus shared in **common** with the apostle and with all other believers who are sound in doctrine. Although Paul was here probably stressing the subjective aspect of Titus's **faith,** it is obvious from this epistle and from accounts in the book of Acts that Paul considered Titus to be sound in doctrine. He would not have left any church in the hands of a leader who was not thoroughly grounded in the Word.

Paul had trusted Titus even to work with the worldly and troublesome church at Corinth. In his second letter to that congregation he speaks of Titus nine times, always favorably. "But God, who comforts the depressed, comforted us by the coming of Titus," he rejoices, "and not only by his coming, but also by the comfort with which he was comforted in you, as he reported to us your longing, your mourning, your zeal for me; so that I rejoiced even more" (2 Cor. 7:6–7). A few verses later he praises the young pastor, saying, "Thanks be to God, who puts the same earnestness on your behalf in the heart of Titus" (8:16) and calling him "my partner and fellow worker among you" (v. 23).

Throughout history, the most powerful and effective leaders in the church have been involved in developing partners and fellow workers who extend and perpetuate the ministry of Jesus Christ. Although Paul was the most highly gifted of the apostles, he never ministered alone, never attempted to carry on a single-handed ministry. Until his death, he was intimately associated with an amazingly large network of preachers, teachers, and other leaders in the church with whom he was a partner in service. He extended himself through others, knowing that the Lord did not call him to function alone. He realized the importance of delegating responsibility and of preparing others to carry on the ministry.

All of Paul's letters carry greetings from and to friends and fellow workers. In the last chapter of his letter to the church at Rome he sends greetings to twenty-seven men and women by name and commends many others who are unnamed. He genuinely loved his fellow believers and workers and built deep personal relationships with them wherever he went. He continually encouraged them and gave himself sacrificially to meeting their needs.

Like Timothy, however, Titus was especially dear to Paul, his spiritual father and mentor. We can but imagine the apostle's profound feeling as he wrote assuringly to his beloved Titus, **grace and peace [to you] from God the Father and Christ Jesus our Savior.**

Grace is the wondrous gift of God that brings salvation, and **peace** is the wondrous blessing that He bestows on those whom He graciously saves. For that reason the phrase **grace and peace** became a common greeting among early Christians, a practice perhaps begun by Paul.

To this greeting he added **from God the Father and Christ Jesus our Savior,** a simple but profound creed that testifies to the source of the believer's **grace and peace.** The apostle has just spoken of "God our Savior" in the previous verse, and now, at the end of the same sentence, he speaks of **Christ Jesus our Savior.**

Although God becomes the heavenly **Father** of all who place their faith in **Christ Jesus,** Paul's emphasis here is on the Father's unique relationship to "His only begotten Son" (John 3:16) and on the truth, mentioned above, that the **Father** and the Son, **Christ Jesus,** are inseparably bound in the work of salvation.

The Qualifications of a Pastor—part 1

2

For this reason I left you in Crete, that you might set in order what remains, and appoint elders in every city as I directed you, namely, if any man be above reproach, the husband of one wife, having children who believe, not accused of dissipation or rebellion. For the overseer must be above reproach as God's steward, not self-willed, not quick-tempered, not addicted to wine, not pugnacious, not fond of sordid gain, but hospitable, loving what is good, sensible, just, devout, self-controlled, holding fast the faithful word which is in accordance with the teaching, that he may be able both to exhort in sound doctrine and to refute those who contradict. (1:5–9)

It would be helpful for every pastor to occasionally read Richard Baxter's classic book *The Reformed Pastor.* That title does not indicate that he deals with what is commonly called Reformed theology but rather refers to the spiritual reformation and reviving of a pastor's personal life. He writes,

> When your minds are in a holy, heavenly frame, your people are likely to partake of the fruits of it. Your prayers and praises and doc-

trine will be sweet and heavenly to them. They will likely feel when you have been much with God. That which is most on your hearts is likely to be most in their ears. . . . When I let my heart grow cold, my preaching is cold; and when it is confused, my preaching is confused; and so I can often observe also in the best of my hearers that when I have grown cold in preaching, they have grown cold too; and the next prayers I have heard from them have been too much like my preaching. . . .

O Brethren, watch therefore over your own hearts; keep out lusts and passions of worldly inclinations. Keep up the life of faith, of love, of zeal. Be much at home and much with God. . . .

Take heed to yourselves, lest your example contradict your doctrine, . . . lest you unsay with your lives what you say with your tongues; and be the greatest hinderers of the success of your own labors. . . .

One proud, surly, lordly word, one needless contention, one covetous action, may cut the throat of many a sermon, and blast the fruit of all that you have been doing. . . . Let your lives condemn sin and persuade men to duty. ([London: Banner of Truth, 1983 ed.], pp. 61–63, 65)

God's standards for leadership in the church are high, a basic and extremely crucial truth that many evangelical churches today either deny or ignore. New Testament standards for pastors are often lowered, selectively applied, or simply disregarded. Some congregations and denominations pick and choose pastoral qualifications that seem most relevant and appropriate for the times, that satisfy personal preferences, and that do not conflict too sharply with contemporary social standards and practices. Some take the liberty to waive biblical standards when they like a pastor and the application of those standards might result in his dismissal. Nothing is more needed in the church than the careful application of the biblical principles of leadership. Yet sound, qualified spiritual leaders are alarmingly scarce in contemporary churches.

No trend in the church is more damaging to Christ's work than that of failing to discipline and permanently disqualify pastors who have committed gross moral sins. And if a pastor is disciplined and removed from the ministry, he often is readily accepted back into leadership as soon as negative publicity subsides. Many of the best-known and most visible church leaders today utterly fail to measure up to biblical standards. While growing in worldly popularity and prestige, a leader can spiritually and morally corrupt the very people who eagerly support and idolize him. Churches can rarely survive a failure of leadership. A pastor who has sunken spiritually, doctrinally, or morally, and is not disciplined and removed, inevitably pulls many of his people down with him.

God offers forgiveness and spiritual restoration to all believers, including pastors and other church leaders, who sincerely confess and renounce their sins, no matter how heinous and public. God's gracious promise is to all Christians: "If we confess our sins, He is faithful and righteous to forgive us our sins and to cleanse us from all unrighteousness" (1 John 1:9). But the Word also makes clear that the Lord does not accept such a person—no matter how gifted, popular, formerly effective, or repentant—back into a position of leadership. Nor should the church.

Lowering God's standards for those He calls into the ministry and who uniquely represent Him before the world, as well as before the church, is tragic. It disobeys and dishonors God and weakens the church. A man who has squandered his integrity, stained the pulpit, and destroyed the trust and confidence of fellow believers does not forfeit salvation or forgiveness, but he does, before God, forfeit the privilege of church leadership. Although moral or doctrinal purity has been publicly forsaken, so has the divine prerogative to preach, teach, or otherwise rule and shepherd Christ's church.

Some Christians argue that falling into a terrible sin and then being forgiven and restored exalts grace and makes a person more sympathetic with and effective in serving others who have committed similar sins. But the implications of that sort of thinking are frightening. It suffers the same kind of logical and theological error as the notion that "we [should] continue in sin that grace might increase" (Rom. 6:1). Paul's response to that depraved absurdity is "May it never be! How shall we who died to sin still live in it?" (v. 2).

Some church members want to lower the standards for ministers in order to make their own sinful living seem more acceptable. Others want to lower the standards because of a distorted and unbiblical concept of love, foolishly thinking that overlooking or excusing a believer's sin will somehow make him more inclined to turn from it and to pursue righteousness. But that approach inevitably makes a person more complacent and becomes a barrier to genuine repentance and holy living.

Godly love is never compatible with sin. "The one who says, 'I have come to know [God],' and does not keep His commandments, is a liar, and the truth is not in him," John declares; "but whoever keeps His word, in him the love of God has truly been perfected. . . . For this is the love of God, that we keep His commandments" (1 John 2:4–5; 5:3; cf. 1 Cor. 13:6). Not only is it *possible* to be loving while not compromising God's standards of righteousness, it is *impossible* to be truly loving if we *do* compromise His standards.

For the greater part of this century, evangelical Christianity has been deeply committed to the battle for doctrinal purity. But in many circles in recent years it has not been as committed to moral purity, even among its leaders. Inevitably the church has experienced erosion of its integrity and spiritual power. The Lord requires leaders in His church who are pure, holy, and above reproach. Anything less is unacceptable to Him and should be unacceptable to His people. Moral compromise, like doctrinal compromise, spells disaster for the church. Important as they are, battles to defend the inerrancy and authority of Scripture lose much of their effectiveness if the defenders of those doctrines fail to also defend and uphold God's equally crucial standards of personal righteousness. And compromisers of the integrity of leadership will much more easily compromise the truth. Unfaithful in the battle for sound living, they are much more likely to fail in the battle for sound doctrine as well.

Paul's central theme in Titus 1:5–9 is that only a man whose character meets divine standards should be allowed to enter or remain in the ministry. Titus was to select such men for leadership in the churches of Crete.

The apostle mentions two reasons for leaving Titus **in Crete.** First, he wanted the young pastor to **set in order what remains.** The verb *epidiorthoō* (**set in order**) is comprised of two prepositions, *epi* ("upon") and *dia* ("through"), attached to *orthoō* ("to make straight"). It is from *orthos* that we derive *orthodontist,* a dental specialist who straightens and aligns crooked teeth. In ancient times, the term was used of setting broken bones and straightening bent limbs, a function of the medical specialty that today we call orthopedics.

Titus was charged with the task of correcting and setting straight certain doctrines (see, e.g., 1:10–11, 13–14; 2:1) and practices (see, e.g., 1:12, 16; 3:9) in the churches **in Crete** that had become defective. The qualifying phrase **what remains** indicates that Paul himself, and perhaps others, had accomplished some of the correcting he now wanted Titus to complete. Judging from the admonitions that followed, the problems were both moral and theological and involved church leaders.

There also were problems of attitude and personal responsibility in the churches. Because some of the older men were not reflecting the maturity that should have come with age, Titus was to admonish them "to be temperate, dignified, sensible, sound in faith, in love, in perseverance" (2:2). Similarly, he was to instruct older women "to be reverent in their behavior, not malicious gossips, nor enslaved to much wine, teaching what is good" (v. 3), to "encourage the young women to love their husbands, to love their children, to be sensible, pure, workers at home, kind, being subject to their own husbands, that the word of God may not be dishonored" (vv. 4–5). He was to counsel "young men to be sensible" (v. 6) and "urge bondslaves to be subject to their own masters in everything, to be well-pleasing, not argumentative" (v. 9).

The major factor in such correction was to **appoint elders in every city as** the apostle had **directed**—indicating that some of the churches there did not yet have their own qualified local leadership. Because many, if not all, of those churches were troubled by "rebellious men, empty talkers and deceivers, especially those of the circumcision" (1:10), and because many of the people had become involved in "foolish controversies and genealogies and strife and disputes about the Law" (3:9), the need for sound spiritual leadership and moral example was all the more urgent. Both of those verses indicate that a large part of the controversy was caused by Judaizers, legalistic Jews who attempted to impose the ceremonial requirements of the old covenant on Christians, even on those who were Gentile.

Paul's pattern of ministry was to lead men and women to Christ, nurture them in the faith, give them the endurance of eternal hope, and provide them with loving, spiritual leaders. That pattern is clearly seen in the book of Acts. After Paul and Barnabas "had preached the gospel to [Derbe] and had made many disciples, they returned to Lystra and to Iconium and to Antioch, strengthening the souls of the disciples, encouraging them to continue in the faith, and saying, 'Through many tribulations we must enter the kingdom of God.' And when they had appointed elders for them in every church, having prayed with fasting, they commended them to the Lord in whom they had believed" (Acts 14:21–23).

Elders translates *presbuteros,* which referred generally to any older man. But the term already had come to be used as an official title for leaders in the early church, as evidenced by the facts that the **elders** were to be appointed and that they were to have the noblest spiritual character and possess the ability to teach. Simply being older—even older in the faith—does not qualify a man for leadership in the church.

From numerous passages in the New Testament it seems certain that elder, overseer (bishop), and pastor refer to the same office, the different terms indicating various features of ministry, not varying levels of authority, as some churches espouse. The qualifications for an *episkopos* (lit., an overseer, or, as sometimes translated, bishop) that Paul gives in 1 Timothy 3:1–7 are clearly parallel to those given here for elders. Both in this first chapter of Titus (vv. 5, 7) and in chapter 20 of Acts (vv. 17, 28), the titles of *presbuteros* and *episkopos* are used of the same men. In Acts 20:28, Paul uses the verb form of still another title (pastor) for the same group of men. "Be on guard for yourselves and for all the flock," he says, "among which the Holy Spirit has made you overseers [*episkopos*], to shepherd [or 'to pastor,' *poimainō*] the church of God which He purchased with His own blood" (v. 28). In Ephesians 4:11, Paul adjoins the divine callings of pastor (*poimēn*) and teacher (*didaskalos*) as a single role of ministry, which properly could be called pastor-teacher.

Although the appointment of **elders** was one of Titus's primary assignments in Crete, the choice of those men was not left to his own human judgment and discretion. He was to seek the leading of the Holy

Spirit. In the same verse (Acts 20:28) just cited twice above, Paul makes clear that the selection of **elders** is the divine prerogative of the Holy Spirit ("the Holy Spirit has made you overseers"). From an earlier account in the book of Acts we learn that, as the prophets and teachers in Antioch of Syria "were ministering to the Lord and fasting, the Holy Spirit said, 'Set apart for Me Barnabas and Saul for the work to which *I have called them*'" (Acts 13:2, emphasis added). Only by the direction of the Holy Spirit, and after further fasting and prayer, did those church leaders send out Paul and Barnabas on their first missionary journey (v. 3). During that trip, "when they had appointed elders for them in every church, having prayed with fasting, they commended them to the Lord in whom they had believed" (Acts 14:23). The appointment of elders by the apostles and by their envoys, such as Timothy and Titus, was always done while seeking the mind and wisdom of the Holy Spirit. Their divine calling was then affirmed by the church.

Every city suggests that much of the island had been evangelized by Paul and that a number of local churches had been established. **As I directed you** indicates that Paul was reiterating a previous instruction. By this written confirmation of apostolic command, the churches would know that appointments by Titus were made under a divine mandate.

In the next four verses (6–9), Paul mentions the divinely revealed, nonnegotiable qualifications for pastors (or elders or overseers). These church leaders are to have unblemished public reputations (v. 6a) and must qualify in four specific areas: sexual morality (v. 6b), family leadership (v. 6c), general character (vv. 7–8), and teaching skill (v. 9). A man who is not qualified in all of those ways is not permitted to be an elder.

PUBLIC REPUTATION

namely, if any man be above reproach, (1:6a)

Anenklētos (**above reproach**) is formed from the negative prefix *a* and the verb *enkaleō* ("to call into account") and carries the idea of being completely blameless. In his *Expository Dictionary of New Testament Words,* W. E. Vine observes that this term "implies not merely acquittal, but the absence of even a charge or accusation against a person." In the legal system of Paul's day, a person who was *anenklētos* was not subject even to indictment, much less trial. Being **above reproach** is of such importance that Paul repeats this qualification in the following verse (7), where he refers to the same church leaders as overseers. Being "beyond reproach" is also required of deacons (1 Tim. 3:10).

At the beginning of the parallel list of qualifications for overseers already mentioned above, Paul uses a related Greek word, *anepilēptos*, which also is translated "above reproach" (1 Tim. 3:2). This word carries the idea of being laid hold of. In other words, an elder, or overseer, should be subject neither to being called to account nor taken into custody, as it were, on any moral or spiritual charge.

Paul is not speaking of sinless perfection but is declaring that leaders of Christ's church must have no sinful defect in their lives that could justly call their virtue, their righteousness, or their godliness into question and indict them. There must be nothing in their lives to disqualify them as models of moral and spiritual character for believers under their care to emulate. They not only must teach and preach rightly but also must live rightly. Paul charged Timothy that "in speech, conduct, love, faith and purity" he was to show himself as "an example of those who believe" (1 Tim. 4:12).

God does not call all elders to be entrepreneurs, men who begin ministries and build them, nor does He call all elders to be producers, men who accomplish a great amount of work in the church, although those are worthy things. Neither does He call all of them to be managers, adept at mobilizing others in the Lord's service, although that, too, is a worthy thing. The Lord *does*, however, call all elders to be godly leaders, men who by their exemplary lives as well as by their sound teaching and preaching set a pattern of virtue and devotion to the Lord for other believers to follow.

Mistakenly, many church leaders view their roles as that of promoter, businessman, executive, psychologist, entertainer, or president. But those roles contrast sharply with those specified in the New Testament. In 2 Timothy 2 and 3, Paul uses eight different figures to depict the "faithful men" (v. 2) who would carry on the ministry. They were to be able teachers (v. 2), soldiers on active duty (vv. 3–4), athletes who compete according to the rules (v. 5), hard-working farmers (v. 6), careful workmen (v. 15), useful vessels (v. 21), and bond servants (v. 24). None of those images are glamorous or self-aggrandizing. All of them exemplify diligent effort and self-sacrifice. And they are called "man of God" (3:17), a technical Old Testament title for one whose calling is to speak for God.

Godly and effective leadership of the church involves many responsibilities. Among them are winning of the lost to Christ, discipling and nourishing believers, preaching and teaching sound doctrine, organizing, wise decision making, careful stewardship of funds, consistent and earnest prayer, discipline of sinning members, and ordination of other qualified elders.

But despite those noble and awesome responsibilities, Christ did not intend the role of pastor or elder to be a mark of status in the church's aristocracy or hierarchy. Like the Lord Himself in His incarnation, church leaders are, above all, to be humble and faithful servants of God and of His people. Jesus' last words to Peter before His ascension included the threefold charge: "Tend My lambs. . . . Shepherd My sheep. . . . Tend My sheep" (John 21:15–17). The word *pastor*, in fact, means "shepherd," a metaphor the Lord used of Himself. "I am the good shepherd," He said; "the good shepherd lays down His life for the sheep. . . . I am the good shepherd; and I know My own, and My own know Me" (John 10:11, 14; cf. v. 16). The writer of Hebrews speaks of Christ as "the great Shepherd of the sheep" (Heb. 13:20). Peter speaks of Him as "the Shepherd and Guardian of [our] souls" (1 Pet. 2:25) and as "the Chief Shepherd" (5:4).

Shepherds have never enjoyed high status. They have always been on the lower rungs of the socioeconomic ladder. Their work is important and fills a necessary function, but it is semiskilled at best, consisting of mundane, repetitive, and unglamorous tasks that most people would shun. If a pastor has a shepherd's heart, he will be as satisfied and faithful with ministering in the least noticeable and least appealing responsibilities as in those that are highly visible and attractive.

During the Last Supper, Jesus

> rose from supper, and laid aside His garments; and taking a towel, He girded Himself about. Then He poured water into the basin, and began to wash the disciples' feet, and to wipe them with the towel with which He was girded. . . . And so when He had washed their feet, and taken His garments, and reclined at the table again, He said to them, "Do you know what I have done to you? You call Me Teacher and Lord; and you are right, for so I am. If I then, the Lord and the Teacher, washed your feet, you also ought to wash one another's feet. For I gave you an example that you also should do as I did to you. Truly, truly, I say to you, a slave is not greater than his master; neither is one who is sent greater than the one who sent him. If you know these things, you are blessed if you do them." (John 13:4, 5, 12–17)

At the end of the supper, however, "there arose also a dispute among [the disciples] as to which one of them was regarded to be greatest" (Luke 22:24). They had utterly forgotten the lesson the Lord had so graphically taught them only a short while before. "And He [Jesus] said to them, 'The kings of the Gentiles lord it over them; and those who have authority over them are called "Benefactors." But not so with you, but let him who is the greatest among you become as the youngest, and the leader as the servant'" (vv. 25–26).

The mark of a godly leader in the church is humble, loving, self-giving service. The Lord does not call them to be celebrities or charismatic personalities, much less domineering taskmasters, but the very opposite—selfless servants who find their greatest fulfillment and joy in emulating the devotion, sacrifice, humility, and love of their Lord, the Great Shepherd of the sheep.

There are ways, of course, in which a pastor's work differs considerably from that of a shepherd. His job is far from being semiskilled. Although he does not have to be highly educated or talented, he must be mature in the faith and exercise the spiritual gift he has received. Even in a small congregation a pastor can face an enormous diversity of problems and challenges. Every pastorate demands effort, energy, devotion, patience, persistence, and wisdom. In the figures Paul uses in 2 Timothy 2 and 3, mentioned above, a pastor/elder must function as a teacher, soldier, athlete, farmer, workman, vessel, bond servant, and man of God. And that list is not exhaustive.

But the emphasis in the present passage is that a pastor, or elder, is not qualified on the basis of intelligence, education, influence, or human talent. He is qualified on the basis of his moral and spiritual character and his ability to impart the Word and on those alone. A minority of God's choice servants throughout history have been highly intelligent, well-educated, and greatly talented, qualities the Lord has chosen to use and bless. As just noted, every pastor should be hardworking. But those are not the foundational qualities that the Lord requires. The foundational and indispensable qualities He requires of highly skilled and eminent pastors are the same as those He requires of the simplest, uneducated pastor who ministers in the primitive backwoods of a rural region or in a developing third-world country. Regardless of where and how they minister, they are to be morally and spiritually pure. Only such men are worthy to be leaders in Christ's church.

Leaders in Christ's church are also to function like parents in a family. Paul frequently referred to those under his care as his children in the faith. "We proved to be gentle among you, as a nursing mother tenderly cares for her own children," he reminded believers in Thessalonica. "Having thus a fond affection for you," he continued, "we were well-pleased to impart to you not only the gospel of God but also our own lives, because you had become very dear to us" (1 Thess. 2:7–8; cf. v. 11). John refers to those to whom he is writing as "My little children" (1 John 2:1). And just as poor parental leadership undermines a family and weakens society as a whole, so does poor pastoral leadership undermine a congregation and weaken the church as a whole.

Like Paul, every elder should be able to say honestly to those to whom he ministers: "Brethren, join in following my example, and observe those who walk according to the pattern you have in us" (Phil. 3:17; cf. 1 Thess. 2:7–12; 5:12; 2 Thess. 3:9). Elders should be remembered by believers in their churches as "those who led [them], who spoke the word of God to [them]," and as those whose conduct and faith were worthy of imitation (Heb. 13:7).

To persecuted Christians scattered throughout the Roman Empire Peter wrote, "Therefore, I exhort the elders among you, as your fellow elder and witness of the sufferings of Christ, and a partaker also of the glory that is to be revealed, shepherd the flock of God among you, exercising oversight not under compulsion, but voluntarily, according to the will of God; and not for sordid gain, but with eagerness; nor yet as lording it over those allotted to your charge, but proving to be examples to the flock" (1 Pet. 5:1–3).

Being above reproach is to be a lifelong characteristic of the faithful elder, overseer, pastor-teacher. Near the end of his first letter to Timothy, Paul admonishes the young pastor to "keep the commandment without stain or reproach until the appearing of our Lord Jesus Christ" (6:14).

After asking rhetorically, "O Lord, who may abide in Thy tent? Who may dwell on Thy holy hill?" David answers his own question, saying, "He who walks with integrity, and works righteousness, and speaks truth in his heart" (Ps. 15:1–2). "Integrity" translates *tamim,* a Hebrew word that carries the idea of being complete, sound, perfect, upright, unblemished, and without defect.

It was Job's integrity toward God that he steadfastly maintained against all accusations and adversities. God Himself said "to Satan, 'Have you considered My servant Job? For there is no one like him on the earth, a blameless and upright man fearing God and turning away from evil. And he still holds fast his integrity [from *tummah,* closely related to *tamim*], although you incited Me against him, to ruin him without cause'" (Job 2:3). It was that integrity that Job's wife foolishly advised him to forsake. "Do you still hold fast your integrity?" she asked. "Curse God and die!" (v. 9). But Job's unswerving testimony was "Till I die I will not put away my integrity from me. I hold fast my righteousness and will not let it go" (Job 27:5–6; cf. 31:6).

Isaiah asked rhetorically, "Who among us can live with the consuming fire? Who among us can live with continual burning?" (Isa. 33:14); that is, who can avoid God's judgment and chastening? In answer, he replies, "He who walks righteously, and speaks with sincerity, he who rejects unjust gain, and shakes his hands so that they hold no bribe; he who stops his ears from hearing about bloodshed, and shuts his eyes from looking upon evil" (v. 15).

David declared, "I will give heed to the blameless way. When wilt Thou come to me? I will walk within my house in the integrity of my heart" (Ps. 101:2). The peerless king of Israel was committed to the Lord in the fullest possible way. He wanted his life to reflect the righteousness and goodness of God, and he wanted his personal relationship with the Lord to be close and sincere. He wanted to live "the blameless way."

David also wanted those who ministered to him to live in that same way. "My eyes shall be upon the faithful of the land," he continues, "that they may dwell with me; he who walks in a blameless way is the one who will minister to me" (v. 6). He did not want to subject himself to the spiritual leadership of any man who did not live a life above reproach. The only person who can truly speak and minister for God is one who has been in God's presence; and the only person who can come into God's presence is one who is inwardly as well as outwardly righteous.

Although the great reproaches of his life, so well chronicled in the Old Testament, were confessed, and he was restored to fellowship with God, who allowed him to continue as king in Israel, David's life is not proof that one can sin scandalously and be restored to the pastorate. Old Testament kings rarely would have qualified. David—with his many wives, adultery, murder, and wayward children—certainly did not.

"Let everyone who names the name of the Lord abstain from wickedness" (2 Tim. 2:19), Paul declares; because only "if a man cleanses himself, . . . will [he] be a vessel for honor, sanctified, useful to the Master, prepared for every good work" (v. 21).

SEXUAL MORALITY

the husband of one wife, (6:b)

The first specific qualification of an elder is his being **the husband of one wife.** The Greek behind that phrase is more literally rendered "a one-woman man," or "one-woman husband."

Because that qualification is so often misinterpreted, it is important to note a number of things it does not signify. Although polygamy is clearly forbidden in the New Testament (cf. 1 Cor. 7:2), that is not Paul's point here. Being married to only one spouse at a time applies to all believers, not just church leaders. Nor is the reference to a widower who has remarried, a practice that is perfectly permissible (Rom. 7:1–3; 1 Cor. 7:39; 1 Tim. 5:14). Nor is Paul saying that an elder must be married. If that were his point, he simply could have stated such. More significantly, Paul himself may well have been an elder in Antioch before he stepped out into the role of apostle (cf. Acts 13:1), and apparently he was not married (cf. 1 Cor. 9:5).

Likewise, the apostle is not here referring explicitly to divorce or he would have mentioned it. It is possible, however, that Paul is including an unbiblical divorce. In New Testament times, divorce was rampant among Jews as well as Gentiles. Although God hates divorce (Mal. 2:16), He graciously permits it under certain circumstances. Jesus declared that the adultery of one spouse permitted the innocent partner to remarry. "I say to you that everyone who divorces his wife, except for the cause of unchastity, makes her commit adultery" (Matt. 5:32). Under divine guidance, Paul taught that, if an "unbelieving [spouse] leaves, let him [or her] leave; the brother or the sister is not under bondage in such cases, but God has called us to peace" (1 Cor. 7:15).

Being **the husband of one wife** refers to the singularity of a man's faithfulness to the woman who is his wife and implies inner as well as outward sexual purity. It is quite possible, and all too common, for a husband to be married to only one woman yet not be a one-woman man, because he has sexual desires for other women besides his wife or engages in impure behavior with another woman. Jesus made clear that "everyone who looks on a woman to lust for her has committed adultery with her already in his heart" (Matt. 5:28). A lustful husband, whether or not he ever commits physical adultery, commits moral adultery if he harbors sexual desire for women other than his wife. He is not a one-woman man. When his unfaithfulness becomes known, he is disqualified.

An elder must have an unsullied, lifelong reputation for devotion to his spouse and to sexual purity. He must be completely free of fornication, adultery, divorce, and remarriage (except after the death of a wife), mistresses, illegitimate children, and all such moral stains that tarnish the reputation of Christ and His church. When a church brings a morally corrupted man into leadership or brings him back into leadership after serious moral sin, it does so in serious contradiction of God's standards and will.

The writer of Proverbs asks rhetorically, "Can a man take fire in his bosom, and his clothes not be burned? Or can a man walk on hot coals, and his feet not be scorched? So is the one who goes in to his neighbor's wife; whoever touches her will not go unpunished" (Prov. 6:27–29). "Men do not despise a thief if he steals to satisfy himself when he is hungry," the writer goes on to say, "but when he is found, he must repay sevenfold; he must give all the substance of his house" (vv. 30–31). But "the one who commits adultery with a woman is lacking sense; he who would destroy himself does it. Wounds and disgrace he will find, and his reproach will not be blotted out" (Prov. 6:32–33). Unlike a thief, a man who commits adultery has no way to make restitution for his sin and can never be free of reproach and, consequently, can never be "above reproach."

Although Reuben was Jacob's "first-born" and was "preeminent in dignity and preeminent in power," he became "uncontrolled as water" and thereby forfeited his "preeminence, because [he] went up to [his] father's bed" and "defiled it" (Gen. 49:3–4). Such a man can never be above reproach.

It should be carefully noted, however, that a man who has never been guilty of sexual sins is not necessarily morally or spiritually superior to a man who has fully confessed and been forgiven of them. It does not mean that a repentant man will never be used effectively by the Lord in Christian service. It simply means that only a sexually pure and faithful man is qualified to be the pastor and example in Christ's church.

David was "a man after [God's] own heart" (1 Sam. 13:14; Acts 13:22), and he "did what was right in the sight of the Lord, and had not turned aside from anything that He commanded him all the days of his life, *except in the case of Uriah the Hittite*" (1 Kings 15:5, emphasis added). David's son Solomon succeeded his father on the throne of Israel, and "among the many nations there was no king like him, and he was loved by his God, and God made him king over all Israel; *nevertheless the foreign women caused even him to sin*" (Neh. 13:26, emphasis added). Both of those godly men were specially loved and blessed by God, yet both were morally disqualified as spiritual shepherds of God's people. Despite their great devotion to the Lord and faithfulness in His service, sexual infidelity gave them a permanent moral stigma.

Despite his apostleship and incomparable service to Christ and His church, Paul knew that he himself was not exempt from possible disqualification. "I buffet my body and make it my slave," he testified, "lest possibly, after I have preached to others, I myself should be disqualified" (1 Cor. 9:27). Earlier in that letter he declares that "every other sin that a man commits is outside the body, but the immoral man sins against his own body. Or do you not know that your body is a temple of the Holy Spirit who is in you, whom you have from God, and that you are not your own?" (1 Cor. 6:18–19). Paul knew that if he succumbed to sexual temptation he no longer would have a life that was above reproach and no longer would be qualified for leadership.

FAMILY LEADERSHIP

having children who believe, not accused of dissipation or rebellion. (1:6c)

The second specific qualification for eldership mentioned here is that of family leadership. A man who cannot spiritually and morally lead his own family is not qualified to lead an entire congregation.

To find out if a man is qualified for leadership in the church, look first at his influence on his own **children.** If you want to know if he is able to lead the unsaved to faith in Christ and to help them grow in obedience and holiness, simply examine the effectiveness of his efforts with his own children.

Children translates *teknon* and refers to offspring of any age. Paul has just referred to Titus, a grown man, as his "true child [*teknon*] in the faith" (v. 4). His immediately following reference to **dissipation** strongly suggests that he has in mind primarily grown or nearly grown children. Even very young children can **believe** in Christ, and they certainly can be rebellious. But they cannot be guilty of **dissipation** in any normal sense of the word.

Pistos is a verbal adjective that passively means "trustworthy," or "faithful" (as KJV), and actively means to **believe,** as rendered here. Some commentators believe that Paul is using only the passive sense here and is simply referring to **children** who are well behaved, who can be trusted to do what is right and are faithful to their parents.

In the New Testament *pistos* is used passively of God's faithfulness (see, e.g., 1 Cor. 1:9; 10:13; 2 Cor. 1:18), of Christ's faithfulness (see, e.g., 2 Thess. 3:3; Heb. 2:17; 3:2), of the faithfulness, or trustworthiness, of God's words (see, e.g., Acts 13:34; 1 Tim. 1:15; 2 Tim. 2:11; Titus 1:9; 3:8). It is also used passively many times of people in general. But it is significant that, except for this sometimes disputed text (Titus 1:6), it always is used of people whom the context clearly identifies as believers (see, e.g., Matt. 25:21, 23; Acts 16:15; 1 Cor. 4:2, 17; Eph. 6:21; Col. 1:7; 4:7; Rev. 2:10, 13; 17:14). Unbelievers are never referred to as faithful. That fact alone argues strongly for the rendering here of **children who believe,** that is, who have placed their faith in Jesus Christ. Even if the idea were that of faithfulness to parents, the use of *pistos* in those other passages would argue for its referring to the faithfulness of *believing* children. In an elder's home, especially, a child who is old enough to be saved, but is not, can hardly be considered faithful. He would be *unfaithful* in by far the most important way.

If a man's children are too young to understand the gospel and to trust in Jesus as Lord and Savior, then the standard given to Timothy applies. An overseer, or elder, "must be one who manages his own household well, keeping his children under control with all dignity (but if a man does not know how to manage his own household, how will he take care of the church of God?)" (1 Tim. 3:4–5; cf. v. 12). As children grow older and the issue is no longer control, the more demanding criteria in Titus 1 come into play.

Many Christian men who work hard to support and manage their households utterly fail in leading their children to salvation, to godliness, and to Christian service. It is not that a faithful and conscientious father is responsible for his children's rejection of the gospel. He may have made every effort to teach them their need of salvation through trust in Jesus Christ and have set a godly example for them to follow. Nevertheless, such men are not qualified to be elders if they do not have **children** not only **who believe** but who also are **not accused of dissipation or rebellion.** Successful spiritual leadership of their own families is their proving ground, as it were, for spiritual leadership in the church, because they are to be models of Christian living.

Asōtia (**dissipation**) carries the ideas of prodigality, profligacy, and even of rioting (as KJV). It was commonly used of drunken revelry at pagan festivals (cf. Eph. 5:18). *Anupotaktos* (**rebellion**) does not in this context refer to political or military insurrection but rather to personal unruliness, refusal to recognize or submit to proper authority, of parents or of society. A man whose children are profligate and unruly, even if they are genuine believers, is not qualified for pastoring or for other elders' duties.

No matter how godly and self-giving a man himself may be in the Lord's service, children of his who do not **believe** and who are known for their **dissipation or rebellion** distract from the credibility of his leadership. If he cannot bring his own **children** to salvation and to godly living, he will not have the confidence of the church in his ability to lead other unbelievers to salvation or to lead his congregation in godly living. Unbelieving, rebellious, or profligate children will be a serious reproach on his life and ministry.

Based on a defective understanding of God's sovereign election, some interpreters argue that Paul could not possibly hold a man responsible for the failure of his children to be saved if God has not elected them. But that sort of thinking is unbiblical. Scriptural predestination is not fatalism or determinism. God's sovereign election, as clearly taught in Scripture, in no way mitigates against Scripture's equally clear teaching that salvation comes only through personal faith in Jesus Christ as Lord and Savior and that the Lord uses believers to witness the gospel to unbelievers by what they say and by how they live.

Jesus commanded, "Let your light shine before men in such a way that they may see your good works, and glorify your Father who is in heaven" (Matt. 5:16). A life that reflects the light of the gospel draws men to that light. It is used to bring salvation to the lost and glory to the Lord. After Pentecost, believers in Jerusalem "were continually devoting themselves to the apostles' teaching and to fellowship, to the breaking of bread and to prayer. . . . And day by day continuing with one mind in the temple, and breaking bread from house to house, they were taking their meals together with gladness and sincerity of heart, praising God, and having favor with all the people. And the Lord was adding to their number day by day those who were being saved" (Acts 2:42, 46–47). Paul testified:

> For though I am free from all men, I have made myself a slave to all, that I might win the more. And to the Jews I became as a Jew, that I might win Jews; to those who are under the Law, as under the Law, though not being myself under the Law, that I might win those who are under the Law; to those who are without law, as without law, though not being without the law of God but under the law of Christ, that I might win those who are without law. To the weak I became weak, that I might win the weak; I have become all things to all men, that I may by all means save some. (1 Cor. 9:19–22; cf. Rom. 11:14)

Paul knew that everything he did, as well as everything he said, had an impact in drawing the unsaved to salvation. Later in that same epistle he admonishes, "Whether, then, you eat or drink or whatever you do, do all to the glory of God. Give no offense either to Jews or to Greeks or to the church of God; just as I also please all men in all things, not seeking my own profit, but the profit of the many, that they may be saved" (1 Cor. 10:31–33; cf. Phil. 2:15–16). "Beloved," Peter wrote, "I urge you as aliens and strangers to abstain from fleshly lusts, which wage war against the soul. Keep your behavior excellent among the Gentiles, so that in the thing in which they slander you as evildoers, they may on account of your good deeds, as they observe them, glorify God in the day of visitation" (1 Pet. 2:11–12). In both of the last two passages the apostles stress the twofold requirement for successful leadership— the negative of not giving cause for reproach and the positive of living a godly example. Paul charged Timothy, his son in the faith and an elder he had appointed in Ephesus: "In speech, conduct, love, faith and purity, show yourself an example of those who believe" (1 Tim. 4:12).

It should be noted that, just as it is not necessary for an elder to be married, neither is it necessary for a married elder to have children. But where there is no marriage or parenthood, a man must prove his spiritual leadership in other areas of family life.

It should also be noted that Paul assumes that, if an elder is married, his wife is a believer. The command "Do not be bound together with unbelievers; for what partnership have righteousness and lawlessness, or what fellowship has light with darkness?" (2 Cor. 6:14) has implications for marriage and applies to all believers, but especially to church leaders. In his comment about having "a right to take along a believing wife, even as the rest of the apostles, and the brothers of the Lord, and Cephas" (1 Cor. 9:5), Paul makes clear that "a believing wife" is the only kind of wife that *any* church leader is to have.

The Qualifications of a Pastor—part 2

3

GENERAL CHARACTER

For the overseer must be above reproach as God's steward, not self-willed, not quick-tempered, not addicted to wine, not pugnacious, not fond of sordid gain, but hospitable, loving what is good, sensible, just, devout, self-controlled, holding fast the faithful word which is in accordance with the teaching, that he may be able both to exhort in sound doctrine and to refute those who contradict. (1:7–9)

A third specific category of qualification for eldership is that of general character. In these two verses, Paul lists five negative and six positive attributes that are to mark the pastor.

WHAT A PASTOR MUST NOT BE

For the overseer must be above reproach as God's steward, not self-willed, not quick-tempered, not addicted to wine, not pugnacious, not fond of sordid gain, (1:7)

As explained in the previous chapter, **overseer** is an alternate title for elder, the term Paul has just used (v. 5) of the same men. *Episkopos* (**overseer**) refers literally to one who sees, or watches, over others. In ancient Greek culture the word was often used of pagan gods, who supposedly watched over worshipers and over their nations. It also was used of human priests who represented a deity. Paul uses the term to emphasize the leadership responsibilities that pastors are to fulfill.

In the role of **overseer,** elders are the spiritual and moral leaders and guardians of the church. They are "to shepherd the church of God which He purchased with His own blood" (Acts 20:28) and, much as in the present text, are to "be above reproach, the husband of one wife, temperate, prudent, respectable, hospitable, able to teach" (1 Tim. 3:2).

Although he did not use the term *episkopos,* the writer of Hebrews was obviously speaking of that very pastoral duty in his command to believers to "obey your leaders, and submit to them; for they *keep watch over* your souls, as those who will give an account" (Heb. 13:17, emphasis added; cf. v. 7). Using the related verb *episkopeō,* Peter exhorted his "fellow elders" to "shepherd the flock of God among you, *exercising oversight,* not under compulsion, but voluntarily, according to the will of God; and not for sordid gain, but with eagerness" (1 Pet. 5:2, emphasis added). He also calls the Lord "the Shepherd and Guardian [*episkopos*] of [our] souls" (1 Pet. 2:25).

Paul again stipulates (see v. 6), this time with an imperative, that **the overseer must be above reproach.** This qualification is not optional but an absolute necessity, because, as noted several times in the previous chapter, pastors not only must teach truth but also must demonstrably lead lives that are godly examples to their flocks.

The overseer fulfills his leadership role **as God's steward.** He is under divine appointment by the Holy Spirit (Acts 20:28) and typically receives affirmation by the church (see Acts 13:2). *Oikonomos* (**steward**) is a compound word, formed from *oikos* ("house") and *nomos* ("law"), or *nemō* ("to arrange," or "to order"). In ancient Greek and Roman societies, a **steward** managed a household on behalf of the owner. Although stewards usually were slaves or freedmen (former slaves), many had considerable responsibility and authority. In addition to caring for all the needs of family members, they could be responsible and accountable for household finances and for making sure, for example, that crops were properly planted, cultivated, and harvested. They often had oversight of all other household servants, to provide for them and to assign and supervise their work. They would make sure that those who were sick or wounded were cared for and even dispensed discipline when necessary.

Paul told Timothy, an elder, "In case I am delayed, I write so that you may know how one ought to conduct himself in the household of God, which is the church of the living God, the pillar and support of the truth" (1 Tim. 3:15). The church is God's household, and elders/overseers/pastors are **God's stewards** in that household. The church belongs to God, but He has given human oversight to elders, who, in His behalf and using their particular giftedness, are responsible to spiritually feed, lead, train, counsel, discipline, and encourage church members. A few verses earlier, Paul reminded Timothy of the importance of an elder's proving himself by properly managing his own family: "If a man does not know how to manage his own household, how will he take care of the church of God?" (1 Tim. 3:5).

As **God's stewards,** elders are accountable to Him for all that they do or fail to do in directing and serving "the church of God which [Christ] purchased with His own blood" (Acts 20:28). "As each one has received a special gift, employ it in serving one another," Peter admonishes, "as good stewards of the manifold grace of God" (1 Pet. 4:10). Elders, like all other believers, do not belong to themselves but "have been bought with a price" (1 Cor. 6:20), but they are uniquely "servants of Christ, and stewards of the mysteries of God" (1 Cor. 4:1); and, Paul goes on to say, "it is required of [them as] stewards that [they] be found trustworthy" (v. 2).

The first specific negative attribute that should characterize the faithful elder is that he is **not self-willed. Self-willed** translates *authadē,* an unusually strong adjective that denotes an arrogant self-interest that asserts its own will with utter disregard for how others might be affected. Proud self-interest is, in one way or another, the root of all sin, because it not only disregards the interests and welfare of other people but, even more important, disregards God's will and replaces His purpose and glory with man's.

Peter describes the wicked extremes and perilous end to which unbridled self-will inevitably leads, saying that the Lord not only

> knows how to rescue the godly from temptation [but also knows how] to keep the unrighteous under punishment for the day of judgment, and especially those who indulge the flesh in its corrupt desires and despise authority. Daring, self-willed [*authadē*], they do not tremble when they revile angelic majesties. . . . These [men], like unreasoning animals, born as creatures of instinct to be captured and killed, reviling where they have no knowledge, will in the destruction of those creatures also be destroyed, . . . having eyes full of adultery and that never cease from sin, enticing unstable souls, having a heart trained in greed, accursed children. . . . These are springs without water, and

mists driven by a storm, for whom the black darkness has been reserved. For speaking out arrogant words of vanity they entice by fleshly desires, by sensuality, those who barely escape from the ones who live in error. (2 Peter 2:9–10, 12, 14, 17–18)

The world usually looks to the aggressive, self-assertive person for leadership. But those characteristics disqualify a man for leadership in the church, where a **self-willed** man has no place. Every believer, and certainly every church leader, must continually fight the battle against fleshly self-will, self-fulfillment, and self-glory.

After rebuking James, John, and their mother for seeking the places of highest honor for those two men next to Jesus in His kingdom, the Lord said, "You know that the rulers of the Gentiles lord it over them, and their great men exercise authority over them. It is not so among you, but whoever wishes to become great among you shall be your servant, and whoever wishes to be first among you shall be your slave; just as the Son of Man did not come to be served, but to serve, and to give His life a ransom for many" (Matt. 20:25–28).

Second, a qualified elder is **not quick-tempered.** *Orgilos* (**quick-tempered**) does not refer to occasional outbursts, bad as those are, but to a propensity to anger. The **quick-tempered** person is irascible. He has a "short fuse" and is easily provoked.

"The Lord's bond-servant," on the other hand, "must not be quarrelsome, but be kind to all, able to teach, patient when wronged" (2 Tim. 2:24). He is not to be "pugnacious, but gentle, uncontentious" (1 Tim. 3:3). As James points out, "the anger of man does not achieve the righteousness of God" (James 1:20). The qualified pastor must carefully guard against a spirit of hostility, resentment, and anger—even when everything in the church seems to be going the wrong way and the people are critical or indifferent. He is a man who can delegate responsibility to others, who may not fulfill a task in the exact way that he would. He can work with others in kindness, patience, and gratitude. He can allow dedicated but inexperienced people around him to fail until they learn to succeed. His own ego is not tied up in everything that is done in the church. He is as quick to share in others' failures as in their successes. He joyfully submits to God and serves all.

Third, a qualified elder is **not addicted to wine.** *Paroinos* (**addicted to wine**) is a compound word, from *para* ("at") and *oinos* (**wine**), and literally means "to be continually alongside, or in the presence of, wine." **Wine** is not to be his companion. Paul uses the same word in his first letter to Timothy, in which he declares that overseers must not be "addicted to wine or pugnacious, but gentle, uncontentious, free from the love of money" (1 Tim. 3:3; cf. v. 8; Titus 2:3).

The **wine** most commonly drunk in Paul's day, as well as in Old Testament times, was either nonalcoholic or had very low alcohol content. Fermented juice was mixed with water (as much as 8 or 10 parts water to 1 part wine) to lessen its power to intoxicate, particularly when the weather was hot and much fluid was consumed. Because water was frequently contaminated, as it is today in many third world countries, the slight alcohol content of common wine acted as a disinfectant and had certain other health benefits. Later in his first letter to Timothy, Paul advised the young elder: "No longer drink water exclusively, but use a little wine for the sake of your stomach and your frequent ailments" (5:23). (For a detailed discussion of alcoholic beverages mentioned in Scripture, see my *Ephesians* volume in this New Testament Commentary series, pp. 235–37.)

In the present passage, Paul is obviously speaking of being **addicted to wine** that was alcoholic enough, or was drunk in sufficient quantity, to cause impaired judgment and even intoxication. Because excessive drinking of **wine** often led to drunkenness and resultant disorderly behavior, the term *paroinos* is sometimes translated "brawler" (as in 1 Tim. 3:3 KJV).

Paul's proscription here doubtless referred to any consumption of **wine** that would cause an elder to lose mental alertness and good judgment. A person in spiritual leadership is to be clear-headed, in control of his senses and judgment at all times.

An overseer, or elder, should not stay around a place where **wine** or other intoxicating beverage is easily available and where he might drink to the point of losing self-control. Even at such proper and joyous events as a wedding feast, he would be careful not to linger at the wine table.

Because nonalcoholic wine is virtually unknown today and because pure water and other safe juices and drinks are so readily available, most elders in modern cultures have no justifiable reason for drinking any alcoholic beverages and putting themselves in the way of temptation. They also have a responsibility, even more than other believers, to avoid exercising a Christian liberty that might "somehow become a stumbling block to the weak" and cause a fellow believer to be "ruined, the brother for whose sake Christ died" (1 Cor. 8:9, 11). "It is good not to eat meat or to drink wine, or to do anything by which your brother stumbles" (Rom. 14:21).

God has always called the leaders of His people to higher standards than other believers. He instructed Aaron and the other high priests, "Do not drink wine or strong drink, neither you nor your sons with you, when you come into the tent of meeting, so that you may not die—it is a perpetual statute throughout your generations" (Lev. 10:9). The Lord had similar high standards for political leaders of His people:

"It is not for kings to drink wine, or for rulers to desire strong drink, lest they drink and forget what is decreed, and pervert the rights of all the afflicted" (Prov. 31:4–5).

The Nazirite vow—associated with such notable figures as Samson, Samuel, and John the Baptist—was a voluntary commitment of special service to the Lord that required considerable self-denial. God commanded Moses, "Speak to the sons of Israel, and say to them, 'When a man or woman makes a special vow, the vow of a Nazirite, to dedicate himself to the Lord, he shall abstain from wine and strong drink; he shall drink no vinegar, whether made from wine or strong drink, neither shall he drink any grape juice, nor eat fresh or dried grapes. All the days of his separation he shall not eat anything that is produced by the grape vine, from the seeds even to the skin'" (Num. 6:2–4). In effect, a Nazirite said to himself and to the world, "I willingly forgo comfort, personal recognition, wealth, popularity, and anything else that would hinder my highest level of dedication to the Lord." Before the birth of John the Baptist, the angel said of him to his father, Zacharias,

> For he will be great in the sight of the Lord, and he will drink no wine or liquor; and he will be filled with the Holy Spirit, while yet in his mother's womb. And he will turn back many of the sons of Israel to the Lord their God. And it is he who will go as a forerunner before Him [Christ] in the spirit and power of Elijah, to turn the hearts of the fathers back to the children, and the disobedient to the attitude of the righteous; so as to make ready a people prepared for the Lord. (Luke 1:15–17)

The fact that Paul gave Timothy the medical advice to "no longer drink water exclusively, but use a little wine for the sake of your stomach and your frequent ailments" (1 Tim. 5:23) strongly suggests that this young elder normally drank no alcoholic beverages of any sort. Although the water was not purified and led to some illness, Timothy was still reluctant to break that abstinence even for health reasons. He probably feared that even modest amounts of **wine** might impair his mind and his judgment to some degree and thereby diminish his faithfulness and effectiveness in the Lord's work.

Fourth, a qualified elder is **not pugnacious,** not a fistfighter. As unnecessary as that prohibition seems to be, apparently it was not uncommon in New Testament times for even grown men to settle disputes with their fists or with a stick or rock. To the contrary, all Christians, especially those in positions of leadership, "must not be quarrelsome, but be kind to all, able to teach, patient when wronged, with gentleness correcting those who are in opposition, if perhaps God may grant them repentance leading to the knowledge of the truth" (2 Tim. 2:24–25).

By extension, **pugnacious** can refer to verbal as well as physical fighting and quarreling. It is possible to hurt a person more deeply and permanently with cruel words than with a fist or club. An elder should have no part in meanness, abusiveness, or retaliation, no matter how cruelly provoked. When conflicts arise, he must make sure that they are settled peacefully, reasonably, and without animosity. "If possible, so far as it depends on you," the apostle admonished Roman believers, "be at peace with all men" (Rom. 12:18).

Fifth, a qualified elder is **not fond of sordid gain,** which translates the single word *aischrokerdē,* a compound of *aischros* ("filthy, shameful, base") and *kerdos* ("gain, profit, greed"). Paul is referring to a person who, without honesty or integrity, seeks wealth and financial prosperity at any cost.

All Christians, including pastors, have a right to make a living for themselves and for their families. Jesus said that "the laborer is worthy of his wages" (Luke 10:7). Paul wrote believers in Corinth, "If we sowed spiritual things in you, is it too much if we should reap material things from you? . . . So also the Lord directed those who proclaim the gospel to get their living from the gospel" (1 Cor. 9:11, 14). A pastor not only has a right to earn a living but has a right to be paid by those to whom he ministers. "Let the elders who rule well be considered worthy of double honor," the apostle said, "especially those who work hard at preaching and teaching" (1 Tim. 5:17). The word *timē* (honor) was used of monetary value as well as esteem and, in this context, doubtless includes the idea of financial remuneration.

Even during the infancy of the church, false teachers had entered the pastorate simply to make an easy living. They were "men of depraved mind and deprived of the truth, who suppose[d] that godliness is a means of gain" (1 Tim. 6:5). They were in the pastorate for the money, not to serve the Lord or His people. "Godliness actually is a means of great gain, when accompanied by contentment," Paul went on to say:

> For we have brought nothing into the world, so we cannot take anything out of it either. And if we have food and covering, with these we shall be content. But those who want to get rich fall into temptation and a snare and many foolish and harmful desires which plunge men into ruin and destruction. For the love of money is a root of all sorts of evil, and some by longing for it have wandered away from the faith, and pierced themselves with many a pang. But flee from these things, you man of God; and pursue righteousness, godliness, faith, love, perseverance and gentleness. (vv. 6–11)

Paul used the term "man of God" as a technical term for pastors and elders (see also 2 Tim. 3:17) in much the same way that it was often used in the Old Testament of prophets (see, e.g., 2 Kings 1:9, 11). Just like those in the early church, false prophets and teachers in Old Testament times were "shepherds who [had] no understanding; they . . . all turned to their own way, each one to his unjust gain, to the last one" (Isa. 56:11). Peter admonished pastors: "Shepherd the flock of God among you," he said, "exercising oversight not under compulsion, but voluntarily, according to the will of God; and not for sordid gain, but with eagerness" (1 Pet. 5:2).

WHAT A PASTOR MUST BE

but hospitable, loving what is good, sensible, just, devout, self-controlled, (1:8)

Turning to the positive features of general character, first, a pastor must be **hospitable.** *Philoxenos* (**hospitable**) is a compound of *philos* ("affection") and *xenos* ("stranger"). A person who is **hospitable** gives practical help to anyone who is in need, friend or stranger, believer or unbeliever. He freely offers his time, his resources, and his encouragement to meet the needs of others.

Jesus elevated hospitality by saying, "When you give a luncheon or a dinner, do not invite your friends or your brothers or your relatives or rich neighbors, lest they also invite you in return, and repayment come to you. But when you give a reception, invite the poor, the crippled, the lame, the blind, and you will be blessed, since they do not have the means to repay you; for you will be repaid at the resurrection of the righteous" (Luke 14:12–14). The Lord was not, of course, saying that we are never to invite friends and relatives over for a meal. He was pointing out that the true test of godly, self-giving hospitality is not what we do for those that we like to be around or who are likely to repay us in some way, but is what we do for others solely out of sincere concern for their welfare.

Paul admonished Christians in Galatia: "While we have opportunity, let us do good to all men, and especially to those who are of the household of the faith" (Gal. 6:10). By showing "hospitality to strangers, . . . some have entertained angels without knowing it" (Heb. 13:2). Every Christian should practice hospitality (Rom. 12:13), especially "to one another" (1 Pet. 4:9). And, as in other ways, church leaders are to set examples for other Christians to follow (cf. 1 Tim. 3:2).

Second, a faithful pastor should be characterized by **loving what is good.** That phrase translates the single Greek word *phila-*

gathos, which carries the idea of having strong affection for that which is intrinsically **good.** A pastor should love those things and those people who are genuinely **good.** "Finally, brethren," Paul told Philippian believers, "whatever is true, whatever is honorable, whatever is right, whatever is pure, whatever is lovely, whatever is of good repute, if there is any excellence and if anything worthy of praise, let your mind dwell on these things" (Phil. 4:8). Those who lead the church should be known as friends of the godly and virtuous.

Third, a pastor is to **be sensible.** *Sōphrōn* (**sensible**) is another compound word, formed from *sōzō* ("to save") and *phrēn* ("mind") and describes a person who is sober minded and coolheaded. In Paul's parallel list of pastoral qualifications, the word is translated "prudent" (1 Tim. 3:2).

The **sensible** person is in command of his mind. He has control of the things he thinks about and does. He does not allow circumstances or the immorality or foolishness of others to distract him and gain his attention and interest. He not only does not become involved in things that are outright immoral and unspiritual but also avoids things that are trivial, foolish, and unproductive. He knows his priorities and is devoted to them.

Fourth, a pastor is to be **just,** from *dikaios,* a common word in the New Testament. It denotes that which is proper, right, and fitting, and is frequently rendered "righteous." Since it could refer to general righteousness, which would make it seem out of place in this list of specifics, it may be best to see it as meaning "fairness," a commitment to and understanding of that which is just and equitable. That quality is crucial to the credibility of a leader. It is used of God Himself. In His high priestly prayer, Jesus addressed His heavenly Father as "O righteous [*dikaios*] Father" (John 17:25). Paul spoke of God as "just [*dikaios*] and the justifier of the one who has faith in Jesus" (Rom. 3:26). John gives us the divine promise that "if we confess our sins, He is faithful and righteous [*dikaios*] to forgive us our sins and to cleanse us from all unrighteousness" (1 John 1:9; cf. 2:29; 3:7). The pastor who is **just,** or righteous, is a man who reflects the just and fair character of God Himself.

The pastor must also be **devout.** *Hosios* (**devout**) is not the most common Greek word (*hagios*) in the New Testament meaning "holy" but is closely related to it and has the same general meaning. It was used to refer to that which was true to divine direction and purpose, to genuine obedience to God's will. In every area of his life, the pastor is to be above reproach.

Like *dikaios* and *hagios,* the term *hosios* is often used of God in the New Testament. Just before the bowl judgments begin, "those who had come off victorious from the beast and from his image and from the number of his name" will sing, "Who will not fear, O Lord, and glorify

Thy name? For Thou alone art *holy,*" and "the angel of the waters [will say], 'Righteous art Thou, who art and who wast, O *Holy* One'" (Rev. 15:2, 4; 16:5, emphasis added). Quoting Psalm 16:10, Peter spoke at Pentecost of Christ as God's "Holy One" (Acts 2:27; cf. 13:35). The writer of Hebrews speaks of Him as our "high priest, holy, innocent, undefiled, separated from sinners and exalted above the heavens" (Heb. 7:26).

In 1 Thessalonians, Paul again connects **just** and **devout.** Using the adverb forms, he testified that his own life exhibited those virtues: "You are witnesses, and so is God, how devoutly [*hosiōs,* 'holily'] and uprightly [*dikaiōs,* 'justly, fairly'] and blamelessly we behaved toward you believers" (1 Thess. 2:10).

A Christian cannot achieve sinless perfection in this life, but every sin is to be confessed. "If we say that we have no sin, we are deceiving ourselves, and the truth is not in us" John declares. But, "if we confess our sins, [the Lord] is faithful and righteous to forgive us our sins and to cleanse us from all unrighteousness" (1 John 1:8–9). By God's grace, mercy, and power, not only pastors but all believers can be cleansed "from all unrighteousness." Like Paul, they can live "devoutly and uprightly," thereby pleasing the Lord, being an example to others, and removing cause for scandal in the church.

The sixth and last positive qualification of a pastor is that of being **self-controlled.** He lives an exemplary life on the outside because he submits to the Holy Spirit's control on the inside.

Accountability to other believers is of great importance in the church, including the accountability of pastors to their congregations. Although Paul cautions that the church should "not receive an accusation against an elder except on the basis of two or three witnesses," any who *are* found to be guilty and who "continue in sin" are to be rebuked "in the presence of all, so that the rest also may be fearful of sinning" (1 Tim. 5:19–20).

But accountability to the church is not Paul's point here. Other believers do not, of course, know about hidden sins. Yet those sins may be more destructive of character and of effective service than many outward sins. A pastor who is not **self-controlled,** who does not continually monitor his own life, submitting his sin to the Lord's cleansing and keeping a clear conscience, is not fit to lead God's people, no matter how outwardly righteous his life may appear to be. If he acts right only when others are looking, he is doing just that—acting.

The **self-controlled** pastor walks with God in the integrity of his heart. He has the continuing grace of God working in his life to the degree that he is spiritually mature and morally pure. He should be able to say with Paul, "Our proud confidence is this, the testimony of our conscience, that in holiness and godly sincerity, not in fleshly wisdom but in the grace of God, we have conducted ourselves in the world, and especially toward you" (2 Cor. 1:12).

It is not that God's basic standards are higher for pastors and elders than for other believers. *Every* believer is "to be perfect, as [their] heavenly Father is perfect" (Matt. 5:48). A Christian who lives a careless, impure life does not forfeit salvation. But Paul's point here is that a Christian man who lives that way *does* forfeit his right to lead God's people. In that sense, God's standards for pastors *are* higher.

In his *Lectures to My Students,* Charles Spurgeon writes,

> [If a pastor] were called to an ordinary position, and to common work, common grace might perhaps satisfy him, though even then it would be an indolent satisfaction; but being elect to extraordinary labours, and called to a place of unusual peril, he should be anxious to possess that superior strength which alone is adequate to his station. His pulse of vital godliness must beat strongly and regularly; his eye of faith must be bright; his foot of resolution must be firm; his hand of activity must be quick; his whole inner man must be in the highest degree of sanity. It is said of the Egyptians that they chose their priests from the most learned of their philosophers, and then they esteemed their priests so highly, that they chose their kings from them. We require to have for God's ministers the pick of all the Christian host; such men indeed, that if the nation wanted kings they could not do better than elevate them to the throne.
>
> For some work we choose none but the strong; and when God calls us to ministerial labour we should endeavour to get grace that we may be strengthened into fitness for our position, and not be mere novices carried away by the temptations of Satan, to the injury of the church and our own ruin. We are to stand equipped with the whole armour of God, ready for feats of valour not expected of others: to us self-denial, self-forgetfulness, patience, perseverance, longsuffering, must be everyday virtues, and who is sufficient for these things? We had need live very near to God, if we would approve ourselves in our vocation. ([Grand Rapids: Zondervan, 1955], pp. 8–9)

TEACHING SKILL

holding fast the faithful word which is in accordance with the teaching, that he may be able both to exhort in sound doctrine and to refute those who contradict. (1:9)

All of the qualifications Paul has mentioned so far (vv. 6–8) have to do with spiritual character and attitudes, with the kind of person a faithful elder is called to *be.* In verse 9 he deals with the primary *minis-*

try of a faithful elder, namely, that of teacher, what a faithful elder is called to *do*. Throughout the pastoral epistles (1 & 2 Timothy, and Titus), the apostle repeatedly emphasizes the critical importance of elders, or overseers, carefully and consistently preaching, teaching, and guarding God's truth.

Preaching and teaching are much alike in content and are distinguished primarily by the nature of presentation. Preaching is the public proclamation of the truth, intended primarily to move the will of the hearers to respond. Teaching is directed more at causing the mind to understand. Preaching involves admonition and exhortation, whereas teaching involves illumination and explanation. Often the two functions overlap and are indistinguishable, as they are in many passages of Paul's letters, as well as in other parts of the New Testament. All good preaching has elements of explanation, and all good teaching includes some exhortation. Some elders clearly have only one of the gifts, whereas others just as clearly have both. Though different in some ways, however, both gifts are crucial to the church and have the common purpose of disseminating God's Word.

Because preaching and teaching of Scripture are spiritual gifts, bestowed sovereignly on servants of God through the Holy Spirit (Rom. 12:7; 1 Cor. 12:28), and because pastors must be "able to teach" (1 Tim. 3:2; 2 Tim. 2:24), it clearly follows that every elder is so gifted in some way and so commissioned by the Holy Spirit. The sine qua non of ministry is preaching and teaching. Giftedness in this area varies, of course, just as the other spiritual gifts vary in degree from believer to believer. But Scripture is unambiguous that *every* true elder is divinely equipped to preach and teach God's Word.

As already noted, "elders who rule well [should] be considered worthy of double honor, especially those who work hard at preaching and teaching" (1 Tim. 5:17). Paul's qualifying phrase "especially those" indicates that, although every elder *ought* to "work hard at preaching and teaching," some of them do not. From the context, it seems obvious that some elders in the early church fell short in this regard. "Work hard" translates *kopiaō*, which carries the idea of diligent effort, of toiling with maximum self-sacrifice in order to fully accomplish a task, to the point of exhaustion if necessary. It has as much to do with the quality of the work as with the quantity. It is important to understand, however, that this quality has nothing to do with the size or influence of a pastor's congregation. Nor is it determined by natural ability or spiritual giftedness. A pastor with limited capabilities who works devotedly without reserve is just as worthy of double honor as an equally hard-working pastor with much greater endowments.

THE NECESSARY FOUNDATION

holding fast the faithful word which is in accordance with the teaching, (1:9a)

The foundation for effective teaching of the Word is the pastor's own understanding of and obedience to that revelation. He must be unwaveringly loyal to Scripture.

Antechō (**holding fast**) means "to strongly cling or adhere to something or someone." Speaking of spiritual allegiance, Jesus said, "No servant can serve two masters; for either he will hate the one, and love the other, or else he will hold to [*antechō*] one, and despise the other. You cannot serve God and mammon" (Luke 16:13; cf. Matt. 6:24). God's preachers and teachers are to cling to **the faithful word** with fervent devotion and unflagging diligence.

Word translates *logos,* which refers to the expression of a concept, thought, or truth. It is frequently used of the revealed truth and will of God. Speaking of the enemies of God, Jesus said, "They have done this in order that the word may be fulfilled that is written in their Law, 'They hated Me without a cause'" (John 15:25). Paul spoke of God's "word of promise" to Abraham: "At this time I will come, and Sarah shall have a son" (Rom. 9:9) and of His judgment: "The Lord will execute His word upon the earth, thoroughly and quickly" (v. 28).

Logos is often used as a synonym for Scripture, the written Word of God. Jesus accused the Pharisees of "invalidating the word of God by [their] tradition which [they had] handed down" (Mark 7:13). To unbelieving Jews in Jerusalem, our Lord clearly identified the Word of God with Scripture, saying, "Has it not been written in your *Law,* 'I said, you are gods'? If he called them gods, to whom the *word of God* came (and the *Scripture* cannot be broken), do you say of Him, whom the Father sanctified and sent into the world, 'You are blaspheming,' because I said, 'I am the Son of God'?" (John 10:34–36, emphasis added).

In the prologue to the book of Revelation, John spoke of himself as one "who bore witness to the word of God and to the testimony of Jesus Christ" (Rev. 1:2; cf. v. 9; cf. 1 Thess. 1:8; 2 Thess. 3:1). In the prologue to his gospel, the same apostle speaks of Jesus as the living Word of God: "In the beginning was the Word, and the Word was with God, and the Word was God. He was in the beginning with God. All things came into being by Him, and apart from Him nothing came into being that has come into being. In Him was life, and the life was the light of men. . . . And the Word became flesh, and dwelt among us, and we beheld His glory, glory as of the only begotten from the Father, full of grace and truth" (John 1:1–4, 14; cf. 1 John 1:1; Rev. 19:13).

Paul spoke of Scripture as "the treasure which [had] been entrusted to" Timothy (2 Tim. 1:14) and as "the sacred writings which are able to give you the wisdom that leads to salvation through faith which is in Christ Jesus. All Scripture is inspired by God," he continues, "and profitable for teaching, for reproof, for correction, for training in righteousness; that the man of God may be adequate, equipped for every good work" (2 Tim. 3:15–17). Paul commended the Ephesian elders to "the word of [God's] grace, which is able to build you up and to give you the inheritance among all those who are sanctified" (Acts 20:32). Peter called Scripture "the pure milk of the word," by which believers "grow in respect to salvation" (1 Pet. 2:2).

Pastors, therefore, are to love **the faithful word** of God, respect it, study it, believe it, and obey it. It is their spiritual nourishment. They are to be "constantly nourished on the words of the faith and of the sound doctrine" (1 Tim. 4:6). That involves more than mere commitment to the inspiration and inerrancy of Scripture, essential as that is. It is commitment to the authority and sufficiency of God's Word as the only source of moral and spiritual truth.

An elder's spiritual leadership in the church is not built on his natural abilities, his education, his common sense, or his human wisdom. It is built on his knowledge and understanding of Scripture, his **holding fast the faithful word,** and on his submission to the Holy Spirit's applying the truths of that **word** in his heart and life. A man who is not himself **holding fast** to God's **faithful word** and committed to live it is not prepared to preach it or teach it. The truth of the Word must be woven into the very fabric of his thinking and living. Like the apostles in the early church, spiritually effective pastors must devote themselves "to prayer, and to the ministry of the word" (Acts 6:4).

It is through the Word that an elder grows in knowledge and understanding of the character of God, the will and purpose of God, the power and glory of God, the love and mercy of God, the principles and the promises of God. It is through the Word that he comes to understand justification, sanctification, and glorification. It is through the Word that he comes to understand the enemy and his powers of darkness, and his own helplessness, even as a pastor, to resist and overcome sin apart from God. It is through the Word that he comes to understand the nature and the purpose of the church and his own role of ministry in the church. All this he teaches his people.

It is failure in the area of **holding fast the faithful word** that is largely responsible for the superficial, self-elevating preaching and teaching in many evangelical churches. Here is the real culprit in the weak, shallow, insipid "sermonettes for Christianettes" that are such common church fare today. Here is the real villain that has led so many to be converted to what they consider relevancy and therefore to preach a pampering psychology or become stand-up comics, storytellers, clever speech-makers or entertainers who turn churches into what John Piper in his most excellent book *The Supremacy of God in Preaching* has called "the slapstick of evangelical worship" ([Grand Rapids: Baker, 1990], p. 21).

Timothy had been "constantly nourished on the words of the faith" and had followed "the sound doctrine" that he learned in Scripture (1 Tim. 4:6). Based on that preparation, he was to *prescribe* and *teach* these things" (v. 11), "*show* [himself] an example of those who believe" (v. 12), "*give attention to* the public reading of Scripture, to exhortation and teaching" (v. 13), "*not neglect* the spiritual gift within [him], which was bestowed upon [him] through prophetic utterance with the laying on of hands by the presbytery" (v. 14), "*take pains* with these things; *be* absorbed in them, so that your progress may be evident to all" (v. 15), "*pay close attention to* [himself] and to [his] teaching," and "*persevere* in these things" (v. 16). The nine emphasized verbs in verses 11–16 all translate Greek imperatives. (As indicated by italics in the NASB, the predicate adjective "absorbed," v. 15, is not in the Greek text but is implied.) Paul was not giving Timothy suggestions or simply personal advice, but divinely revealed apostolic orders.

Later in that letter Paul said, "Let the elders who rule well be considered worthy of double honor, especially those who work hard at preaching and teaching" (1 Tim. 5:17). Preaching and teaching are the primary responsibilities of elders. Timothy was to "teach and preach these principles" that Paul laid out (1 Tim. 6:2), to "instruct those who are rich in this present world not to be conceited or to fix their hope on the uncertainty of riches, but on God," and to "instruct them to do good, to be rich in good works, to be generous and ready to share" (vv. 17–18).

The apostle spoke of himself as "a preacher and an apostle and a teacher," (2 Tim. 1:11; cf. v. 8); and he charged Timothy: "Retain the standard of sound words which you have heard from me, in the faith and love which are in Christ Jesus. Guard, through the Holy Spirit who dwells in us, the treasure which has been entrusted to you. . . . And the things which you have heard from me in the presence of many witnesses [that is, his apostolic teaching of divinely revealed truths], these entrust to faithful men, who will be able to teach others also" (vv. 13–14; 2:2). Timothy was to carefully safeguard and uphold the things he had been taught and then was to teach them to other elders, who, in turn, would teach them to still other elders, and so on. That is the Lord's plan for teaching and preaching in His church.

Paul went on to remind Timothy, "All Scripture is inspired by God and profitable for teaching," as well as "for reproof, for correction, for training in righteousness" (2 Tim. 3:16). It is God's Word, under the guidance and illumination of the Holy Spirit, that makes "the man of

God"—the spiritual leader, in particular the pastor-teacher—"adequate, equipped for every good work" (v. 17). He is divinely commissioned to "preach the word; be ready in season and out of season; reprove, rebuke, exhort, with great patience and instruction" (4:2). He is to "speak the things which are fitting for sound doctrine" (Titus 2:1).

This duty to Scripture is in accord with the **teaching** (*didaskalia*), which refers to the content of that which is taught, to doctrine, divinely revealed truth.

Believers in the early church "were continually devoting themselves to the apostles' teaching" (Acts 2:42). After God's revelation was completed through their teaching, it was recorded in what we now know as the New Testament. That truth is absolutely trustworthy and sufficient. It is not to be redacted, edited, updated, or modified.

THE NECESSARY DUTY

that he may be able both to exhort in sound doctrine and to refute those who contradict. (1:9b)

Because he personally knows deeply and is exclusively loyal to God's Word, the pastor becomes qualified, under the direction and power of the Holy Spirit, to exercise his gift of preaching and teaching that Word in the church.

Positively, the pastor is **to exhort** believers **in sound doctrine.** He is to strengthen God's people in their knowledge of and obedience to the Word. *Parakaleō* (**to exhort**) means "to urge, beseech, and encourage." Literally, it means "to call alongside of" for the purpose of giving strength and help. The term was used of defense counsel in a court of law, the advocate who pleaded the cause of the accused.

In the Upper Room discourse, Jesus refers to the Holy Spirit as "another Helper [*paraklētos*]," or Advocate, who would stand beside the Twelve after Jesus ascended to His Father. This "Helper, the Holy Spirit, whom the Father will send in My name, He will teach you all things," the Lord promised, "and [will] bring to your remembrance all that I said to you" (John 14:16, 26; cf. 15:26; 16:7; cf. 1 John 2:1). That promise was fulfilled in a unique way in regard to the apostles, who authoritatively taught and established God's New Testament Word. But every pastor who is genuinely called by the Lord is to become **able . . . to exhort in sound doctrine.**

Sound translates *hugiainō*, from which we derive the English *hygienic.* It has the basic meaning of being healthy and wholesome, referring to that which protects and preserves life. In his preaching and teaching, it should be the pastor's sole objective to enlighten his congregation in **doctrine** that protects and preserves their spiritual health. It is an awesome and demanding task, and for that reason James warns, "Let not many of you become teachers, my brethren, knowing that as such we shall incur a stricter judgment" (James 3:1). Speaking to those under the pastor's care, the writer of Hebrews says, "Obey your leaders, and submit to them; for they keep watch over your souls, as those who will give an account" (Heb. 13:17). No reasonable, sensible Christian man would presume to take the role of pastor-teacher on himself without the Lord's calling. Nor would he attempt, when divinely called, to fulfill that calling by preaching and teaching whatever ideas might come to his own mind. He will preach and teach nothing but **sound doctrine.**

It is for that reason that preaching and teaching must be expositional, setting forth as clearly, systematically, and completely as possible the truths of God's Word and only those truths. Like Ezra, the faithful pastor will "set his heart to study the law of the Lord, and to practice it, and to teach His statutes and ordinances" (Ezra 7:10). Like Apollos, he will be "mighty in the Scriptures" (Acts 18:24). The pastor who recognizes that Scripture alone is inerrant and is our sole, complete, and sufficient authority knows exactly what he is called to preach and teach. He will "preach the word; be ready in season and out of season; reprove, rebuke, exhort, with great patience and instruction" (2 Tim. 4:2). He will "fully carry out the preaching of the word of God" (Col. 1:25). That is the commission of every preacher and teacher.

Contrary to what is offered in much popular preaching today, the Bible is not a resource for truth but is the divinely revealed *source* of truth. It is not a supplementary text but the only text. Its truths are not optional but mandatory. The pastor's purpose is not to make Scripture relevant to his people but to enable them to understand doctrine, which becomes the foundation of their spiritual living. The Bible is "user friendly" to those who humbly submit to its profound truth.

Sinners will be intolerant of the uncomfortable truths. That is to be expected. On the other hand, they will want to hear comfortable lies. They may seek what is sensational, entertaining, ego-building, nonthreatening, and popular. But what we preach is dictated by God, not by the crowds we face. Psychiatrist and Christian writer John White has penned some compelling words that need to be heard:

> Until about fifteen years ago psychology was seen by most Christians as hostile to the gospel.
> [But today] let someone who professes the name of Jesus baptize secular psychology and present it as something compatible with Scripture truth, and most Christians are happy to swallow theological hemlock in the form of psychological insights.

Over the past fifteen years there has been a tendency for churches to place increasing reliance on trained pastoral counselors. . . . To me it seems to suggest weakness or indifference to expository preaching within evangelical churches. . . . Why do we have to turn to the human sciences at all? Why? Because for years we have failed to expound the whole Scripture. Because from our weakened exposition and our superficial topical talks we have produced a generation of Christian sheep having no shepherd. And now we are damning ourselves more deeply than ever by our recourse to the wisdom of the world.

What I do as a psychiatrist and what my psychologist colleagues do in their research or their counseling is of infinitely less value to distressed Christians than what God says in his Word. But pastoral shepherds, like the sheep they guide, are following (if I may change my metaphor for a moment) a new Pied Piper of Hamelin who is leading them into the dark caves of humanistic hedonism.

A few of us who are deeply involved in the human sciences feel like voices crying in a godless wilderness of humanism, while the churches turn to humanistic psychology as a substitute for the gospel of God's grace. (*Flirting with the Word* [Wheaton, Ill.: Harold Shaw, 1982), pp. 114–17)

About that same problem, John Stott writes,

Expository preaching is a most exacting discipline. Perhaps that is why it is so rare. Only those will undertake it who are prepared to follow the example of the apostles and say, "It is not right that we should give up preaching the Word of God to serve tables. . . . We will devote ourselves to prayer and to the ministry of the Word" (Acts 6:2, 4). The systematic preaching of the Word is impossible without the systematic study of it. It will not be enough to skim through a few verses in daily Bible reading, nor to study a passage only when we have to preach from it. No. We must daily soak ourselves in the Scriptures. We must not just study, as through a microscope, the linguistic minutiae of a few verses, but take our telescope and scan the wide expanses of God's Word, assimilating its grand theme of divine sovereignty in the redemption of mankind. "It is blessed," wrote C. H. Spurgeon, "to eat into the very soul of the Bible until, at last, you come to talk in Scriptural language, and your spirit is flavoured with the words of the Lord, so that your blood is Bibline and the very essence of the Bible flows from you." (*The Preacher's Portrait* [Grand Rapids: Eerdmans, 1961], pp. 30–31)

The second duty of the pastor who teaches faithfully is negative. Not only is he to exhort believers in sound doctrine but he is also **to re-**

fute those—especially **those** within the church—**who contradict** healthy, life-protecting, life-preserving doctrine.

Pastors have an obligation to God to give their people an understanding of the truth that will create the discernment necessary to protect them from the ubiquitous error that incessantly assaults them. *Antilegō* (**to refute**) means literally "to speak against." The Lord's preachers and teachers are to be polemicists against unsound doctrine that goes under the guise of biblical truth. Not long after Paul himself ministered in Crete, "many rebellious men, empty talkers and deceivers, especially those of the circumcision," were causing trouble and confusion in the churches there (Titus 1:10). They were not to be ignored, much less tolerated, but were to "be silenced because they [were] upsetting whole families, teaching things they should not teach, for the sake of sordid gain" (v. 11). They were particularly dangerous because they arose from within the congregations. "They profess to know God," Paul said, "but by their deeds they deny Him, being detestable and disobedient, and worthless for any good deed" (v. 16).

Even the spiritually mature church at Ephesus was not immune to false teaching. "I know that after my departure," Paul warned elders from that church, "savage wolves will come in among you, not sparing the flock; and from among your own selves men will arise, speaking perverse things, to draw away the disciples after them" (Acts 20:29–30).

Although false teachers in the church exist under many guises, they all, in one way or another, **contradict** biblical truth. They are the enemies of sound doctrine and therefore of God and His people. Simply to accept Scripture as the inerrant Word of God does not protect against its being misunderstood or even perverted. To give certain personal insights and decisions of church councils equal authority beside Scripture is to **contradict** God's Word—just as surely as is denying the deity of Christ or the historicity of His resurrection. The final warning of Scripture is: "I testify to everyone who hears the words of the prophecy of this book: if anyone *adds to them,* God shall add to him the plagues which are written in this book; and if anyone *takes away* from the words of the book of this prophecy, God shall take away his part from the tree of life and from the holy city, which are written in this book" (Rev. 22:18–19, emphasis added).

The dual role of the godly preacher and teacher is to proclaim and to defend God's Word. In the eyes of the world and, tragically, in the eyes of many genuine but untaught believers, to denounce false doctrine, especially if that doctrine is given under the guise of evangelicalism, is to be unloving, judgmental, and divisive. But compromising Scripture in order to make it more palatable and acceptable—whether to believers or to unbelievers—is not "speaking the truth in love" (Eph.

4:15). It is speaking falsehood and is the farthest thing from godly love. It is a subtle, deceptive, and dangerous way to **contradict** God's own Word. The faithful pastor must have no part in it. He himself tolerates, and he teaches his people to tolerate, only sound doctrine.

Men Who Must Be Silenced

4

For there are many rebellious men, empty talkers and deceivers, especially those of the circumcision, who must be silenced because they are upsetting whole families, teaching things they should not teach, for the sake of sordid gain. One of themselves, a prophet of their own, said, "Cretans are always liars, evil beasts, lazy gluttons." This testimony is true. For this cause reprove them severely that they may be sound in the faith, not paying attention to Jewish myths and commandments of men who turn away from the truth. To the pure, all things are pure; but to those who are defiled and unbelieving, nothing is pure, but both their mind and their conscience are defiled. They profess to know God, but by their deeds they deny Him, being detestable and disobedient, and worthless for any good deed. (1:10–16)

One of Titus's major responsibilities in overseeing the churches on Crete was to prepare them to counteract the false teaching and immoral living of certain leaders. Paul charged Titus, and through him the churches, not simply to correct their false doctrine and denounce their immoral behavior but to silence them and remove such spiritual cancers from the fellowships.

These false teachers were much like those in Ephesus about whom Paul had warned Timothy. The young elder was admonished to "instruct certain men not to teach strange doctrines, nor to pay attention to myths and endless genealogies, which give rise to mere speculation rather than furthering the administration of God which is by faith," men who had "turned aside to fruitless discussion, wanting to be teachers of the Law, even though they do not understand either what they are saying or the matters about which they make confident assertions" (1 Tim. 1:3–4, 6–7). Obviously, the apostle believed that those particular men may have been salvageable, perhaps even as teachers.

Some of the false teachers in Crete, however, were beyond reclamation, because, as Paul asserts at the end of the present passage, "They profess to know God, but by their deeds they deny Him, being detestable and disobedient, and worthless for any good deed" (Titus 1:16).

In general, the tongue is a devastating force for evil, and in the mouths of false teachers who need to be silenced, it has always been a severe danger, not only to God's people but also to society in general. "The tongue is a small part of the body," James reminds us, "and yet it boasts of great things. Behold, how great a forest is set aflame by such a small fire! And the tongue is a fire, the very world of iniquity; the tongue is set among our members as that which defiles the entire body, and sets on fire the course of our life, and is set on fire by hell" (James 3:5–6). Left unchecked, the tongue spews forth the filth and evil of a depraved heart and mind and can cause immeasurable damage. Nothing better demonstrates man's fallenness and depravity than the wicked things that come out of his mouth. "With their tongues they keep deceiving, the poison of asps is under their lips," Paul says of those who speak evil; their mouths are "full of cursing and bitterness" (Rom. 3:13–14; cf. Pss. 5:9; 140:3). Isaiah referred to his sinfulness as "unclean lips" (Isa. 6:5). God promises that one day "the mouths of those who speak lies will be stopped" (Ps. 63:11; cf. 107:42; Rom. 3:19).

Sometimes God sovereignly silences a person's tongue by sickness or death. Sometimes He chooses to close a blasphemous mouth by other means. Countless times He has silenced a wicked tongue by graciously bringing its owner to Himself in salvation. Sometimes He says to His own people what He said to Ezekiel, one of His choice servants: "I will make your tongue stick to the roof of your mouth so that you will be dumb, . . . But when I speak to you, I will open your mouth" (Ezek. 3:26–27). The day will come when God will intervene and forever silence all false preachers and teachers.

In the meanwhile, however, it is the task of the church, and especially of its godly leaders, to silence those who associate with the Body of Christ in an effort to pervert God's truth and confuse and corrupt His people. "Evil men and impostors will proceed from bad to worse, deceiving and being deceived," Paul assured Timothy (2 Tim. 3:13). But, like Timothy, faithful pastors and elders have standing orders to "guard what has been entrusted to [them], avoiding worldly and empty chatter and the opposing arguments of what is falsely called 'knowledge'" (1 Tim. 6:20).

First, spiritual leaders are to oppose false teachers by overpowering them with the truth taught so clearly, precisely, and powerfully that those who spread error hide in humiliation when their falsehood is exposed.

Jesus combated the lies and deceptions of Satan and of his ungodly human servants by declaring divine truth. He thwarted Satan in the wilderness by countering each temptation with a quotation from Scripture (Matt. 4:1–11). When the unbelieving Sadducees tried to confound Jesus by asking Him what they thought was an unanswerable question about marriage in heaven, He "answered and said to them, 'You are mistaken, not understanding the Scriptures, or the power of God. For in the resurrection they neither marry, nor are given in marriage, but are like angels in heaven'" (Matt. 22:29–30). Simply by stating the truth, "He had put the Sadducees to silence" (v. 34).

Thinking they could succeed where the Sadducees had failed, the Pharisees had one of their scribes, "a lawyer, [ask] Him a question, testing Him, 'Teacher, which is the great commandment in the Law?'" (Matt. 22:35–36). He replied that the greatest commandment was to "love the Lord your God with all your heart, and with all your soul, and with all your mind," and that "a second is like it, 'You shall love your neighbor as yourself'" (vv. 37, 39). He then turned the tables and questioned them about the relationship of the Messiah to King David. When He pointed out from Scripture that their answer was defective, "no one was able to answer Him a word, nor did anyone dare from that day on to ask Him another question" (v. 46).

False teachers are not, of course, always silenced by God's truth, certainly not permanently. After the occasion just mentioned, the scribes, Pharisees, Sadducees, and other enemies of Jesus stopped confronting Him directly, but they hardly stopped opposing Him. Nor will false teachers today always or permanently be silenced when confronted by God's truth. Yet that truth will always be the primary weapon for combating error. Truth is the spiritual weapon that is able to destroy fortresses and speculations (false ideologies) and "every lofty thing" that is raised up against the truth of God (see 2 Cor. 10:4–5).

Second, we are to oppose false teachers by revoking their right to preach, teach, or otherwise have leadership in the church. In modern times, that revocation includes refusing to support or encourage spurious teaching that they promulgate through magazines, books, radio, television, tape ministries, conferences, teaching positions, or any other means.

Third, false teachers are to be opposed by believers living holy lives. Error promotes sin, and people who teach ungodly ideas inevitably live ungodly lives. God's truth also is impugned when those who teach that truth do not live accordingly. On the other hand, righteous living undergirds the truth, and it "is the will of God that by doing right [we] may silence the ignorance of foolish men" (1 Pet. 2:15).

In Titus 1:10–16, Paul first gives a general description of false teachers in the church who are to be silenced (vv. 10–13a). He then specifies what the reaction to such men should be (vv. 13b–14) and evaluates their lives (vv. 15–16).

THE DESCRIPTION OF THE MEN WHO MUST BE SILENCED

For there are many rebellious men, empty talkers and deceivers, especially those of the circumcision, who must be silenced because they are upsetting whole families, teaching things they should not teach, for the sake of sordid gain. One of themselves, a prophet of their own, said, "Cretans are always liars, evil beasts, lazy gluttons." This testimony is true. (1:10–13a)

In describing the false teachers who were to be restrained and removed from the churches, the apostle points out their proliferation (v. 10a), their behavior, which included rebelliousness, empty talk, and deceit (v. 10b), their effect on believers in the churches (v. 11a), their motive (v. 11b), and their character, which was lying, savage, and gluttonous (vv. 12–13a).

THEIR PROLIFERATION

For there are many (1:10a)

The fact that **there [were] many** false teachers in the churches of Crete made Titus's responsibility to oppose them all the more urgent. It was also for that reason, among others, that he needed to carefully "appoint elders in every city," as Paul already had directed (v. 5). No matter how diligent and persuasive Titus might have been, no one man would have had time to deal with the growing number of heretics and apostates. Most believers in those churches were new in the faith and had little defense against erroneous doctrine.

Paul had given similar warning to Timothy, saying that "the Spirit explicitly says that in later times some will fall away from the faith, paying attention to deceitful spirits and doctrines of demons, by means of the hypocrisy of liars seared in their own conscience as with a branding iron" (1 Tim. 4:1–2). The "later times" about which the Spirit spoke had already begun.

Perhaps a year after Paul wrote to Titus, Peter warned churches throughout the empire that "there will also be false teachers among you, who will secretly introduce destructive heresies, even denying the Master who bought them, bringing swift destruction upon themselves. And many will follow their sensuality, and because of them the way of the truth will be maligned; and in their greed they will exploit you with false words" (2 Pet. 2:1–3).

The greatest spiritual danger always comes from within the church. "Now I urge you, brethren," Paul counseled the church at Rome, "keep your eye on those who cause dissensions and hindrances contrary to the teaching which you learned, and turn away from them. For such men are slaves, not of our Lord Christ but of their own appetites; and by their smooth and flattering speech they deceive the hearts of the unsuspecting" (Rom. 16:17–18). Paul warned the Ephesian elders: "I know that after my departure savage wolves will come in among you, not sparing the flock; and from among your own selves men will arise, speaking perverse things, to draw away the disciples after them" (Acts 20:29–30).

By definition, dissension comes from within a group. In the church, deceivers disguise themselves as believers and as true teachers of the gospel. At all costs and by every godly means, they are to be silenced. The danger of false gospels is so great that Paul said that even if he "or an angel from heaven, should preach to you a gospel contrary to that which we have preached to you, let him be accursed" (Gal. 1:8).

THEIR BEHAVIOR

rebellious men, empty talkers and deceivers, especially those of the circumcision, (1:10b)

First of all, the false teachers on Crete were **rebellious,** as such people always are. They are spiritual and moral insurgents—the enemies of God, His truth, and His people. Being a law unto themselves and representing the rebel Satan, they do not recognize the authority of God's Word or of His Spirit, much less that of His divinely called preachers and teachers. Even when their erroneous doctrine and immoral living are exposed, they are inclined to defy correction and discipline by the true church.

Second, the false teachers were **empty talkers.** In the words of Shakespeare, they are "full of sound and fury, signifying nothing." Their talk is often captivating and persuasive. Their words are smooth and they cleverly disguise their falsehoods in terms that make them seem truthful, frequently using biblical words and phrases that are distorted and taken out of context. But what they teach is bereft of truth. Their preaching and teaching is based on the musings of their own warped imaginations, speculations, and knowledge set up against the Word of God.

Third, those false teachers were **deceivers.** As already noted, they typically disguise their deceit in biblical terminology. And unfortunately, they seldom lack for an audience. Almost from its beginning, the church has included some people who, buying into that deception, "will not endure sound doctrine; but wanting to have their ears tickled, . . . will accumulate for themselves teachers in accordance to their own desires; and will turn away their ears from the truth, and will turn aside to myths" (2 Tim. 4:3–4; cf. 1 Tim. 4:1–2).

God hates all lying and deceit. "'Let none of you devise evil in your heart against another, and do not love perjury; for all these are what I hate,' declares the Lord" (Zech. 8:17; cf. Mal. 3:5). But He holds special hatred for lying and deceit that is done in His name, most specially when it is directed at His people.

As Paul was the peerless apostle against false teaching, so Jeremiah was the peerless Old Testament prophet against it. He declared:

> Then the Lord said to me, "The prophets are prophesying falsehood in My name. I have neither sent them nor commanded them nor spoken to them; they are prophesying to you a false vision, divination, futility and the deception of their own minds." . . . Therefore thus says the Lord God of Israel concerning the shepherds who are tending My people: "You have scattered My flock and driven them away, and have not attended to them; behold, I am about to attend to you for the evil of your deeds. . . . I did not send these prophets, but they ran. I did not speak to them, but they prophesied. . . . Behold, I am against those who have prophesied false dreams," declares the Lord, "and related them, and led My people astray by their falsehoods and reckless boasting." (Jer. 14:14; 23:2, 21, 32)

Prophesying falsehood in the name of a false god is evil enough, but false prophesying in the name of the true God is immeasurably worse. "Moreover, among the prophets of Samaria I saw an *offensive* thing: They prophesied by Baal and led My people Israel astray. Also among the prophets of Jerusalem I have seen a *horrible* thing: The committing of adultery and walking in falsehood; and they strengthen the hands of evildoers, so that no one has turned back from his wickedness. All of them have become to Me like Sodom, and her inhabitants like Gomorrah" (Jer. 23:13–14, emphasis added). The falsehoods of the pagan prophets in Samaria were *offensive,* but those of the pretended prophets of the Lord in Jerusalem were *horrible.*

Because so many of the early Christians were Jews, churches in New Testament times were **especially** plagued by **those of the circumcision,** that is, by Jews within the church. Some of them, called Judaizers because of their attempt to obligate all believers to Jewish legalism, wanted to impose Old Testament ceremonial standards and sometimes even rabbinical traditions. From ancient records it is known that many Jews lived on the island of Crete (cf. Acts 2:11), and from the apostle's comments here, a number of them apparently were Judaizers.

Some fifteen years earlier, the Council of Jerusalem was convened to respond to "certain ones of the sect of the Pharisees who [said], 'It is necessary to circumcise them, and to direct them to observe the Law of Moses'" (Acts 15:5). As first spokesman for the council, Peter asked, "Why do you put God to the test by placing upon the neck of the disciples a yoke which neither our fathers nor we have been able to bear?" (v. 10). After considerable discussion by the group and reports by Paul and Barnabas about the "signs and wonders God had done through them among the Gentiles," James proposed that they "not trouble those who are turning to God from among the Gentiles, but . . . write to them that they abstain from things contaminated by idols and from fornication and from what is strangled and from blood" (see vv. 12–20). The rest of the council agreed, and letters to that effect were sent "to the brethren in Antioch and Syria and Cilicia" (vv. 22–23), where the problem at that time was the most serious.

That the influence of Judaizers in the church continued to be powerful for many years after that, however, is seen in Peter's own temporarily distancing himself from Gentile believers because of his "fearing the party of the circumcision" (Gal. 2:12), a compromise for which Paul "opposed him to his face" (v. 11).

As Paul notes later in this chapter, the men **of the circumcision** in the Cretan churches were spreading "Jewish myths and commandments of men who turn away from the truth" (v. 14). And, although they "[professed] to know God, . . . by their deeds they [denied] Him, being detestable and disobedient, and worthless for any good deed" (v. 16). The apostle does not describe the exact form of this heresy, and the particulars are not important. All false teaching must be opposed, in whatever way and to whatever degree it departs from Scripture.

THEIR EFFECT

who must be silenced because they are upsetting whole families, teaching things they should not teach, (1:11a)

These particular heretics apparently were not doing most of their teaching during worship services or other church meetings but in the homes of the people. Several reasons for such a tactic are obvious. For one thing, a large group is more likely to include believers who are spiritually perceptive and well grounded in Scripture, making false teaching more likely to be recognized and contested. An isolated small group such as a single family, on the other hand, not only is less likely to include a biblically grounded believer but also, because of its size, is often more easily intimidated. It is largely for those reasons that many cults focus on person-to-person and door-to-door ministries to capture converts. Speaking of just such activity, Peter wrote that, "speaking out arrogant words of vanity," false teachers "entice by fleshly desires, by sensuality, those who barely escape from the ones who live in error" (2 Pet. 2:18).

Deceivers in the church **must be silenced,** Paul said, **because they are upsetting whole families.** Paul warned Timothy about ungodly and immoral men "who enter into households and captivate weak women weighed down with sins, led on by various impulses" (2 Tim. 3:6). Earlier in that letter he had admonished the young pastor at Ephesus to charge believers there "not to wrangle about words, which is useless, and leads to the ruin of the hearers," and to "avoid worldly and empty chatter, for it will lead to further ungodliness" (2 Tim. 2:14, 16). Peter tells us that "untaught and unstable" leaders in the early church distorted the teachings of Paul, "as they do also the rest of the Scriptures, to their own destruction" (2 Pet. 3:16).

THEIR MOTIVE

for the sake of sordid gain. (1:11b)

With perhaps a few fanatical exceptions, false teachers carry on their destructive work **for the sake of sordid gain.**

Sordid gain refers primarily to ill-gotten financial profit. The motives and objectives of ungodly leaders are in direct contrast to those who are godly. Whereas godly elders are morally pure and faithful to their wives (v. 6), ungodly leaders are immoral and unfaithful. The sinful attributes of self-will, a quick temper, addiction to wine, belligerence, and loving money that should *not* be found in elders (v. 7) are the very things that ungodly men cherish. On the other hand, the righteous attitudes of self-control, hospitality, and loving what is good, sensible, just, and devout that *are* found in godly elders (v. 8) are things that ungodly leaders repudiate and despise. The faithful word of sound doctrine that godly elders teach and defend is what the ungodly seek to destroy. And it is a distinct mark of false teachers that they love money.

Throughout the history of the church, false preachers and teachers have used their positions and slanted their messages to promote their own financial **gain.** They not only have "a morbid interest in controversial questions and disputes about words, out of which arise envy, strife, abusive language, evil suspicions," but they also "suppose that godliness is a means of gain" (1 Tim. 6:4–5). "Godliness actually is a means of great gain, when accompanied by contentment," Paul goes on to say (v. 6), but that is not the kind of **gain** that false teachers crave. Peter warns all pastors to "shepherd the flock of God among you, exercising oversight not under compulsion, but voluntarily, according to the will of God; and not for sordid gain" (1 Pet. 5:2).

THEIR CHARACTER

One of themselves, a prophet of their own, said, "Cretans are always liars, evil beasts, lazy gluttons." This testimony is true. (1:12–13a)

The immorality, greed, and untrustworthiness of the false teachers about whom Paul warns were characteristic of the island's inhabitants in general, as testified by **one of themselves, a prophet of their own.** Although that **prophet,** the poet Epimenides, may have been exaggerating, his basic assessment was on target. He was a highly respected Greek intellectual of the sixth century B.C. and in ancient times was considered to be one of the seven great wise men of Greece. As a native of Crete, he knew the people well and was not speaking out of malice as an enemy.

The Cretans' most famous falsehood, doubtless also a self-deception, was the claim that the god Zeus was buried on their island. Even in light of their own pagan belief, that claim was foolish, because Zeus was considered to be immortal. The truth of the assertion that **Cretans are always liars** also is reflected in the ancient phrase "to Cretanize," which was used as a figure of speech for lying.

Cretans also had the reputation of being **evil beasts [and] lazy gluttons.** The idea behind **evil beasts** is that of behaving like a wild animal, living solely on the level of sensual appetites and passions. Such people are malicious and often savage and rapacious. The meaning of **lazy gluttons** is self-evident. Cretans hated to work but loved to eat. They were self-indulgent, greedy, lustful, overfed, and perhaps in poor physical condition. Paul affirmed that the six-hundred-year-old **testimony** of Epimenides about the Cretans was still **true.**

REACTION TO THE MEN WHO MUST BE SILENCED

For this cause reprove them severely that they may be sound in the faith, not paying attention to Jewish myths and commandments of men who turn away from the truth. (1:13b–14)

For this cause, that is, because of the reasons just given, Titus was to forcefully and immediately confront the heretical teaching and ungodly living of the false teachers.

REPROVE THEM

reprove them severely that they may be sound in the faith, (1:13b)

Because of the extreme spiritual danger that those men posed if they infected the church, Titus was to **reprove them severely. Severely** translates *apotomōs,* a compound adverb formed from the preposition *apo* and the verb *tennō,* which means "to cut," as with a knife or ax. The reproof was to cut with penetrating force.

The severity of such a rebuke should be remedial. Titus was not to condemn the men but seek to correct their doctrinal error and personal sinfulness, in order **that they may be sound in the faith.** As someone has observed, "The surgeon of the soul only cuts to achieve a cure." Like Timothy, therefore, Titus was to "reprove, rebuke, [and] exhort with great patience and instruction" (2 Tim. 4:2). "The Lord's bond-servant must not be quarrelsome, but be kind to all, able to teach, patient when wronged, with gentleness correcting those who are in opposition, if perhaps God may grant them repentance leading to the knowledge of the truth" (2 Tim. 2:24–25).

Paul himself was remarkably patient, as is particularly evident in his relationship with the immature, immoral, and doctrinally confused believers in Corinth, among whom he had personally ministered for about a year and a half. "I am writing these things while absent," he told them in his second letter, "in order that when present I may not use severity [*apotomōs*], in accordance with the authority which the Lord gave me, for building up and not for tearing down" (2 Cor. 13:10). The spirit of kindness and humility that characterized Paul should characterize every leader in Christ's church, as it was so perfectly by the Lord Himself in His incarnation. All believers, in fact, are to "have this attitude in [themselves] which was also in Christ Jesus, [who] emptied Himself, taking the form of a bond-servant, and being made in the likeness of men. And being found in appearance as a man, He humbled Himself by becoming obedient to the point of death, even death on a cross" (Phil. 2:5, 7–8).

REPUDIATE THEM

not paying attention to Jewish myths and commandments of men who turn away from the truth. (1:14)

Paying attention to carries the sense of giving heed to or devoting oneself to, in this case, heeding and devoting oneself to error. This is forbidden of all church leaders. Paul made this point most firmly in 2 Corinthians 6:14–18:

> Do not be bound together with unbelievers; for what partnership have righteousness and lawlessness, or what fellowship has light with darkness? Or what harmony has Christ with Belial, or what has a believer in common with an unbeliever? Or what agreement has the temple of God with idols? For we are the temple of the living God; just as God said, "'I will dwell in them and walk among them; and I will be their God, and they shall be My people. Therefore, come out from their midst and be separate,' says the Lord. 'And do not touch what is unclean; and I will welcome you. And I will be a father to you, and you shall be sons and daughters to Me,' Says the Lord Almighty."

That command not to be associated with unbelievers is in the context of religious and spiritual matters. Only evil is to be gained by linking up with those who teach or practice any form of false religion—precisely what the Corinthian believers were doing (see 1 Cor. 10:20–21).

In particular for the churches on Crete, such danger came from **Jewish myths and commandments of men who turn away from the truth.** The apostle gave an almost identical warning to Timothy, telling him not "to pay attention to myths and endless genealogies, which give rise to mere speculation rather than furthering the administration of God which is by faith" (1 Tim. 1:4; 4:7).

Paul does not identify the particular **Jewish myths** and man-made **commandments** that were being promulgated. Some insight can be gained by remembering that ancient Hebrew had no numerals as such, but instead used a complex system that assigned a numerical value to each letter in the alphabet and to various combinations of letters, which, until the eighth or ninth century A.D., included no written vowels.

The first Hebrew word (*brshth,* "in the beginning") in Genesis 1:1, for example, had the numerical value of 913. *Brm* ("Abram") had the value of 318. A century or so after the Babylonian Captivity, many rabbis began adapting gnostic Greek numerology—the practice of assigning mystical meanings to numbers—to the Hebrew language. Under one such scheme (and there were many), it was believed that the secret in the letter-numbers in Abram's name meant that he had 318 servants.

Hebrew numerology was applied not only to the Hebrew Scriptures but also to the Talmud, a collection of authorized rabbinical interpretations of Scripture, especially the Mosaic Law, that began during the time of Ezra (ca. 450 B.C.) and continued until about A.D. 500. By New Testament times, many rabbis and other learned Jews—especially those who lived in areas where Greek philosophy was still dominant (as it was on Crete)—mixed ideas from Hebrew and Greek numerology and added their own allegorical fancies, making the resulting interpretations more bizarre than ever.

For several centuries, **Jewish** rabbis had been developing many traditional laws, identified here as the **commandments of men.** Those **commandments** probably referred to, and certainly included, legalistic ordinances and standards—most of them doubtless from the Talmud—that added to and often contradicted or nullified Scripture.

When a group of Pharisees and scribes (interpreters and teachers of the Law) asked Jesus, "'Why do Your disciples not walk according to the tradition of the elders, but eat their bread with impure hands?' He answered, 'Rightly did Isaiah prophesy of you hypocrites, as it is written, "This people honors Me with their lips, but their heart is far away from Me. But in vain do they worship Me, teaching as doctrines the precepts of men." Neglecting the commandment of God, you hold to the tradition of men.' He was also saying to them, 'You nicely set aside the commandment of God in order to keep your tradition'" (Mark 7:5–9; cf. Isa. 29:13; Matt. 15:9).

Paul probably did not specify particular heresies because there were so many varieties. Had he failed to mention a certain heresy, some immature and undiscerning believers might have concluded that it was therefore excluded from this warning. The apostle rather admonished that everything that was taught in the name of Christ be measured against the Old Testament Scriptures and the teaching of the apostles.

The fact that false teachers in the Cretan churches were identified as **men who [turned] away from the truth** indicates that they had been exposed to **the truth** and had once acknowledged it, but later rejected it in favor of Satan-inspired and man-made myths, precepts, and traditions.

EVALUATION OF THE MEN WHO MUST BE SILENCED

To the pure, all things are pure; but to those who are defiled and unbelieving, nothing is pure, but both their mind and their conscience are defiled. They profess to know God, but by their deeds they deny Him, being detestable and disobedient, and worthless for any good deed. (1:15–16)

Paul gives two divinely inspired evaluations of false teachers in the Cretan churches, evaluations that apply to false teachers in any age. First he assesses their inner lives and finds them to be corrupt. He then assesses their outer lives and finds them to be hypocritical and debauched.

THEIR INNER LIVES

To the pure, all things are pure; but to those who are defiled and unbelieving, nothing is pure, but both their mind and their conscience are defiled. (1:15)

When a certain "Pharisee asked [Jesus] to have lunch with him, . . . He went in, and reclined at the table. And when the Pharisee saw it, he was surprised that He had not first ceremonially washed before the meal. But the Lord said to him, 'Now you Pharisees clean the outside of the cup and of the platter; but inside of you, you are full of robbery and wickedness. You foolish ones, did not He who made the outside make the inside also? But give that which is within as charity, and then all things are clean for you'" (Luke 11:37–41). In other words, when a person is **pure** in heart and mind, his perspectives on **all things are pure,** and that inner purity always produces outer purity.

Jewish legalism, like every other form of legalism, presumed that a person can make himself acceptable to God by meticulously observing certain ceremonies and traditions that were considered good and obligatory and by just as meticulously avoiding those that were considered evil. The idea that, by doing or not doing certain things, a person is able, by his own power and merit, to please and reconcile himself to God has always been the basic heresy of sacramental, sacerdotal, or ritualistic religion, whatever its form—Jewish, Catholic, Protestant, Orthodox, Islamic, or other. The basic heresy of every false religious system is works righteousness. Paul describes those who promote that foundational heresy in his letter to the church at Rome, saying of them, " For not knowing about God's righteousness, and seeking to establish their own, they did not subject themselves to the righteousness of God" (Rom. 10:3).

In every age of human history since the Fall, men have been made right with God only through saving faith in Him. And, on the other hand, those who are not accepted by Him remain unsaved because they are **unbelieving.** Such things as lighting candles, burning incense, genuflecting, counting beads, repeating prescribed prayers, facing a certain direction when praying, having visions or mystical experiences, and even being baptized or partaking of the Lord's Supper have absolutely no saving power. To the contrary, unless a practice, even one that is biblically commanded, is done as the fruit of a believing heart, it can become a formidable barrier to salvation and blessing.

In the words of the nineteenth-century Scottish theologian Patrick Fairbairn, those who trust in sacramentalism or other form of works righteousness "have a fountain of pollution which spreads itself over and infects everything about them. Their food and drink, their possessions, their employment, their comforts, their actions—all are in the reckoning of God tainted with impurity, because they are putting away from them that which alone has for the soul regenerating and cleansing efficacy" (Quoted in D. Edmond Hiebert, *Titus and Philemon,* Everyman's Bible Commentary [Chicago: Moody, 1957], pp. 44–45).

To those who are defiled and unbelieving, Paul says, **nothing is pure,** or can be pure, because **both their mind and their conscience are defiled.** All their perspectives and actions are infected with their inner defilement.

It is "not what enters into the mouth [that] defiles the man," Jesus said, "but what proceeds out of the mouth, this defiles the man" (Matt. 15:11). When Peter asked Him to explain what He meant, the Lord replied, "Are you still lacking in understanding also? Do you not understand that everything that goes into the mouth passes into the stomach, and is eliminated? But the things that proceed out of the mouth come from the heart, and those defile the man. For out of the heart come evil thoughts, murders, adulteries, fornications, thefts, false witness, slanders. These are the things which defile the man; but to eat with unwashed hands does not defile the man" (vv. 15–20). A person is morally and spiritually **defiled** by sin in his heart and mind, not by material things that he handles or eats.

It was not until several years after Pentecost that Peter came to fully understand that truth. After his three-time vision of the sheet filled with unclean animals and the heavenly command to "Arise, . . . kill and eat!" the apostle "was greatly perplexed in mind as to what the vision which he had seen might be" (Acts 10:10–17). Only after he obeyed the Spirit's command to witness to Cornelius, a Gentile and a Roman centurion, and observed the salvation of that man and his household and their being filled with the Holy Spirit (vv. 20–48) did he finally comprehend that Gentiles were not ceremonially "unclean" and that the gospel was offered as freely to them as to Jews. "If God therefore gave to them the same gift as He gave to us also after believing in the Lord Jesus Christ," he later testified, "who was I that I could stand in God's way?" (11:17).

"If you have died with Christ to the elementary principles of the world," Paul asked Colossian believers, "why, as if you were living in the world, do you submit yourself to decrees, such as, 'Do not handle, do not taste, do not touch!' (which all refer to things destined to perish with the using)—in accordance with the commandments and teachings of men? These are matters which have, to be sure, the appearance of wisdom in self-made religion and self-abasement and severe treatment of the body, but are of no value against fleshly indulgence" (Col. 2:20–23). "Everything created by God is good, and nothing is to be rejected, if it is received with gratitude; for it is sanctified by means of the word of God and prayer" (1 Tim. 4:4–5).

THEIR OUTER LIVES

They profess to know God, but by their deeds they deny Him, being detestable and disobedient, and worthless for any good deed. (1:16)

Only God, of course, can evaluate a person's heart. But by the way they live, unbelievers usually betray their unbelief. By their words, **they profess to know God, but by their deeds they deny Him.**

People who trust in their works righteousness also tend to have an air of superiority about them, believing, like the ancient Greek gnostics, that they are "in the know" about religious matters and live on a level above other people. They not only **profess to know God** but to know Him better than others. The truth, however, is that they do not know Him at all, much less have a saving relationship to Him. **By their deeds, they deny Him,** and because of their unbelief (v. 15), He denies them (cf. Matt. 10:33). They hold "to a form of godliness, [but] they have denied its power" (2 Tim. 3:5). That is precisely what Jesus taught when He said of false teachers, "You will know them by their fruits" (Matt. 7:16).

Self-righteous false teachers not only are proud and feel superior to others but are utterly **detestable and disobedient, and worthless for any good deed.** The noun form of the adjective *bdeluktos* (**detestable**) was used by Jesus to describe Antichrist, "the abomination [*bdelugma*] of desolation which was spoken of through Daniel the prophet, standing in the holy place" (Matt. 24:15). John declares that "nothing unclean and no one who practices abomination [*bdelugma*] and lying, shall ever come into it, but only those whose names are written in the Lamb's book of life" (Rev. 21:27). **Detestable** false teachers will have no place in heaven.

Disobedient lives betray a professed faith in God. The ungodly continue to walk "according to the course of this world, according to the prince of the power of the air, of the spirit that is now working in the sons of disobedience" (Eph. 2:2). Because they attempt to "deceive [God's people] with empty words, . . . the wrath of God comes upon the sons of disobedience" (Eph. 5:6; cf. Col. 3:6). And, as Jeremiah had proclaimed many centuries earlier, "they [do not] furnish [God's] people the slightest benefit" (Jer. 23:32). They are **worthless for any good deed.** The term for **worthless** is *adokimos,* which means "disqualified or rejected" (cf. 2 Tim. 3:8).

The Character of a Healthy Church—part 1 **5**

But as for you, speak the things which are fitting for sound doctrine. Older men are to be temperate, dignified, sensible, sound in faith, in love, in perseverance. Older women likewise are to be reverent in their behavior, not malicious gossips, nor enslaved to much wine, teaching what is good, that they may encourage the young women to love their husbands, to love their children, to be sensible, pure, workers at home, kind, being subject to their own husbands, that the word of God may not be dishonored. Likewise urge the young men to be sensible; in all things show yourself to be an example of good deeds, with purity in doctrine, dignified, sound in speech which is beyond reproach, in order that the opponent may be put to shame, having nothing bad to say about us. Urge bondslaves to be subject to their own masters in everything, to be well-pleasing, not argumentative, not pilfering, but showing all good faith that they may adorn the doctrine of God our Savior in every respect. (2:1–10)

In chapter 2, the subject changes from pastors to congregations, from leadership to laity. The entire chapter deals with the evangelistic impact of a spiritually healthy congregation and gives direct, practical instruction about how believers are to live for the purpose of showing sinners the power and joy of salvation.

But as for you indicates a transition by contrast between the false teachers in the churches, who, although they professed to know God, denied Him by their unholy living and were therefore "detestable and disobedient, and worthless for any good deed" (Titus 1:16). Those men had been tested and found to be useless, even dangerous. Titus therefore was commissioned by Paul to challenge their false teaching and false living and to **speak the things which are fitting for sound doctrine,** in order to strengthen the testimony of the churches for the gospel of salvation.

Speak translates a present imperative of *laleō,* which refers to ordinary conversation. The present tense carries the idea of continuity and persistence, and the imperative makes the verb a command. Titus, and the elders he appointed (1:5), were commanded to **speak** about right living as well as right **doctrine.** They were not to deviate, capitulate, or be intimidated. They were to be as aggressive in their teaching of **sound doctrine** and its corresponding godly lifestyle as the false teachers in the Cretan churches were in their unsound doctrine and its consequent ungodly lifestyle. They were to give regular and careful pastoral instruction about practical Christian living and about the godly attitudes and actions that result from believing and obeying divine truth. They were to live lives that properly reflected their salvation from sin and were a worthy affirmation of the transforming power of their Savior.

About a year later, the apostle would admonish Timothy to "preach the word; be ready in season and out of season; reprove, rebuke, exhort, with great patience and instruction. For the time will come," he continued, "when they will not endure sound doctrine; but wanting to have their ears tickled, they will accumulate for themselves teachers in accordance to their own desires; and will turn away their ears from the truth, and will turn aside to myths" (2 Tim. 4:2–4). The churches and their leaders on Crete faced the same dire prospect as would those at Ephesus.

It is important to note that the apostle is not here focusing on the teaching and preaching of **sound doctrine** itself, as he does in 1:9. He is rather focusing on practical instruction about **the things which are fitting for,** that is, based on and appropriate to, the **sound doctrine** that already has been taught. *Prepō* **(fitting)** carries the basic meaning of "being prominent or conspicuous" and came to be used of a distinguishing characteristic. Eventually it was used to describe that which is **fitting,** appropriate, proper, seemly. Truth requires certain behaviors that reflect and are appropriate to it. "Do not let immorality or any impurity or greed even be named among you," Paul admonished Ephesian believers, "as is proper [*prepō*] among saints" (Eph. 5:3).

Sound translates a participle form of the verb *hugiainō*, which has the basic meaning of "being well and healthy" and is the term from which we derive "hygiene." Paul uses a form of this word nine times in the pastoral epistles, five of those times in Titus, and always in relation to personal righteousness and spiritual well-being. He repeatedly emphasizes that sound doctrine (1 Tim. 1:10; 2 Tim. 4:3; Titus 1:9; 2:1) eventuates in sound faith and sound speaking (1 Tim. 6:3; 2 Tim. 1:13; Titus 1:13; 2:2, 8). Healthy doctrine produces healthy spiritual living.

The Bible never divorces doctrine from duty, truth from behavior. After presenting eleven chapters of basic New Testament doctrine, Paul then said to believers at Rome, "I urge you therefore, brethren, by the mercies of God, to present your bodies a living and holy sacrifice, acceptable to God, which is your spiritual service of worship. And do not be conformed to this world, but be transformed by the renewing of your mind, that you may prove what the will of God is, that which is good and acceptable and perfect" (Rom. 12:1–2). He followed the same pattern in his letters to believers in Ephesus (see Eph. 4:1), Philippi (see Phil. 4:8–9), and Colossae (see 3:2–10). Quoting Leviticus 11:44, Peter said, "It is written, 'You shall be holy, for I am holy'" (1 Pet. 1:16). Those who claim the name of God have always been commanded to live godly lives.

What is true of individual believers is, of course, also true of the church as a body. A church that is grounded in spiritual truth and protected from spiritual falsehood is to be spiritually healthy and productive through the way in which its members live. The fruit of right doctrine is righteous living.

Pastors are to concentrate on the spiritual depth of their congregations and allow God to take care of the breadth. "I planted, [and] Apollos watered," Paul said, "but God was causing the growth" (1 Cor. 3:6). "He who supplies seed to the sower and bread for food," he reminded believers in Corinth, "will supply and multiply your seed for sowing and increase the harvest of your righteousness" (2 Cor. 9:10; cf. Col. 2:19).

In Titus 2:2–10, the Holy Spirit prescribes a series of binding requirements that are necessary for members of a healthy church to have an evangelistic impact. In 2:11–14, the reason for such holy living is magnificently declared to be bound up in God's redemptive plan. The admonition of verse 1 is then repeated and reinforced in verse 15: "These things speak and exhort and reprove with all authority. Let no one disregard you" (Titus 2:15).

The injunctions in verses 2–10 are strong, straightforward, and specific. Because they are so contrary to proud and self-willed human nature, they often have been unpopular and controversial, even in the church. At no time have they been more unpopular and controversial than in many churches today, where personal opinion and cultural standards take precedence over God's truth and self-fulfillment is more important than holy living.

The patterns of holy living that make for effective witness are here given as the distinguishing marks of the Christian groups addressed in these verses: older men (v. 2), older women (vv. 3–4a), young women (vv. 4b–5), young men (vv. 6–8), and bondslaves/employees (vv. 9–10).

OLDER MEN

Older men are to be temperate, dignified, sensible, sound in faith, in love, in perseverance. (2:2)

Old age is often associated with such things as maturity, wisdom, and patience. Ideally, "Wisdom is with aged men, [and] with long life is understanding" (Job 12:12). But that is not always the case. Increased age typically brings decreased energy, diminished vision and hearing, more aches and pains, and often more depression, hopelessness, and cynicism. In the last chapter of Ecclesiastes we are told, "Remember also your Creator in the days of your youth, before the evil days come and the years draw near when you will say, 'I have no delight in them'; before the sun, the light, the moon, and the stars are darkened, and clouds return after the rain; in the day that the watchmen of the house tremble, and mighty men stoop" (12:1–3).

As we grow older, change can become harder to accept. Life can become less fulfilling, less satisfying, and more disillusioning. It is easy to become a creature of habit, and the longer a habit is practiced, the more deeply entrenched and formidable it becomes. Besetting sins can become such an integral part of daily living that they cease to be recognized as sins at all.

For a Christian, however, old age should bring greater love for God, for the people of God, and for the sacred things of God. Those who have walked with Christ for many years should rejoice in that privilege and in the prospect of one day seeing Him face to face. A church should value and honor those who have spent many years in fellowship with the Lord, in the study of His Word, and in service to and through His church. A church is blessed when it has believers who can say with Paul, "I have fought the good fight, I have finished the course, I have kept the faith" (2 Tim. 4:7) and who can pray, "O God, Thou hast taught me from my youth; and I still declare Thy wondrous deeds" (Ps. 71:17).

Moses was 80 years old when God called him to lead Israel out of bondage in Egypt and to the land of promise. But, like his poor speaking ability (Ex. 4:10–12), advanced age did not excuse him from the Lord's work.

At the age of 83—after having traveled some 250,000 miles on horseback, preached more than 40,000 sermons, and produced some 200 books and pamphlets—John Wesley regretted that he was unable to read and write for more than 15 hours a day without his eyes becoming too tired to work. After his 86th birthday, he admitted to an increasing tendency to lie in bed until 5:30 in the morning!

Godly older saints who bring strength, stability, and wisdom to a church should be cherished. Ancient Israel was told by the Lord, "You shall rise up before the grayheaded, and honor the aged" (Lev. 19:32; cf. Prov. 16:31). The godly are assured that they "will still yield fruit in old age" (Ps. 92:14) and that "the path of the righteous is like the light of dawn, that shines brighter and brighter until the full day" (Prov. 4:18).

In itself, however, old age does not make a believer more godly, more faithful, more satisfied, or more effective in service to God. As Paul's injunctions in this verse indicate, even **older men** sometimes need to be admonished to exemplify certain basic virtues.

Both the Old and New Testaments teach that **older men** and women, whether believers or not, are to be treated with special respect and consideration by those who are younger. That principle applied with special force in regard to children and their parents. As Paul pointed out to believers in Ephesus, the command to "honor your father and mother . . . is the first commandment with a promise" (Eph. 6:2; cf. Ex. 20:12). Under the old covenant, striking a parent was a capital offense (Ex. 21:15).

It is not, of course, that older people are beyond correction. But when an older person commits an offense, he is to be reproved with respect and care. "Do not sharply rebuke an older man," Paul warned Timothy, "but rather appeal to him as a father" (1 Tim. 5:1).

Older men translates the single Greek term *presbutēs,* which Paul used of himself (Philem. 9) when he was in his sixties. The only other time it is used in the New Testament is of Zacharias, the father of John the Baptist, who questioned the angel about his becoming a father, saying, "for I am an old man, and my wife is advanced in years'" (Luke 1:18). Zacharias obviously thought that both he and his wife were then past normal childbearing age. In ancient Greek literature the word sometimes was used of men as young as 50.

Paul does not use the word "admonish" in his injunction to **older men,** older women, or younger women, as he does in regard to young men and bondslaves (vv. 6, 9). But the use of "likewise urge" in verse 6 clearly indicates that the apostle expected Titus to personally admonish believers in the first three groups as well.

All **older men** are to live holy, exemplary lives before the Lord, before the church, and before the world. They are to abandon the recklessness, impetuosity, thoughtlessness, and instability that are characteristic of youth.

First, they are to be **temperate.** The adjective *nēphalios* (**temperate**) carries the root idea of being free from intoxication. In the New Testament it is used metaphorically of someone who is moderate (see also 1 Tim. 3:2, 11). A **temperate** person avoids extravagance and overindulgence. Paul and Peter used a related word in admonishing believers to be sober-minded (1 Cor. 15:34; cf. 1 Pet. 1:13; 4:7).

The **temperate** older man is able to discern more clearly which things are of the greatest importance and value. He uses his time, his money, and his energy more carefully and selectively than when he was younger and less mature. His priorities are in the right order, and he is satisfied with fewer and simpler things.

Second, **older men** are to be **dignified.** *Semnos* (**dignified**) originally carried the idea of revered and venerable, but later came to be used generally of a person or thing that is honorable and **dignified.** The word does not carry the idea of haughtiness or high class but of somberness in its best sense. The **dignified** person is never frivolous, trivial, or superficial. He never laughs at immorality, vulgarity, or anything else that is sinful and ungodly. Nor does he laugh at that which is tragic or at the expense of others.

Older believers have lived long enough to see many people, including good friends and close family members, experience serious misfortune, suffer great pain, and perhaps die at an early age. They may have seen a spouse or a child suffer leukemia or some other form of cancer or debilitating disease. They have learned the value of time and opportunity. They better accept and comprehend their own mortality, the imperfections of this present world, and the inability of material things to give lasting, deep satisfaction. They have seen utopian ideas fail and have learned how short-lived and disappointing euphoric emotional experiences can be, even those—or perhaps especially those—that purport to be of a higher spiritual order.

Third, **older men** are to be **sensible.** They should have the discernment, discretion, and judgment that comes from walking with God for many years. They control their physical passions and they reject worldly standards and resist worldly attractions. Like Paul, by God's grace they "think so as to have sound judgment" (Rom. 12:3).

Fourth, **older men** are to be characterized by three positive attributes. They should be **sound in faith, in love, [and] in perseverance.**

Sound is from the same verb (*hugiainō*) used in the previous verse in regard to doctrine. It refers to that which is healthy, proper, whole, to that which is as it ought to be.

First of all, **older men** who have been through 50, 60, 70, or more years of life are to be **sound in faith,** having learned that God indeed can be trusted in every way. They do not question His wisdom or power or love, and they do not lose trust in His goodness and grace or lose confidence in His divine plan and divine wisdom. They do not doubt the truth or sufficiency of His Word or waver in their divinely assured hope that His sovereign plan will be fulfilled.

Second, **older men** are to be **sound . . . in love**—toward God, toward His people, and toward those who do not yet know Him. They **love** by bearing one another's burdens and thereby fulfilling the law of Christ (Gal. 6:2). They have learned to love when their love is not deserved and to continue loving when it is rejected and even when they suffer because of it. They lovingly forgive and they lovingly serve.

In his first letter to believers in the church at Corinth, Paul explained what godly love is and what it is not, what it does and what it does not do. "Love is patient, love is kind, and is not jealous; love does not brag and is not arrogant, does not act unbecomingly; it does not seek its own, is not provoked, does not take into account a wrong suffered, does not rejoice in unrighteousness, but rejoices with the truth; bears all things, believes all things, hopes all things, endures all things" (1 Cor. 13:4–7).

The godly older man believes and practices the truth that we are to "love one another, for love is from God; and everyone who loves is born of God and knows God" (1 John 4:7; cf. v. 11). He knows that "the one who does not love does not know God, for God is love" (v. 8) and that he has "passed out of death into life, because [he loves] the brethren" (3:14). He has come to know and believe "the love which God has for us," that God is love, and [that] the one who abides in love abides in God, and God abides in him" (4:16). He is not afraid, because "there is no fear in love; [and] perfect love casts out fear" (v. 18). He knows that he is able to love because the Lord "first loved us" (v. 19) and that the mark of our love for God is the keeping of "His commandments," which "are not burdensome" (5:3).

Third, **older men** are to be **sound . . . in perseverance.** They are to exhibit the ability to endure hardship, to accept disappointment and failure, to be satisfied despite thwarted personal desires and plans. They have learned to graciously live with such difficulties as physical weakness, loneliness, and being misunderstood and unappreciated. They do not lose heart when things do not turn out the way they had hoped and expected, but have the perfect confidence "that God causes all things to work together for good to those who love God, to those who are called according to His purpose" (Rom. 8:28).

OLDER WOMEN

Older women likewise are to be reverent in their behavior, not malicious gossips, nor enslaved to much wine, teaching what is good, that they may encourage the young women (2:3–4a)

Like older men, **older women** in the church are to be awarded special respect and deference because of their age. As noted above, "the first commandment with a promise" requires honor of both mother and father (Eph. 6:2; cf. Ex. 20:12), and the penalty under the old covenant for striking either parent was death (Ex. 21:15). Even when an **older** woman does something that is seriously wrong, she should be lovingly rebuked as a mother (1 Tim. 5:2).

In the passage just cited, Paul puts no qualification on such respect, which applies even to an older person who is immature and inconsiderate. When the apostle himself found it necessary to publicly reprove Euodia and Syntyche, he graciously urged them "to live in harmony in the Lord" and asked an unidentified "true comrade . . . to help these women who have shared my struggle in the cause of the gospel" (Phil. 4:2–3).

Paul does not specify the age a woman would have to be to qualify as **older.** But childbearing typically ends at about 40–45 years of age and, correspondingly, child-rearing ends at about 60–65. It therefore seems reasonable to take **older women** as referring to women that are at least 60 years old. That is the age that Paul mentions in his first letter to Timothy in regard to widows who qualified for being put on the list to receive financial support from the church (1 Tim. 5:9).

Such godly **older women** are a rich spiritual resource in the church and deserve special esteem and consideration. Paul therefore declared that a Christian widow more than 60 years old who had no family to support her and who "has fixed her hope on God, and continues in entreaties and prayers night and day," who was a faithful and godly wife and mother, and who "has shown hospitality to strangers, . . . washed the saints' feet, . . . assisted those in distress, and . . . devoted herself to every good work" not only should be honored by the church but financially supported as well (1 Tim. 5:3–10).

In New Testament times, **older women** served the church in numerous ways. As Paul mentions later in the present passage, a key function of older women was to teach and encourage younger women in the things of the Lord. They also ministered to each other and to women in the church of any age, single, married, or widowed. They visited the sick and those in prison. They provided hospitality to Christian travelers, especially those in some form of ministry.

In towns that were strongly pagan, Christian women would go through the streets and marketplaces searching for abandoned newborns who were unwanted and had been left to die by their parents. Since abortion was both dangerous and expensive and birth-control devices did not exist, an unwanted baby was simply abandoned at birth. Some male babies were raised to be slaves or gladiators, and some girls were trained for prostitution. Christian women who rescued these infants would give them to church families for adoption.

Paul states several qualities that should characterize **older women.** First, they **are to be reverent in their behavior. Reverent in . . . behavior** translates the single Greek word *hieroprepēs,* used only here in the New Testament. The word has the root meaning of being priestlike and came to refer to that which is appropriate to holiness. **Older women** are to be godly examples of holiness.

Anna illustrates such virtue. Having been "a widow to the age of eighty-four, . . . she [had] never left the temple, serving night and day with fastings and prayers" (Luke 2:37). Because she had lived so faithfully in the Lord, the Holy Spirit enabled her to immediately recognize the infant Jesus when Joseph and Mary brought Him to the temple. The moment she saw Him, "she came up and began giving thanks to God, and continued to speak of Him to all those who were looking for the redemption of Jerusalem" (v. 38).

Women who are **reverent in their behavior** "adorn themselves with proper clothing, modestly and discreetly, not with braided hair and gold or pearls or costly garments; but rather by means of good works, as befits women making a claim to godliness," and they "quietly receive instruction with entire submissiveness" (1 Tim. 2:9–11). They are women who, through the bearing of children, have removed the stigma of Eve's sin and have lived "in faith and love and sanctity with self-restraint" (v. 15).

Second, **older women** are **not [to be] malicious gossips.** They refuse to listen to, much less propagate, slanderous or demeaning words about others. Just as men are more inclined to abuse others physically, women are more inclined to abuse others verbally, which can be even more destructive.

Paul is not referring simply to unfavorable idle chatter about a person, bad as that is. **Malicious gossips** translates *diabolos,* which means "slanderer, or false accuser" and is used thirty-four times in the New Testament as a title of Satan, whom Jesus describes as "the father of lies" (John 8:44).

Third, **older women** are not to be **enslaved to much wine,** a strong phrase that refers to drunkenness. As many of them have done throughout history, older people on Crete sometimes turned to drink as a stimulant and a means of ameliorating the pains, frustrations, and loneliness of old age. *Douloō* means literally to be **enslaved,** "to be held and controlled against one's will," and addiction to **much wine** becomes more a prison than a means of escape. Worse still, an older believer who becomes so addicted brings dishonor to the Lord's name, sullies the reputation of the church, and, more often than not, leads others into following his or her ungodly example.

Fourth, and in a positive vein, **older women** are to be known for **teaching what is good.** *Kalodidaskalos* (**teaching what it good**) refers to instruction in that which is noble, excellent, and lofty. In this context, it includes the **teaching** of **what is** holy and godly. Having taught their own children well, older women now have the responsibility for **teaching** younger women in the church and encouraging them to also be righteous and godly wives and mothers (vv. 4–5).

That they may encourage the young women is the first of four purpose (*hina*) clauses in this passage (see also vv. 5, 8, 10). Older women are to teach and model godliness in order to **encourage the young women** in the church in the particular ways that Paul mentions here. *Sōphronizō* (to **encourage**) literally means "to cause someone to be of sound mind and to have self-control." It is closely related to the words translated "sensible" in 1:8 and 2:5 and "sensibly" in 2:12. A related noun in 1 Timothy 2:15, also applied to Christian women, is rendered "self-restraint." The subjunctive verb in the present text refers to helping others cultivate good judgment and sensibilities. It is therefore another form of teaching, which, when accepted and heeded, will **encourage** those who are taught, in this case, **young women.**

Although women are forbidden to teach or have authority over men (1 Tim. 2:12), they do have the God-given responsibility to formally and informally teach children, especially their own, and younger women in the church. When godly Christian women do not infuse the younger generation with the things of God, the church comes to dire straits.

YOUNG WOMEN

[encourage the young women] to love their husbands, to love their children, to be sensible, pure, workers at home, kind, being subject to their own husbands, that the word of God may not be dishonored. (2:4b–5)

Although Paul uses the term **young women,** it is clear from the context that he is here speaking only to wives, to **young women** who are married. It is not God's plan that all men or women marry. To some believers He gives the gift of singleness (cf. 1 Cor. 7:8–9, 17). But the apostle is here speaking first to *all* **young women** who are married

(v. 4b), then to those who have children, natural or adopted (v. 4c), and then again to all young wives (v. 5).

As already noted, in this passage Paul addresses two broad age categories of both men and women. Because older women would include those 60 years of age and older, **young women** therefore would include those of marriageable age until about 60.

No biblical standard is more viciously attacked today than the God-ordained role of women in society. And no passage is more ridiculed or reinterpreted by assailants within the church than these two verses.

As with many worldly influences, the feminist movement has made great inroads in the church, including the evangelical church. In the name of women's rights, the Word of God is dishonored as being sexist, chauvinistic, and unfairly limiting. Some feminists maintain that standards set forth in these and similar passages were culturally oriented to New Testament times or were simply Paul's personal beliefs. In either case, they are considered irrelevant and nonbinding for Christians today.

The God-ordained institutions of marriage and family, which are the primary foundation of a healthy society, are attacked as archaic and outrageous or, at best, unnecessary. Tragically, many unthinking, poorly taught Christians are seduced by feminist rhetoric into believing that traditional roles of women—in the family, in society, and in the church— are outdated and oppressive. The phrase "women's liberation" has an attractive, democratic ring, which, on the surface, seems reasonable and justified. It has special appeal, of course, to women who feel unappreciated, restricted, exploited, victimized, and trapped by the traditional roles and opportunities for women.

It should be understood that the basic tenets of feminism did not originate in modern society and were not produced simply by the self-centered ambitions of contemporary women who want to be free to be whatever they want to be and do whatever they want to do. Radical feminism is not uniquely a twentieth-century phenomenon nor the product of Western egalitarianism. The feminist agenda is ancient and, at root, satanic. It is a primeval heresy that is part of Satan's strategy to undermine and destroy God's plan for mankind. It began in the Garden of Eden, with Satan's temptation and Eve's rebellion, first against God and then against her husband. When she chose to follow her own independent way, she led the whole race into sin and made effective Satan's first ploy against marriage and the family.

The distinctions of headship and submission were ordained by God at Creation. As a consequence of Eve's disobedience to God's command and her failure to consult with Adam about the temptation, God told her, "Your desire shall be for your husband, and he shall rule over you" (Gen. 3:16). The desire spoken of here is not sexual or psychological, both of which Eve had for Adam before the Fall as his specially created helper. It is rather the same desire spoken of in the next chapter, where the same Hebrew word (t'shûqâ) is used. The term comes from an Arabic root that means "to compel, impel, urge, or seek control over." The Lord warned Cain, "Sin is crouching at your door; it *desires* to have you [that is, control you], but you must master it" (4:7 NIV; emphasis added). Sin wanted to master Cain, but God commanded Cain to master sin. The curse on Eve was that a woman's desire would henceforth be to usurp the place of man's headship and that he would resist that desire and even more strongly exercise his control over her. The Hebrew word here translated "rule" is not the same as that used in 1:28. Rather it represented a new, despotic kind of authoritarianism that was not in God's original plan for man's headship.

With the Fall and its curse came the distortion of woman's proper submissiveness and of man's proper authority. That is where the battle of the sexes began, where women's liberation and male chauvinism came into existence. Women have a sinful propensity to usurp men's authority, and men have a sinful propensity to put women under their feet. The divine decree that man would rule over woman in this way was part of God's curse on humanity, and it takes a manifestation of grace in Christ by the filling of the Holy Spirit to resolve the created order and harmony of proper submission in a relationship that has become corrupted and disordered by sin.

The core ideas of feminism, including reversal of sexual roles, are found in virtually all ancient religions, including the mother-god legends of Babylonian and Persian mythology. By New Testament times, the foremost proponent of feminism was Greek gnosticism (from the Greek *gnōsis,* "to know"), a general philosophical belief system that prided itself in its unique and superior knowledge about all matters of importance. Despite the attempts of some gnostics to incorporate their beliefs into Judaism and later into Christianity, gnosticism was a malevolent system designed by Satan that was anti-God, anti-Christ, and anti-biblical. In his outstanding book *The Gnostic Empire Strikes Back,* Peter Jones observes that "Gnosticism is a broad term to describe false anti-God religion developed before the birth of Christianity—as the meeting of the mysticism of the Eastern religions and the rationalism of the Greek west" ([Phillipsburg, N.J.: Presbyterian & Reformed, 1992], p. 15). The gnostics combined the humanistic musings of man's mind and the esoteric and fanciful notions of eastern mysticism to produce a hybrid, and purportedly superior, system of truth. But they succeeded only in developing a more sophisticated, and especially deceptive and dangerous, form of paganism.

In all genuinely gnostic literature, the creation of the physical universe is portrayed as an act of arrogant, foolish pride by a powerful but subordinate god who tragically corrupted the heretofore perfect universe of the spirit. A recently discovered ancient gnostic text depicts the creator god as being blind, ignorant, arrogant, the source of envy, and the father of death. Much ancient gnostic literature mocked the Creator God of Scripture with a disdain that bordered on contempt. But that sub-god, or demiurge, also somehow managed to endow the men he had created with a spark of divinity, which, when properly fanned, makes a person fully divine.

Ancient gnosticism also elevated women, considering Eve to have been a spirit-endowed woman who actually saved Adam *from* the bungling male deity called God. Similarly, salvation for all of mankind will be brought through female power. Dame Wisdom, the Heavenly Eve, was a mystical goddess who was the source of all wisdom. She was presumed to have entered the serpent in the Garden of Eden and instructed Eve in the ultimate wisdom of self-actualization and self-fulfillment, a wisdom she passed on to Adam. As Peter Jones observes, gnosticism took redemptive history and stood it on its head, like an upside-down satanist cross in a black mass.

Although gnosticism has taken many forms during its long history of deception, its core doctrine is the consubstantiality of the human self with God. Man's purpose is to make himself fully God, and the means to that end is elevation of self through developing self-esteem, self-knowledge, and self-realization. "It follows," comments Jones, "that part of self-redemption is the rejection of biblical norms and the promotion of the distortion of biblical sexuality" (p. 26).

In the mythology of gnosticism, the supreme deity is androgynous, that is, both male and female. But the female role is always supreme. Consequently, biblical sexual roles for mankind are reversed, and female dominance and lesbianism are exalted.

The modern heir of gnosticism is the New Age movement, which, like its ancient progenitor, has many forms and facets. But it has the same disdain for Scripture and the God of Scripture and the same elevation of self. As just noted, it also is characterized by female domination and lesbianism. Although Hinduism has many forms and countless gods and goddesses, many of its basic tenets are gnostic, and its supreme deity is a goddess.

Radical feminism, with its homosexuality, sexual freedom, and assault on gender differences and definitions of family, has strongly influenced major Christian denominations, as seen in the rapidly growing practice of ordaining women to the priesthood and pastorate and in the publishing of gender-neutral, and even female-deity, versions of the Bible. As already noted, such unbiblical ideas are not primarily the contrivance of women to make them feel better about themselves but are no less than satanic religion. (For a more complete treatment of this subject, see Jones, *The Gnostic Empire Strikes Back*, pp. 19–72.)

Roman Catholic theologian Carol Christ has written, "I found God in myself and I loved her fiercely." Peter Jones writes that New Age author Charlene Spretnak's book *The Politics of Women's Spirituality*

> is a call to bring to an end Judeo-Christian religion by a feminist movement nourished on goddess-worship paganism, and witchcraft that succeeds in overthrowing the global rule of men.
>
> Feminism is demanding revenge. Such a movement gets rid of certain expressions of unjustifiable male oppression, but its real ideological goal is to efface any recollection of creational structures. It is surprising that a non-Christian (at least he lays no claim to being a Christian in his books), once-feminist thinker, George Gilder, has (since 1973) recognized this ideological agenda whereas the thinking of so many Christians appears naively oblivious.

Gilder notes:

> The revolutionary members of the women's movement . . . say that our sexual relationships are fundamental to all other institutions and activities. If one could profoundly change the relations between the sexes, they contend, one could radically and unrecognizably transform the society. (Jones, p. 61)

That is exactly the kind of rebellion and resultant divine judgment of which Paul speaks:

> For the wrath of God is revealed from heaven against all ungodliness and unrighteousness of men, who suppress the truth in unrighteousness. . . . For even though they knew God, they did not honor Him as God, or give thanks; but they became futile in their speculations, and their foolish heart was darkened. Professing to be wise, they became fools, and exchanged the glory of the incorruptible God for an image in the form of corruptible man and of birds and four-footed animals and crawling creatures. Therefore God gave them over in the lusts of their hearts to impurity, that their bodies might be dishonored among them. For they exchanged the truth of God for a lie, and worshiped and served the creature rather than the Creator, who is blessed forever. Amen. For this reason God gave them over to degrading passions; for their women exchanged the natural function for that which is unnatural, and in the same way also the men abandoned the natural function of the woman and burned in their desire toward one another, men with men committing indecent acts and receiving in their own persons the due penalty of their error. And just as they did not see fit to acknowledge God any longer, God gave them over to a depraved mind, to do those things which are not proper. (Rom. 1:18, 21–28)

Sodom and Gomorrah did not survive homosexuality run rampant, nor did the Roman Empire.

How extremely different is God's plan. He has a magnificent and wonderful design for women. It is a design that will fulfill their created purpose, maximize their uniqueness, make them a blessing to the world, and bring fulfillment to their own lives and glory to God. That design is succinctly stated in Titus 2.

Paul continues by saying that, by their godly teaching and example, older women in the church are to **encourage the young women to love their husbands.** Paul is not speaking of romantic or sexual love, which certainly have a proper place in marriage, but of a committed **love** that godly wives choose to have for their husbands, just as godly husbands choose to have for their wives (Eph. 5:25, 28). *Philandros* is a noun, here rendered **to love . . . husbands,** and refers to willing, determined **love** that is not based on a husband's worthiness but on God's command and that is extended by a wife's affectionate and obedient heart. Even unlovable, uncaring, unfaithful, and ungrateful husbands are to be loved. This sort of **love** of husbands and wives for each other involves unqualified devotedness and is a friendship that is strong and deep.

If a wife does not truly love her husband, she must, in obedience to the Lord, train herself to love him. Contrary to popular thinking, love that is carefully built and nurtured is not artificial. It is much more common that spontaneous, "bells and whistles" romances prove to be the ones that are artificial and short-lived. The principle is reciprocal and applies equally to husbands.

Training yourself to love involves doing loving things for the other person, whether or not you feel like doing them. It involves putting their interests and welfare above your own. It involves sacrificial giving of yourself to others for their sakes, not for the sake of appreciation or returned love or favor. "For if you love those who love you," Jesus asked, "what reward have you? Do not even the tax-gatherers do the same?" (Matt. 5:46).

"Make my joy complete," Paul wrote believers at Philippi, "by being of the same mind, maintaining the same love, united in spirit, intent on one purpose. Do nothing from selfishness or empty conceit, but with humility of mind let each of you regard one another as more important than himself; do not merely look out for your own personal interests, but also for the interests of others" (Phil. 2:2–4). That general admonition to all Christians applies in a special way to Christian husbands and wives. When you sacrificially serve others, it becomes almost impossible *not* to love them. Where there is genuine practical love, genuine emotional love is sure to follow.

That is the opposite of what society is saying today to **young women,** who are not encouraged **to love their husbands** but rather to love and to follow their own way and to "love" whomever they want whenever they want. At best, marriage is held to be a matter of convenience and preference, which, when it becomes inconvenient and unpreferred, is abandoned.

This set of commands for **young women,** like those to the other groups in Titus 2, has immense and far-reaching ramifications for the kingdom. Even the most uneducated unbeliever can understand the meaning of what Paul is saying here.

The first command is simple and unambiguous: **Young women,** which in this context refers to young wives, are **to love their husbands.** There are no conditions or exceptions. It is not simply that love of **husbands** is a virtue but that not loving them is a sin.

Jesus said, "If you love Me, you will keep My commandments" (John 14:15), and "He who has My commandments and keeps them, he it is who loves Me; and he who loves Me shall be loved by My Father, and I will love him, and will disclose Myself to him" (14:21; cf. 15:10; 1 John 5:3). A healthy church will have a strong witness in the world because its members are obedient to the will of their Lord.

On the other hand, an unsaved person who sees professing Christians who have no concern about their own sin and who openly follow the world's standards instead of God's, can hardly be expected to see the need for his or her own salvation from sin. In particular, unsaved young women who see inconsistency and hypocrisy in their Christian counterparts will have little reason to love and be faithful to their husbands, or even to bother with marriage at all. Nor will they see the power of divine transformation and love at work.

Some people, including some evangelicals, point to Paul's declaration in Galatians that "there is neither male nor female" and claim that the apostle here teaches the total equality of the sexes. But equality in salvation, in spiritual standing before God, has no bearing on God's order for marriage and for church leadership. The same apostle who wrote those words to the Galatian churches also wrote this letter to Titus.

A new generation of young women has been brought up in a society, including an education system and media, that touts feminism and belittles biblical standards for men and women. In many cases, **young women** even in evangelical churches have not had the benefit of careful "teaching [of] what is good" (v. 3) or the godly example of older women in the church, including that of their own mothers. Nor have they been exposed to the clear teaching of Scripture in Sunday School, in youth group, or from the pulpit.

Second, **young women** who are mothers are to be encouraged **to love their children.** Whether the **children** are born to the couple or are adopted, they are to be loved with a love that, like the love of spouses for each other, should be selfless and sacrificial. As with love for their husbands, love for their children is not an option. It is not based on the children's physical attractiveness or personalities or intelligence but on their need. The most important responsibility of **love** for believing parents is to lead their **children** to a saving knowledge of Jesus Christ. But Paul's admonition here is inclusive. Young mothers are **to love their children** in *every* way—practical, physical, social, moral, and spiritual—with a **love** that has no conditions and no limits. This love, to be fully expressed, is extremely demanding as the mother seeks to fulfill her obligation to raise godly children (see 1 Tim. 2:15).

Third, married **young women** are **to be sensible.** This is the same quality that should characterize elders (1:8), all older men (2:2), and, in fact, all believers (2:12). Common sense and good judgment should improve with age, but they should be evident even in early adulthood.

Fourth, **young women** are to be **pure.** *Hagnos* (**pure**) refers primarily to moral purity, and, especially in this context, to sexual purity, marital faithfulness. Like older women, in fact like all Christian women, young wives are "to adorn themselves with proper clothing, modestly and discreetly, not with braided hair and gold or pearls or costly garments; but rather by means of good works, as befits women making a claim to godliness" (1 Tim. 2:9–10). "Modesty" refers to a healthy sense of shame at saying anything, doing anything, or dressing in any way that would cause a man to lust. "Discreetly" refers to moral control, to keeping passions, especially sexual passions, subdued.

Also addressing Christian women, Peter said,

> Let not your adornment be merely external—braiding the hair, and wearing gold jewelry, or putting on dresses; but let it be the hidden person of the heart, with the imperishable quality of a gentle and quiet spirit, which is precious in the sight of God. For in this way in former times the holy women also, who hoped in God, used to adorn themselves, being submissive to their own husbands. Thus Sarah obeyed Abraham, calling him lord, and you have become her children if you do what is right without being frightened by any fear. (1 Pet. 3:3–6)

Fifth, married **young women** are to be **workers at home.** One of the hardest things for many contemporary wives to do is be satisfied with being a homemaker. Part of the reason is that modern appliances and other conveniences greatly simplify and reduce housework, and time that is not used for something constructive inevitably produces boredom, dissatisfaction, and often increased temptations.

But the greatest pressure on young wives today is the saturation of our culture by the ungodly precepts of radical feminists, who believe that wives being homebound is an egregious form of bondage by males, from which all women need to be freed. They unequivocally insist that women should be as free as men to work outside the home at whatever job and to whatever extent they want.

For many years in the United States, more than 50 percent of mothers with children under six years of age have held jobs outside the home. For those with older children, the percentages are much higher. It is estimated that, by the year 2000, 90 percent of all women between the ages of 16 and 65 will have jobs outside the home. That trend is frightening even to many secular observers, who recognize the damage being done to young children who spend a large part of their time with and receive a large part of their training, or lack of training, from adults other than their parents. Statistics also make clear that extramarital affairs increase exponentially with women who work outside the home, simply because of greatly increased exposure to temptation. In addition to that, they often find themselves under the authority of a man other than their husband (cf. Eph. 5:22, especially the word "own) and in an environment that is antithetical to Christian standards of morality and sexual roles.

It is tragic that many young mothers are forced to hold outside jobs because their husbands have died, been imprisoned, or have left them and pay no child support, or because they have never been married and their own families are unable, or unwilling, to help. It is also tragic that many churches and Christian friends forsake their obligation to help young women who find themselves in such straits. And when the mother is away from home, younger children most often are cared for away from home. They need to be at home as much as possible and not be deprived of their mother's companionship and instruction.

Women who have no children or whose children are grown obviously have fewer obligations in the home and therefore much more time available, and the point is not so much that a woman's place is in the home as that her responsibility is for the home. She may have a reasonable outside job or choose to work in the church or to minister in a Christian organization, a hospital, a school, or many other ways. But the home is a wife's special domain and always should be her highest priority. That is where she is able to offer the most encouragement and support to her husband and is the best place for extending hospitality— to Christian friends, to unbelieving neighbors, and to visiting missionaries or other Christian workers.

In regard to being **workers at home,** young Christian wives today must take special care to be sensible, as they are admonished earlier in this verse. In consultation with their husbands, they must use good judgment in deciding how much time can justifiably and wisely be spent in activities outside the home, whether at a paying job or in some form of service. When they have a genuine desire to obey and honor the Lord in all things and to conscientiously seek guidance from His Word and in prayer, they can be assured that He will provide the necessary wisdom and resolution.

The true female victims today are not women who are willingly bound by love to the Lord, to their husbands, and to their children. The true victims are rather those women who have been deceived by unbiblical and satanic feminist ideas about being liberated from God and from the home.

The home is where a wife can provide the best expressions of love for her husband. It is where she teaches and guides and sets a godly example for her children. It is where she is protected from abusive and immoral relationships with other men and where, especially in our day, she still has greater protection from worldly influences—despite the many lurid TV programs, magazines, and other ungodly intrusions. The home is where she has special opportunity to show hospitality and devote herself to other good works. The home is where she can find authentic and satisfying fulfillment, as a Christian and as a woman.

Sixth, **young women** are to be **kind,** the meaning of which is obvious. They are to be gentle, considerate, amiable, congenial, and sympathetic, even with those who are undeserving and unkind to them. To be **kind** is to be godlike, "for [God] Himself," Jesus said, "is kind to ungrateful and evil men" (Luke 6:35). Similarly, Paul admonishes believers to "be kind to one another, tender-hearted, forgiving each other, just as God in Christ also has forgiven you" (Eph. 4:32).

Seventh, and finally, married **young women** are to be **subject to their own husbands.** Like all other Christian wives, they are to "be subject to [their] own husbands, as to the Lord. For the husband is the head of the wife, as Christ also is the head of the church, He Himself being the Savior of the body. But as the church is subject to Christ, so also the wives ought to be to their husbands in everything" (Eph. 5:22–24; cf. 1 Tim. 2:11–14).

Charles Spurgeon wrote the following beautiful tribute to his wife, Susannah:

> She delights in her husband, in his person, his character, his affection; to her, he is not only the chief and foremost of mankind, but in her eyes, he is all in all. Her heart's love belongs to him and to him only. He is her little world, her paradise, her choice treasure. She is glad to sink her individuality in him; she seeks no renown for herself; his honor is reflected upon her, and she rejoices in it. She will defend his name with her dying breath; safe enough is he where she can speak

for him. His smiling gratitude is all the reward she seeks. Even in her dress she thinks of him, and considers nothing beautiful which is distasteful to him.

He has many objects in life, some of which she does not quite understand; but she believes them all, and anything she can do to promote them, she delights to perform. Such a wife, as a true spouse, realizes the model marriage relation, and sets forth what our oneness with the Lord ought to be.

That the word of God may not be dishonored is the second of four purpose clauses in this passage (see also vv. 4, 8, 10). This one and the one in verse 10 focus on glorifying God's Word.

In his first letter to Timothy, Paul gives a similar admonition, with a negative objective, to young widows, whom he wanted "to get married, bear children, keep house, [in order to] give the enemy no occasion for reproach, for some have already turned aside to follow Satan" (1 Tim. 5:14–15; cf. 3:7; 6:1). Whenever and in whatever way Satan's will is accomplished, God's glory is tarnished and His **word** is **dishonored.**

Dishonored translates *blasphēmeō*, which means "to blaspheme or defame." William Kelley translates this phrase, "so that God's Word may suffer no scandal." Paul's point is that not only the evil things we say and we do, but also the good things that we fail to say and do, dishonor God and His Word before the church and before the world. Unbelievers judge the genuineness and value of our faith more by our living than by our theology. In doing so, they judge the truth and power of **the word of God** by the way in which we live. The world judges the gospel, which is the heart of **the word of God,** by the character of the people who believe and claim to be transformed by it. The nineteenth-century German philosopher Heinrich Heine said, "Show me your redeemed life and I might be inclined to believe in your Redeemer."

Many husbands have rejected **God** and mocked His **word** because of the ungodly behavior of a Christian wife who is not loving and submissive (cf. 1 Pet. 3:1–2). It is equally true, of course, that the hypocritical lives of Christian husbands, children, parents, and other relatives and friends have had, and continue to have, the same tragic effect.

Because of his adultery with Bathsheba and his causing her husband, Uriah, to be killed, the Lord said to David through the prophet Nathan, "Why have you despised the word of the Lord by doing evil in His sight? . . . Now therefore, the sword shall never depart from your house, because you have despised Me and have taken the wife of Uriah the Hittite to be your wife. . . . Behold, I will raise up evil against you from your own household" (2 Sam. 12:9–11). Even after David confessed and was forgiven, the Lord promised still greater punishment. "Because by this deed you have given occasion to the enemies of the Lord to blaspheme," Nathan explained, "the child also that is born to you shall surely die" (2 Sam. 12:14).

Paul excoriated unfaithful Israel, saying, "If you bear the name 'Jew,' and rely upon the Law, and boast in God, and know His will, and approve the things that are essential, being instructed out of the Law, and are confident that you yourself are a guide to the blind, a light to those who are in darkness, . . . you, therefore, who teach another, do you not teach yourself? . . . You who boast in the Law, through your breaking the Law, do you dishonor God? . . . For 'the name of God is blasphemed among the Gentiles because of you,' just as it is written'" (Rom. 2:17–19, 21, 23–24; cf. Isa. 52:5).

Because "the house of Israel [while] living in their own land, . . . defiled it by their ways and their deeds," the Lord reminded His people, "I scattered them among the nations, and they were dispersed throughout the lands. According to their ways and their deeds I judged them. When they came to the nations where they went, they profaned My holy name, because it was said of them, 'These are the people of the Lord; yet they have come out of His land'" (Ezek. 36:17, 19–20). Because Israel lived like immoral and ungodly pagans, their true and holy God was despised, held in derision, and thought to be no more righteous or powerful than the false and debauched pagan gods.

The positive concern that corresponds to living so as not to dishonor God and His Word, and thereby put a barrier between the unsaved and the gospel, is that of living so as to attract the unsaved to our gracious Lord.

Jesus commands His followers: "Let your light shine before men in such a way that they may see your good works, and glorify your Father who is in heaven" (Matt. 5:16). Paul said of believers in Corinth, "You are our letter, written in our hearts, known and read by all men; being manifested that you are a letter of Christ, cared for by us, written not with ink, but with the Spirit of the living God, not on tablets of stone, but on tablets of human hearts" (2 Cor. 3:3). Whether they intend to be or not, Christians are "living letters" of Christ and sometimes are the only testimony to the Lord and to His saving gospel that the world has.

There seems to be an almost limitless number of strategies, methodologies, and techniques that have been developed to win people to Jesus Christ. In most cases, the goal is noble and the desire is admirable. And although our human ideas, methods, and planning have a proper place in the work of Christ's church, they must always be consistent with and subordinate to the foundational requirements and principles for evangelism that God sets forth in His Word. Those include a clear proclamation of every man's innate sinfulness and lostness and his need for salvation, which can be attained only through faith in the atoning, substitutionary work of Jesus Christ, who paid the full penalty for sin and whose righteousness is credited to the penitent and forgiven believer.

The only platform from which Christians are to so preach and witness is a transformed life marked by godly virtue. We are to live in a way that will "prove [ourselves] to be blameless and innocent, children of God above reproach in the midst of a crooked and perverse generation, among whom [we are to] appear as lights in the world" (Phil. 2:15). As children of God, we should be godly, just as He commands: "You shall be holy, for I am holy" (1 Pet. 1:16). We "are a chosen race, a royal priesthood, a holy nation, a people for God's own possession, that [we] may proclaim the excellencies of Him who has called [us] out of darkness into His marvelous light" (1 Pet. 2:9).

For a person to be convinced that God can save him from sin, he needs to be shown someone who has been saved from sin and who, as far as possible, lives a life separated from sin. For a person to be convinced of God's hope, he must be shown someone who has hope where there was once despair. For a person to be convinced that God can miraculously provide us with love, peace, and happiness, he needs to be shown someone who now radiates those blessings.

The Character of a Healthy Church—part 2

Likewise urge the young men to be sensible; in all things show yourself to be an example of good deeds, with purity in doctrine, dignified, sound in speech which is beyond reproach, in order that the opponent may be put to shame, having nothing bad to say about us. (2:6–8)

As with young women, the general age group for young men would be from marriageable age to 60 years old or so.

EXHORTATION

Likewise urge the young men to be sensible; in all things (2:6–7a)

Urge translates *parakaleō,* which means "to strongly entreat someone." As in verses 2 and 5, **sensible** carries the broad meaning of having common sense, good judgment, and self-control. Just as older men and young women are to be **sensible,** so **likewise** are **young men.**

Paul exhorted his young friend Timothy to "flee from youthful lusts, and pursue righteousness, faith, love and peace, with those who call on the Lord from a pure heart" (2 Tim. 2:22). Peter commands young men to "be subject to your elders; and all of you, clothe yourselves with humility toward one another, for God is opposed to the proud, but gives grace to the humble" (1 Pet. 5:5).

The phrase **in all things** properly belongs at the end of verse 6. It refers to being **sensible** and emphasizes the broad scope of this admonition. **Young men,** who frequently are impulsive, passionate, ambitious, volatile, and sometimes arrogant, are to exercise self-control and show good sense and judgment **in all things.**

"Everyone who competes in the games exercises self-control in all things," Paul reminded believers in Corinth. "They then do it to receive a perishable wreath, but we an imperishable" (1 Cor. 9:25). Because self-control is so important in living for and serving the Lord, even that great apostle, after many years of faithful, sacrificial service to his Lord, went on to say of himself, "Therefore, I run in such a way, as not without aim; I box in such a way, as not beating the air; but I buffet my body and make it my slave, lest possibly, after I have preached to others, I myself should be disqualified" (1 Cor. 9:26–27).

Self-control, a synonym for **sensible,** is a fruit of the Spirit (Gal. 5:23). With the Spirit's help, therefore, **young men,** like all other believers, are enabled to master all areas of their lives in a way that is pleasing to the Lord.

THE EXAMPLE

show yourself to be an example of good deeds, with purity in doctrine, dignified, sound in speech which is beyond reproach, (2:7b–8a)

Having given a general admonition for Titus to pass on to other young men under his care in Crete, Paul then gives that young spiritual leader a personal charge to **show [himself] to be an example** for them, as well as for all other believers in the churches, to follow. He was to confront them not only with spiritual words but with a spiritual life that corresponded to those words. Even the most forceful and compelling counsel will fall on deaf ears if the one who gives it fails to live by it.

Tupos (**example**) literally refers to a mark or impression left by an instrument such as a pen, a sword, or a hammer. Thomas refused to believe that Jesus was raised from the dead unless he saw "in His hands the imprint [*tupos*] of the nails" (John 20:25). It also came to be used figuratively of a pattern, mold, model, or copy of the original of something, whether a physical object, such as a statute, or a principle or virtue.

If **example** does not follow advice, the one giving it will be viewed rightly as a hypocrite, and hypocrisy never promotes righteousness, no matter how sound and biblical a person's teaching and counsel may be. Others may be inclined to accept the principles intellectually but will see no reason for living by them, and will themselves, like their teacher, become hypocrites.

Jesus' harshest words were to religious hypocrites. To some Pharisees and scribes in Jerusalem, He said, "You hypocrites, rightly did Isaiah prophesy of you, saying, 'This people honors Me with their lips, but their heart is far away from Me'" (Matt. 15:7–8). When another group of Pharisees tried to trick Him into treason, "Jesus perceived their malice, and said, 'Why are you testing Me, you hypocrites?'" (Matt. 22:18). The evil effect of their hypocrisy went far beyond their own lives. "Woe to you, scribes and Pharisees, hypocrites," the Lord castigated them, "because you shut off the kingdom of heaven from men; for you do not enter in yourselves, nor do you allow those who are entering to go in" (Matt. 23:13). Hypocrites "say things," He said, but "do not do them" (Matt. 23:3).

In his sorrowful meeting with the Ephesian elders on the seashore near Miletus, Paul gave them the parting advice to "help the weak and remember the words of the Lord Jesus, that He Himself said, 'It is more blessed to give than to receive'" (Acts 20:35b). We can be sure that his counsel was taken fully to heart by those men. He reminded them—doubtless unnecessarily—that, while he was among them, he had "coveted no one's silver or gold or clothes. You yourselves know," he continued, "that these hands ministered to my own needs and to the men who were with me. In everything I showed you [these principles] by working hard in this manner [myself]" (vv. 33–35a).

With perfect confidence, the apostle could exhort believers at Corinth to "be imitators of me, just as I also am of Christ" (1 Cor. 11:1; cf. 4:16) and the brethren in Philippi to "join in following my example, and observe those who walk according to the pattern you have in us" (Phil. 3:17). In his second letter to the church at Thessalonica, he said, "We [did not] eat anyone's bread without paying for it, but with labor and hardship we kept working night and day so that we might not be a burden to any of you" (2 Thess. 3:8). It was "not because we do not have the right to this," he went on to explain, "but in order to offer ourselves as a model for you, that you might follow our example" (v. 9). Paul did not want to give even the appearance of using his ministry as a means to financial gain or of his life being in the least way inconsistent with his teaching (cf. 1 Thess. 5:22).

Consistency of life with teaching is perhaps the most important aspect of effective spiritual leadership. The writer of Hebrews could confidently admonish his readers to imitate "those who led you, who spoke the word of God to you," because the conduct of those leaders corresponded to their counsel (Heb. 13:7). Paul informed Timothy that the surest way to overcome the perceived disadvantage of his youthfulness was to make sure that, "in speech, conduct, love, faith and purity," he showed himself "an example of those who believe" (1 Tim. 4:12). Members of the church at Ephesus might resist the bare words that he taught, but they could not deny the power of the truths that were faithfully exemplified in his life. If his *speech* in daily living, not just "from the pulpit," was godly; if the *conduct* of his personal life was moral and self-less; if his *love* for the Lord and for fellow believers was genuine; if his *faith* was manifested in genuine trust in the Lord; and if his life was characterized by moral *purity;* he could be sure that his ministry would be effective, that it would be blessed and bear fruit.

There were several categories in which exemplary behavior was to be manifest. First, Titus was to be **an example** in doing **good deeds.** *Kalos* (**good**) does not refer to that which is superficial or cosmetic but to what is genuinely and inherently **good,** righteous, noble, and excellent. Titus's **deeds** were to be true reflections of what he preached and taught. Christians are the Lord's divine workmanship and are "created in Christ Jesus for good works, which God prepared beforehand, that we should walk in them" (Eph. 2:10).

Second, Titus was to be an example of **purity in doctrine.** Perhaps Paul was urging this young elder to make sure that he preached pure, orthodox **doctrine,** which he has already mentioned in 1:9 and 2:1. On the other hand, there may be another explanation. *Aphthoria* (**purity**) is a negative form of a term that carries the basic idea of being morally corrupt and vile, which in extrabiblical literature was often used of morally depraved people such as rapists, seducers, and abortionists. A related form of the word is used by Peter, who says that false teachers promise "freedom while they themselves are slaves of *corruption;* for by what a man is overcome, by this he is enslaved" (2 Pet. 2:19, emphasis added). Paul may have used this term to admonish Titus to live a life of moral **purity** that corresponds to the pure **doctrine** that he proclaimed.

Third, Titus was to set the example of a **dignified** life, a serious life that is fixed on God and honors whatever honors Him. As noted previously in relation to older men (v. 2), being **dignified** does not preclude a sense of humor, laughter, or enjoyment. It does mean that they should be able to distinguish between that which is important and that which is trivial.

Fourth, Titus was to set an example by being **sound in speech that is beyond reproach. Sound** is the same word (*hugiainō*) that is found in verse 1 and has the basic meaning of "being well, healthy, and whole." *Logos* (**speech**) is often translated "word" and frequently refers to the Word of God, both written Scripture (see, e.g., Mark 7:13; Rev. 1:2, 9) and the living Christ (see, e.g., John 1:1; Rev. 19:13). But the Greek term has a number of other connotations, including those of "talk" and "language." In Ephesians 4:29 it is rendered "word," referring to conversation, and in Ephesians 6:19 as "utterance."

The issue here is not doctrine or theology but conversation, day-by-day **speech.** Titus's speaking, whether formal teaching or informal conversation, was to be **sound,** healthy, edifying, life-giving, appropriate, and **beyond reproach.** Such virtuous and consistent conversation is surely the mark of a genuinely spiritual man.

The writer of Ecclesiastes says, "Rejoice, young man, during your childhood, and let your heart be pleasant during the days of young manhood. And follow the impulses of your heart and the desires of your eyes. Yet know that God will bring you to judgment for all these things" (Eccles. 11:9). The guard against foolishness and sinfulness is to "remember also your Creator in the days of your youth, before the evil days come and the years draw near when you will say, 'I have no delight in them'" (12:1).

THE EFFECT

in order that the opponent may be put to shame, having nothing bad to say about us. (2:8b)

The phrase **in order that the opponent may be put to shame** is the second purpose clause in this passage that reflects a reason for such high standards of holy living (see also vv. 5, 10) and refers back to the admonitions in verses 2–8a. The godly lives of older men, older women, young women, and young men all have, as part of their purpose, the putting **to shame** of the critics of Christ, His church, and His people. The opponents on Crete obviously included the "many rebellious men, empty talkers and deceivers, especially those of the circumcision" whom Paul mentions in 1:10.

When an **opponent** makes a rash, unfounded charge against a believer, the obvious and public testimony of that believer's life should be so commonly known that the accuser is embarrassed by his false criticism.

The true effectiveness of evangelism does not come from man-made methods, strategy, or marketing techniques adapted from the culture, but from the genuine virtue, moral purity, and godliness of be-lievers whose lives give proof of the truth of God's Word and the power of Christ to redeem men from sin. That is what silences the critics and makes the gospel believable.

It is for that reason that Peter admonished believers to "abstain from fleshly lusts" for the sake of their own spiritual well-being, because those lusts "wage war against the soul" (1 Pet. 2:11). He then urges them to "keep [their] behavior excellent among the Gentiles" for the sake of those to whom and before whom they witness, "so that in the thing in which they slander you as evildoers, they may on account of your good deeds, as they observe them, glorify God in the day of visita-tion" (v. 12; cf. 2:15). He means that, when the Lord returns, they will be among those who glorify God because they have come to salvation through the testimony of godly saints (cf. Matt. 5:16).

When an unbeliever criticizes us, our righteous living should make it clear that he really has **nothing bad to say about us.** Hopefully our godly testimony will arouse his curiosity, then his consideration, and ultimately his receiving Christ as Savior and Lord.

Us may simply refer to Christians in general, because people of-ten judge a local church, or the Christian faith, by what they know about Christians. But it seems likely in this context that Paul includes himself in this **us.** All believers on Crete, and doubtless a large number of un-believers as well, knew of Paul's close association with Titus. Therefore, if Titus did not lead an exemplary spiritual life, his failure would reflect negatively on the apostle as well. And, on the other hand, Titus's faithful living would also reflect positively on the noble apostle.

SLAVES/EMPLOYEES

Urge bondslaves to be subject to their own masters in every-thing, to be well-pleasing, not argumentative, not pilfering, but showing all good faith that they may adorn the doctrine of God our Savior in every respect. (2:9–10)

Unlike the first four, the fifth category of believers about which Paul admonishes Titus is not based on age but on social standing. *Dou-loi* (**bondslaves**) refers to slaves, those who were owned and con-trolled by **their own masters.**

The Roman Empire depended on bondslaves for most of its la-bor, and they were an essential part of society and the economy. Many, if not most, slaves were abused and often brutalized. For even minor in-fractions, or simply for displeasing their owners in some way, they could be severely beaten or killed. Many of them, however, were given great responsibility and authority in running a household and some-times a family farm or other business. Some of them—frequently those who were captured in war—were highly educated and cultured, in many cases having superior education to that of their owners. Slaves were al-lowed to marry and raise their own families, their children becoming slaves like their parents. A slave sometimes was given a small parcel of land on which to grow crops to feed his family and perhaps earn a small income.

But Paul does not address the condition of slavery. He offers no judgment about its basic fairness or morality. He simply recognizes that it exists and deals with the attitude that Christian **bondslaves** should have toward **their own masters,** whether those **masters** were believ-ers or unbelievers.

Although slavery was carefully regulated under Mosaic law, nei-ther the Old nor New Testaments condemns slavery as such. Social strata are recognized and even designed by God for man's good. Some people will be served and some will serve others. That is the nature of human society. How they treat each other is what concerns God. Slave/master relationships and responsibilities are dealt with much as those of employer/employee, and both testaments give considerable instruction about God's plan for these relationships and associated responsibili-ties. As I have written in the *Ephesians* volume in this New Testament commentary series,

> Although slavery is not uniformly condemned in either the Old or New Testaments, the sincere application of New Testament truths has repeatedly led to the elimination of its abusive tendencies. Where Christ's love is lived in the power of His Spirit, unjust barriers and rela-tionships are inevitably broken down. As the Roman empire disinte-grated and eventually collapsed, the brutal, abused system of slavery collapsed with it—due in great measure to the influence of Christian-ity. In more recent times the back of the black slave trade was broken in Europe and America due largely to the powerful, Spirit-led preach-ing of such men as John Wesley and George Whitefield and the godly statesmanship of such men as William Wilberforce and William Pitt.
>
> New Testament teaching does not focus on reforming and re-structuring human systems, which are never the root cause of human problems. The issue is always the heart of man—which when wicked will corrupt the best of systems and when righteous will improve the worst. If men's sinful hearts are not changed, they will find ways to op-press others regardless of whether or not there is actual slavery. On the other hand, Spirit-filled believers will have just and harmonious rela-tionships with each other, no matter what system they live under. Man's basic problems and needs are not political, social, or economic but spiritual. . . .

Throughout history, including in our own day, working people have been oppressed and abused by economic intimidation that amounts to virtual slavery—regardless of the particular economic, social, or political system. Paul's teaching therefore applies to every business owner and every worker. ([Chicago: Moody, 1986], p. 324. For additional treatment of biblical teaching about slavery, see pp. 323–28 in that volume.)

Nowhere in Scripture is rebellion or revolution justified in order to gain freedom, opportunity, or economic, social, or political rights. The emphasis is rather on the responsibility of slaves to serve their human masters faithfully and fully, in order to reflect the transforming power of God in their lives.

In his letter to the church at Ephesus, Paul wrote unambiguously, "Slaves, be obedient to those who are your masters according to the flesh, with fear and trembling, in the sincerity of your heart, as to Christ; not by way of eyeservice, as men-pleasers, but as slaves of Christ, doing the will of God from the heart" (Eph. 6:5–6). After giving similar instruction to believers at Colossae (Col. 3:22–23), the apostle added, "knowing that from the Lord you will receive the reward of the inheritance. It is the Lord Christ whom you serve" (v. 24). And to Timothy he wrote, "Let all who are under the yoke as slaves regard their own masters as worthy of all honor so that the name of God and our doctrine may not be spoken against" (1 Tim. 6:1).

For many Christians today, as throughout church history, the most important and fertile field for evangelism is the place where they work. That is their mission field. As in almost no other place, unbelievers have the opportunity to observe believers in day-by-day situations and activities. They see whether the believer is patient or impatient, kind or uncaring, selfless or selfish, honest or dishonest, clean or vulgar in his talk. They have the opportunity to see how well the Christian lives up to the faith he professes and the principles of the Scripture he claims to hold dear. Inviting unsaved friends to church certainly has a place in witnessing for Christ, but it will be useless and even counterproductive if one's attitude, reliability, and honesty on the job are questionable.

As Paul points out in the passages just cited above, the primary purpose for working hard and for respecting our employer, even more than leading someone to faith, is to bring honor to Christ. And our most important compensation is not the possible praise or increase in pay we may receive from our employer but the assured reward that we will receive from our Lord. He is the One who determines and assures what the eternal compensation will be (cf. Rev. 20:12–13).

In Titus 2:9–10 Paul gives five character qualities that should distinguish every **bondslave** and every other believer who is employed by someone else. As clearly indicated from the apostle's comments in the above passages from Ephesians, Colossians, and 1 Timothy, these characteristics are to be genuine and from the heart, and are to be without reservation, not superficial or hypocritical.

SUBMISSIVE

Urge bondslaves to be subject to their own masters in everything, (2:9a)

First, Christian workers are to be submissive, **subject to their own masters,** their own employers. *Hupotassō* (**to be subject to**) was often used by the military to designate a soldier's relationship to his superior officers. The relationship is not conditional or optional but an absolute and inescapable given.

In God's sight, the obligation of Christian workers to their bosses is just as unconditional and universal. **To be subject to** translates a passive imperative verb, and is therefore a command to submit oneself. Regardless of how unreasonable a boss may be or how oppressive a work situation may be, the faithful believer willingly submits himself **in everything** as long as he is employed in that job. If a situation becomes intolerable, he should look for work elsewhere.

Proper submission to authority is essential in a family, in which children are subject to their parents (Eph. 6:1; Col. 3:20). It is essential in government, in which citizens are to respect and honor their leaders (Rom. 13:1–7; Titus 3:1). It also is essential in the work place. A Christian worker who is first of all concerned about his personal rights and who participates in noncompliance efforts and work stoppages against his employer dishonors God.

Masters translates *despotēs,* from which we get the English "despot," which denotes a person with absolute authority and power. If **bondslaves** are obligated to submit to **their** absolute and often cruel and arbitrary **masters,** how much more are "free" believers obligated to submit to an employer, even one who is mean, unreasonable, and overbearing (cf. 1 Pet. 2:18–19).

COMMITTED TO EXCELLENCE

to be well-pleasing, (2:9b)

Second, a Christian worker should **be well-pleasing,** committed to excellence in his work. **Well-pleasing** translates *euarestos,* which, in the New Testament, is almost always used of being acceptable and pleasing to God. Paul urges believers "to present your bodies a living and holy sacrifice, acceptable to God, which is your spiritual service of worship. And do not be conformed to this world, but be transformed by the renewing of your mind, that you may prove what the will of God is, that which is good and acceptable and perfect" (Rom. 12:1–2). Later in that letter, he says that whoever has "righteousness and peace and joy in the Holy Spirit . . . serves Christ [and] is acceptable to God and approved by men" (14:17–18). It was always the apostle's "ambition, whether at home or absent, to be pleasing to Him [Christ]" (2 Cor. 5:9). He declared that the sacrificial giving of Philippian believers was "a fragrant aroma, an acceptable sacrifice, well-pleasing to God" (Phil. 4:18). It should be the purpose of every Christian "to learn [and to believe and to do] what is pleasing to the Lord" (Eph. 5:10).

Even in the workplace, Christ is our ultimate overseer, and in His Word He makes clear that being well-pleasing to our heavenly Master includes being **well-pleasing** to our earthly **master,** or boss. Some Christians reason that, if their employer is a Christian, they have less obligation to respect and please him, because we "are all one in Christ Jesus" (Gal. 3:28). But equality in the spiritual realm does not translate to equality in the earthly. "Let those who have believers as their masters not be disrespectful to them because they are brethren," Paul says, "but let them serve them all the more, because those who partake of the benefit are believers and beloved" (1 Tim. 6:1–2).

It is not wrong to work hard, do excellent work, and seek to please our employer in order to advance in a company and increase our income. In the right spirit, those motives are legitimate. But they should never be a Christian's highest objectives. Above all else—far above all else—should be the sincere desire, even on the job, to do that which is pleasing and acceptable to our Lord.

RESPECTFUL

not argumentative, (2:9c)

Third, a Christian worker should be respectful to his employer in such a way that he is **not argumentative.** *Antilegō* (to be **argumentative**) means literally "to speak against," in the sense of talking back or contradicting. It carries the ideas of "mouthing off," of being contentious or obstructionist—at least partly, if not entirely, just for the sake of being disagreeable. Being **argumentative** is the opposite of being submissive and well-pleasing.

Paul used the same verb in 1:9 in regard to church members who want to contradict sound teaching. In Romans 10:21, the word is translated "obstinate." And in Pisidian Antioch, when Jewish leaders saw that "many of the Jews and of the God-fearing [Gentile] proselytes followed Paul and Barnabas," and that "nearly the whole city assembled to hear the word of God . . . they were filled with jealousy, and began *contradicting* the things spoken by Paul, and were blaspheming" (Acts 13:43–45, emphasis added).

The noun form (*antilogia*) of that verb is rendered twice in the book of Hebrews as "dispute" (6:16; 7:7). Later in that letter it is used of the "hostility" that Christ endured "by sinners against Himself" (12:3), and it is used by Jude in referring to the "rebellion of Korah" against Moses (Jude 11; cf. Num. 16).

In our day of self-centeredness and self-elevation, being **argumentative** is almost a way of life for some people, including, unfortunately, some Christians. The prohibition does not refer to standing up for our convictions, for what we believe is right, proper, and God-honoring, but rather to standing up merely for our own self-interest and preferences.

If a worker has opportunity to express his opinions in a proper forum, that is certainly permissible. Workers today obviously have legitimate means for expressing grievances to an employer that slaves of New Testament times could not have imagined. We have many more appropriate means for doing so than workers in free societies even a century ago. But when management makes a final decision, that decision should be accepted and fully complied with by workers, no matter how disappointing and unfair it may appear to be. As already noted, if a policy or requirement is too onerous, involves doing something immoral or unbiblical, or in any other way is unacceptable to our conscience, the only permissible alternative at that point is to find another place of employment.

HONEST

not pilfering, (2:10a)

Fourth, a Christian worker is to show honesty by **not pilfering.** **Pilfering** (from *nophizō*) literally means "to put aside for oneself or misappropriate" and came to be used of stealing by embezzlement.

Because household stewards, or business managers, in New Testament times were frequently slaves, they had considerable opportunity to misappropriate money, food, jewelry, or other valuables entrusted to their care. In modern times, many workers have access to company funds and property that is easily converted to personal use. Many others pilfer by such means as submitting inflated time sheets and expense reports, taking office supplies home for personal use, making unauthorized calls on the office phone, and taking unauthorized trips in the company car. When Christians do such things, their actions not only are unethical and damage their employer financially but also are unspiritual and do damage to the Lord's name and to their testimony.

In effect, Ananias and Sapphira embezzled money that belonged to the church, and therefore to the Lord. After selling a piece of property, they gave only part of the proceeds to the apostles but claimed they had given the full amount. As Peter explained to Ananias, they were not obligated to sell the property or to give any of the proceeds to the Lord's work. But by giving less than they claimed, they lied not only to men but to God (Acts 5:1–4). Their deception amounted to **pilfering** and was so serious in the Lord's eyes that it cost the couple their lives and caused "great fear [to] came upon the whole church, and upon all who heard of these things" (vv. 5–11).

LOYAL

but showing all good faith (2:10b)

Fifth, **showing all good faith** describes that most cherished virtue of loyalty. *Pistos* can be translated **faith,** but in this context it seems preferable to render it as "faithfulness," referring to faithfully doing whatever work a believer is supposed to do. It refers to trustworthiness and reliability, the quality of being utterly dependable, even when one is not being watched by the master or the employer.

Showing is from *endeiknumi,* which means "to show forth for the purpose of demonstrating or proving something." The Christian employee is not to leave his loyalty in doubt but is to give ample evidence of it. Tragically, **good faith** loyalty to one's employer, and to one's fellow employees, is a common casualty of the modern "work ethic," even that of some Christians.

THE RESULT

that they may adorn the doctrine of God our Savior in every respect. (2:10c)

This last clause in verse 10 is the third purpose clause in this passage that gives a reason for such a call to holy living (see also vv. 5,

8) and, like the one in verse 5, focuses on honoring and glorifying God's Word.

Adorn is from *kosmeō,* from which we get "cosmetics," the vast array of substances, both natural and artificial, that women (and men) use to make themselves more physically attractive. The root idea of the term is that of arranging something in proper order to give it symmetry, comeliness, and beauty. In ancient times it was used of arranging jewels in a brooch, necklace, ring, or crown in a way that best displayed the beauty of the gems.

Paul of course, was not speaking about physical and superficial adornment. What makes the church attractive and influential in the world for the Lord is not its strategy or its programs but the virtue and holiness of its people. His people therefore are to **adorn the doctrine of God our Savior** by their submissiveness, by the excellence of their work, by their respectful attitude, by their honesty, and by their loyal service to their employer—whether he is a fellow Christian or a rank pagan, fair or unfair, pleasant or unpleasant, deserving or undeserving.

Our supreme message to the unsaved about **God** is that He is **our Savior** and desires to be their **Savior** as well, because He is "not wishing for any to perish but for all to come to repentance" (2 Pet. 3:9). We are to let them know—by what we say, by what we do, and by the way we work at our job—that God "is a rewarder of those who seek Him" (Heb. 11:6).

Saving Grace

7

For the grace of God has appeared, bringing salvation to all men, instructing us to deny ungodliness and worldly desires and to live sensibly, righteously and godly in the present age, looking for the blessed hope and the appearing of the glory of our great God and Savior, Christ Jesus; who gave Himself for us, that He might redeem us from every lawless deed and purify for Himself a people for His own possession, zealous for good deeds. (2:11–14)

Actors, musicians, athletes, entertainers, politicians, and other celebrities who have achieved exceptional media exposure, popularity, or success often are called *stars.* Because they have risen to great prominence in their fields, they stand out brightly in the world's eyes and are accorded great acclaim and deference. Most of those stars, however, are far from being luminaries in God's sight.

In Daniel's final vision, the angel said to him, "Those who have insight will shine brightly like the brightness of the expanse of heaven, and those who lead the many to righteousness, like the stars forever and ever" (Dan. 12:3). Daniel himself was such a star of righteousness, as were Noah, Abraham, Sarah, Moses, Rahab, and all the other godly men

2:11–14   TITUS

and women of the Old Testament who gained God's approval through their faith (Heb. 11:4–39). A few of them, such as Moses and David, also achieved worldly prominence. But often the lives of those ancient saints, including Moses and David, were characterized much less by worldly success than by physical weakness, torture, mocking, scourging, chains, imprisonment, affliction, destitution, and even execution (vv. 34–37). The world considered them unworthy of respect or admiration. But in God's sight "the world was not worthy" of them (v. 38).

Those who hold to divine truth and have divine wisdom are able to discern the sinfulness, hopelessness, and futility of the world's wisdom and standards. Because they choose God's way above man's, they not only live righteously themselves but also "lead the many to righteousness." And for their faithfulness they "will shine brightly like the brightness of the expanse of heaven, . . . like the stars forever and ever."

Speaking of John the Baptist, the angel declared to his father Zacharias that "he will be great in the sight of the Lord, and he will drink no wine or liquor; and he will be filled with the Holy Spirit, while yet in his mother's womb. And he will turn back many of the sons of Israel to the Lord their God. And it is he who will go as a forerunner before Him in the spirit and power of Elijah, to turn the hearts of the fathers back to the children, and the disobedient to the attitude of the righteous; so as to make ready a people prepared for the Lord" (Luke 1:15–17). In the final verse of his letter, James assures us that any believer "who turns a sinner from the error of his way will save his [the sinner's] soul from death, and will cover a multitude of sins" (James 5:20). It should be our constant purpose to "prove [ourselves] to be blameless and innocent, children of God above reproach in the midst of a crooked and perverse generation, among whom [we are to] appear as lights in the world" (Phil. 2:15). Those who follow the instructions in vv. 2–10 and are godly in this life will become heavenly luminaries in the life to come.

The promise given through Daniel is based on character, not accomplishment. It is faithful believers who know, live, and reflect God's redeeming truth so that others are led to belief who will shine like stars forever in His heavenly kingdom. It is God's gracious plan to demonstrate His saving power through His saved people. Just as "the Son of Man has come to seek and to save that which was lost" (Luke 19:10), so should the purpose be of those whom the Son has already sought and saved. The sovereign purpose of all exhortations to holy living in Scripture is to honor and glorify God through the righteous living of His people, leading to the salvation of more sinners.

Paul wanted to reinforce this central reality of redemptive purpose and therefore culminates this practical instruction with a monumental section about the saving work of God. He begins where we should always begin—with **the grace of God.** God's **grace** is His un-merited favor toward wicked, unworthy sinners, by which He delivers them from condemnation and death. But **the grace of God** is more than a divine attribute; it is a divine Person, Jesus Christ. Jesus Christ not only was God incarnate but was **grace** incarnate. He Himself personifies and expresses **the grace of God,** the sovereign, eternal, and unmerited divine gift of Him who **has appeared, bringing salvation to all men.**

Has appeared is from *epiphainō,* which carries the meaning of coming to light, especially that of becoming manifest in a way that previously was unseen. Jesus brought God's saving purpose out of the shadows, as it were, into full light. God "has saved us, and called us with a holy calling," Paul reminded Timothy, "not according to our works, but according to His own purpose and grace which was granted us in Christ Jesus from all eternity, but now has been revealed by the *appearing* of our Savior Christ Jesus, who abolished death, and brought life and immortality to light through the gospel" (2 Tim. 1:9–10, emphasis added). As Paul again declares later in this letter to Titus, it was in the very person of Jesus Christ that salvation appeared. "When the *kindness* of God our Savior and His *love* for mankind appeared, *He* saved us" (3:4–5, emphasis added). He not only was **grace** incarnate, but also love and kindness incarnate.

As the godly Simeon took the infant Jesus in his arms, he "said, 'Now Lord, Thou dost let Thy bond-servant depart in peace, according to Thy word; for my eyes have seen Thy salvation'" (Luke 2:28–30). Just as Isaiah prophesied, in the incarnate Son of God, "all flesh [would] see the salvation of God" (Luke 3:6; Isa. 40:5). In Jesus Christ "the Word became flesh, and dwelt among us, and we beheld His glory, glory as of the only begotten from the Father, full of grace and truth. . . . For of His fulness we have all received, and grace upon grace" (John 1:14, 16).

Speaking of the incarnation, the noted German theologian Erich Sauer wrote, "Of all times it is the turning point, of all love it is the highest point, of all worship it is the central point, of all salvation it is the starting point."

The very point of the redemptive **grace of God** through Jesus Christ is to save men from the corruption and damnation of sin—sin that debilitates and crushes human life, that separates sinners from a holy God, and that persists in unredeemed mankind like an incurable and fatal disease.

In Titus 2:11–14, Paul condenses the eternal plan of God in Christ by grace. He gives four aspects, or realities, of God's redemptive grace: salvation from the penalty (v. 11b), the power (v. 12), the presence (v. 13), and the possession (v. 14) of sin.

SALVATION FROM THE PENALTY OF SIN

bringing salvation to all men, (2:11b)

The single word **salvation** sums up the longing of God that is manifested in His redemptive work, because it denotes deliverance, rescue, and release from sin. What verses 11 and 12 imply, verse 14 makes explicit: Jesus "gave Himself for us, that He might redeem us from every lawless deed."

In His sovereign grace, God often saves from physical danger and affliction, even death. Daniel, for example, was divinely delivered from a den of lions (Dan. 6:19–22), just as his compatriots, Shadrach, Meshach, and Abed-nego, had been delivered from a fiery furnace (3:24–27). During a storm on the Sea of Galilee, Jesus saved the Twelve from almost certain drowning (Mark 4:39). But unless the context clearly indicates otherwise, when Scripture, either Old or New Testament, refers to **salvation,** or redemption, it is always in regard to deliverance from sin and its consequences (spiritual death and separation from God) and from its penalty (eternal damnation). "The wages of sin [always] is death" (Rom. 6:23). Jesus scathingly warned, "You shall die in your sins; for unless you believe that I am He, you shall die in your sins" (John 8:24; cf. v. 21). "Do not fear those who kill the body, but are unable to kill the soul," He had warned on another occasion; "but rather fear Him who is able to destroy both soul and body in hell" (Matt. 10:28).

Hell, "where their worm does not die, and the fire is not quenched" (Mark 9:44; cf. Isa. 66:24), is the certain, inescapable destiny of those who die unforgiven in their sins. It is from that dreadful prospect that God's sovereign and supreme grace brings eternal **salvation** to those who place their trust in His Son, Jesus Christ.

If, as some Christians maintain, salvation can be forfeited, it then would be obvious that God's grace lacks everlasting power, that the life He bestows on believers is not eternal. A believer's hope could only be temporary. He would be in continual danger of losing salvation, because it would be dependent on his own faithfulness and power to avoid sin that would cast him back into lostness. If that were true, one's own power to sin would be greater than God's power to save, and any testimony given to unbelievers to bring them to salvation would be undermined.

Without qualification, Jesus declared that "all that the Father gives Me shall come to Me, and the one who comes to Me I will certainly not cast out" (John 6:37) and that "I give eternal life to them, and they shall never perish; and no one shall snatch them out of My hand"

(10:28). The Lord *will* *not* revoke a believer's salvation, and anyone else—whether the believer himself, another human being, or even Satan —*cannot* revoke it (cf. Rom. 8:28–38).

Or if, as others maintain, a believer cannot lose his salvation but can lose his faith, disregard Christ's lordship, turn from Him to complete disobedience, and continue to live in sin, his testimony is equally impaired, because his life gives no evidence of God's saving power. As Paul states later in the present text, Jesus "gave Himself for us, that He might *redeem* us from every lawless deed and *purify* for Himself a people for His own possession" (Titus 2:14, emphasis added). A person who is not being purified from sin has no claim on being saved from it.

Those twin truths have significance not only in regard to personal salvation but also in regard to world evangelization. If God is unable to keep a believer saved or to purify his life after he is saved, He has nothing by which to demonstrate His saving grace to a lost and condemned world.

To all men does not, as some maintain, refer to universal salvation but rather to the universal opportunity for salvation. In his first letter to Timothy, Paul speaks of "the living God, who is the Savior of all men, especially of believers" (1 Tim. 4:10). God "is Savior of all men" in the sense of delaying their deserved judgment for sin and of granting them countless temporal blessings that they do not deserve but nevertheless receive because of His gracious love.

Contrary to what many people think, the Old Testament does not portray a God of judgment and wrath and the New Testament a God of love and mercy. In both testaments, He is above all a God of infinite grace who desires the salvation of all mankind. By His very nature, God is a Savior. Over six centuries before the birth of Christ, the Lord declared through Isaiah: "There is no other God besides Me, a righteous God and a Savior; there is none except Me" (Isa. 45:21; cf. 43:11). Earlier the prophet professed, "Behold, God is my salvation, I will trust and not be afraid; for the Lord God is my strength and song, and He has become my salvation" (Isa. 12:2).

As noted above, God delivers all sorts of people—individuals and nations, Jews and Gentiles, believers and unbelievers—from various physical dangers and afflictions, including death. Paul told Jewish members of the church at Corinth, "I do not want you to be unaware, brethren, that our fathers were all under the cloud, and all passed through the sea; and all were baptized into Moses in the cloud and in the sea; and all ate the same spiritual food; and all drank the same spiritual drink, for they were drinking from a spiritual rock which followed them; and the rock was Christ" (1 Cor. 10:1–4). All of the people were guided by the cloud that went before them; all of them were saved from death or reenslavement by the Egyptians after passing through the Red

Sea; all of them were saved from thirst and starvation by God's gracious provision of manna to eat and water to drink in the wilderness; and all of them had the blessing of knowing God's righteous standards through the law. "Nevertheless," Paul goes on to say, "with most of them God was not well-pleased" (1 Cor. 10:5). Although all of the Israelites were blessed by God, most of them did not trust in Him and were not spiritually saved.

In his book *The Five Points of Calvinism,* R. L. Dabney writes: "Christ's sacrifice has certainly purchased for the whole human race a merciful postponement of the doom incurred by our sins, including all the temporal blessings of our earthly life, all the gospel restraints upon human depravity, and the sincere offer of heaven to all. For, but for Christ, man's doom would have followed instantly after his sin, as that of the fallen angels did" ([Harrisburg, Pa.: Sprinkle Publications, 1992], p. 62).

"Do you think lightly of the riches of [God's] kindness and forbearance and patience," Paul asks rhetorically, "not knowing that the kindness of God leads you to repentance?" (Rom. 2:4). God graciously delays judgment and showers unbelieving mankind with every sort of blessing in order that they might repent and come to Him in saving faith. His temporal manifestations of grace, however, are not permanent or eternal. One day they will end. "Because of your stubbornness and unrepentant heart," Paul goes on to warn unbelievers, "you are storing up wrath for yourself in the day of wrath and revelation of the righteous judgment of God" (Rom. 2:5).

In His atoning death, Christ did not save all men spiritually but provided the *means* of **salvation to all men** who would be saved. In His matchless grace, God "desires all men to be saved and to come to the knowledge of the truth" (1 Tim. 2:4). Emphasizing that same truth, Peter wrote, "The Lord is not slow about His promise, as some count slowness, but is patient toward you, not wishing for any to perish but for all to come to repentance" (2 Pet. 3:9). As our Lord Himself declared in His beautiful and familiar promise: "God so loved the world, that He gave His only begotten Son, that *whoever* believes in Him should not perish, but have eternal life" (John 3:16, emphasis added; cf. John 6:51). The gospel is good news **to all men,** not because they are all elected or because Christ died for each one of them in particular, but because, as Jesus promised, *"anyone* [who] enters through Me, he shall be saved" (John 10:9, emphasis added).

When God calls on all sinners to believe, He does not command them to believe that they are divinely chosen or that Christ died especially for them. He commands them to believe that Jesus Christ died for all sinners in the world. He does not offer salvation to a person either as elect or not elect but simply as a sinner.

Scripture nowhere teaches what is commonly called double predestination. God does not deterministically elect some men to salvation and others to damnation. In a way that is inscrutable and incomprehensible to our finite minds, God's Word makes clear that every believer was chosen by God "in Him [Christ] before the foundation of the world, that we should be holy and blameless before Him" (Eph. 1:4). Scripture makes equally clear that those who do not believe are responsible and guilty for their rejection of Christ (cf. John 3:17–20). Jesus gives us the marvelous assurance that "all that the Father gives Me shall come to Me, and the one who comes to Me I will certainly not cast out. . . . And this is the will of Him who sent Me, that of all that He has given Me I lose nothing, but raise it up on the last day" (John 6:37, 39; cf. 17:2). With that assurance, He also gives the promise that "he who comes to Me shall not hunger, and he who believes in Me shall never thirst, . . . and the one who comes to Me I will certainly not cast out" (John 6:35, 37).

In his letter to the church at Rome, Paul further explains that "whom [God] foreknew, He also predestined to become conformed to the image of His Son, that He might be the first-born among many brethren; and whom He predestined, these He also called; and whom He called, these He also justified; and whom He justified, these He also glorified" (Rom. 8:29–30). A bit later the apostle gives the immortal promises that "whoever believes in Him will not be disappointed" and "whoever will call upon the name of the Lord will be saved" (Rom. 10:11, 13).

But Scripture does not teach what might seem to be the corollary of that truth—that God predestines unbelievers to hell. As noted above, God is by nature a Savior, and it is unbelievers alone who are responsible for the sin that sends them to hell. The Lord "desires *all* men to be saved and to come to the knowledge of the truth" (1 Tim. 2:4, emphasis added), "not wishing for any to perish but for *all* to come to repentance" (2 Pet. 3:9, emphasis added). Men are not condemned because God has not chosen them but because they have not chosen Him. The Lord says to all unbelievers what He said to unbelieving Jews in Jerusalem: "Truly, truly, I say to you, he who hears My word, and believes Him who sent Me, has eternal life, and does not come into judgment, but has passed out of death into life. . . . And you do not have His word abiding in you, for you do not believe Him whom He sent. . . . and you are unwilling to come to Me, that you may have life" (John 5:24, 38, 40; cf. 8:24). All men are not saved for the single reason that "not all have faith" in Jesus Christ (2 Thess. 3:2).

It is not the extent of the atonement that excludes some people from salvation. As John makes clear in his second letter, Jesus "Himself is the propitiation for our sins; and not for ours only, but also for those of the *whole world*" (1 John 2:2, emphasis added). Jesus tasted death for everyone (Heb. 2:9). The atonement was sufficient because Christ was divine perfection and completely satisfied God. If God had chosen every person who ever lived, no further atonement would be needed than Christ's.

In his *Discourses and Sayings of Our Lord Jesus Christ*, the noted eighteenth-century Scottish Puritan John Brown wrote,

> There can be no doubt in the mind of a person who understands the doctrine of personal election, that those who are actually saved are the objects of a special love on the part of God; and that the . . . Savior had a special design in reference to them. But there can be little doubt that the atonement of Christ has a general reference to mankind at large; and that it was intended as a display of love on the part of God to our guilty race.
>
> Not merely was the atonement offered by Christ Jesus sufficient for the salvation of the whole world, but it was intended and fitted to remove out of the way of the salvation of sinners generally, every bar which the perfections of the divine moral character and the principles of the divine moral government presented. . . . In consequence of that atonement, every sinner may be, and if he believe in Jesus certainly shall be, pardoned and saved. . . . The revelation of mercy made in the gospels refers to men as sinners, not as elect sinners. ([New York: Robert Carter & Bros., 1855], 1:33)

The problem, therefore, is not in the sufficiency or the scope of God's grace. "There is one God, and one mediator also between God and men, the man Christ Jesus, who gave Himself as a ransom for *all*" (1 Tim. 2:5–6, emphasis added). Without any exception, God calls all men to faith in His Son, Jesus Christ, whose atoning sacrifice was more than sufficient to cover every sin that has been or ever will be committed.

The Holy Spirit revealed that great truth to the prophet Isaiah, who declared that "all of us like sheep have gone astray, each of us has turned to his own way" and then foretold of Christ that "the Lord has caused the iniquity of us all to fall on Him" (Isa. 53:6). John the Baptist testified of Jesus, "Behold, the Lamb of God who takes away the sin of the world!" (John 1:29). Paul explains more fully that, "if by the transgression of the one the many died, much more did the grace of God and the gift by the grace of the one Man, Jesus Christ, abound to the many. . . . So then as through one transgression there resulted condemnation to all men, even so through one act of righteousness there resulted justification of life to all men. . . . And the Law came in that the transgression might increase; but where sin increased, grace abounded all the more" (Rom. 5:15, 18, 20; cf. 2 Cor. 5:14–15). The abundance of God's grace more than exceeds the whole of man's depravity.

But not all men trust in God's gracious and sufficient provision of salvation. That is always the reason, and the only reason, that Scripture gives for a person's not being saved. Jesus' beautiful promise in John 3:16–17 is followed by the dire warning that "he who does not believe has been judged already, because he has not believed in the name of the only begotten Son of God" (v. 18). Part of the Holy Spirit's work is to "convict the world concerning sin, and righteousness, and judgment; concerning sin, because they do not believe in Me" (John 16:8–9). In an appearance after His resurrection, Jesus reiterated that truth, saying, "He who has believed and has been baptized shall be saved, but he who has disbelieved shall be condemned" (Mark 16:16). It might be said that Christ's atonement is *sufficient* for the whole world but is *efficient* only for those who believe.

God calls His people, those who are already saved, to demonstrate His saving power in their lives and thereby show Him to be a saving God, to glorify Him and to draw others to Him. "Now all these things are from God," Paul declares, "who reconciled us to Himself through Christ, and gave us the ministry of reconciliation, namely, that God was in Christ reconciling the world to Himself, not counting their trespasses against them, and He has committed to us the word of reconciliation. Therefore, we are ambassadors for Christ, as though God were entreating through us; we beg you on behalf of Christ, be reconciled to God" (2 Cor. 5:18–20).

SALVATION FROM THE POWER OF SIN

instructing us to deny ungodliness and worldly desires and to live sensibly, righteously and godly in the present age, (2:12)

As ultimately important as salvation from the penalty of sin is, Paul's major emphasis in this passage is on salvation from its power. In Jesus Christ, God's redeeming grace breaks sin's power and dominion in our lives and gives us a new nature that desires holiness.

Instructing is from *paideuō,* which carries the closely related meanings of teaching, training, discipling, educating, and nurturing. It is the term from which we get *pedagagy.* The subject of **instructing** is "the grace of God," which, as has been pointed out, is personified in Jesus Christ, the incarnation of God's grace, who has appeared and brought salvation (v. 11). Revealed and personified in Christ, God's sovereign saving grace not only is a deliverer but also a teacher, a guide, a counselor. When we were saved, we immediately came under the tutelage of God through His Holy Spirit and through His Word. "Now we have received, not the spirit of the world," Paul explained to believers in

Corinth, "but the Spirit who is from God, that we might know the things freely given to us by God, which things we also speak, not in words taught by human wisdom, but in those taught by the Spirit, combining spiritual thoughts with spiritual words" (1 Cor. 2:12–13). "We have," the apostle goes on to say, the very "mind of Christ" (v. 16).

In chapter 3 of his letter to the church at Rome, Paul describes the total depravity of every human being apart from Jesus Christ. Quoting from the Psalms, he says: "There is none righteous, not even one; there is none who understands, there is none who seeks for God; all have turned aside, together they have become useless; there is none who does good, there is not even one" (Rom. 3:10–12; cf. Pss. 14:1–3; 53:1–4). Because of that total bondage to sin, "There is no fear of God before their eyes" (v. 18; cf. Ps. 36:1). "A natural man *does not accept* the things of the Spirit of God; for they are foolishness to him, and he *cannot understand* them, because they are spiritually appraised" (1 Cor. 2:14, emphasis added).

Paul reminded believers in Ephesus of their former condition of uninterrupted sinfulness, saying, "You were dead in your trespasses and sins, in which you formerly walked according to the course of this world, according to the prince of the power of the air, of the spirit that is now working in the sons of disobedience. Among them we too all formerly lived in the lusts of our flesh, indulging the desires of the flesh and of the mind, and were by nature children of wrath, even as the rest" (Eph. 2:1–3). It was only because of God's "being rich in mercy, because of His great love with which He loved us, even when we were dead in our transgressions, [that He] made us alive together with Christ (by grace you have been saved), and raised us up with Him, and seated us with Him in the heavenly places, in Christ Jesus" (vv. 4–6). The person who "is in Christ, . . . is a new creature; the old things [have] passed away; behold, new things have come" (2 Cor. 5:17).

As emphasized in two of my books, *The Gospel According to Jesus* (Zondervan, 1988) and *Faith Works* (Word, 1993), when a person is genuinely saved, truly converted and given new life in Jesus Christ, there is a transformation not only of nature but of living. It is not possible—as those who oppose what they call "lordship salvation" strongly insist—to be saved from the penalty of sin and not be saved from its power and dominion. Because of a Christian's new nature and the indwelling Holy Spirit, he simply cannot continue to live in unmitigated sin, bereft of any outward evidence of his new, holy, and righteous nature and of the presence of Christ's own Holy Spirit within him.

By His divine grace, Jesus Christ completely reprograms our computers, as it were. He throws away the old disks and deletes the previous programs and files—all of which were permeated with errors and destructive "viruses"—and graciously replaces them with His own divine truth and righteousness. "I have been crucified with Christ," Paul testified to the churches of Galatia, "and it is no longer I who live, but Christ lives in me; and the life which I now live in the flesh I live by faith in the Son of God, who loved me, and delivered Himself up for me" (Gal. 2:20).

Scripture does not teach that sinless perfection is possible in the earthly lives of believers. Although Paul could say sincerely, "I am conscious of nothing against myself," he immediately went on to say, "yet I am not by this acquitted" (1 Cor. 4:4). He clearly testified that he had not "already become perfect." But "I press on," he said, "in order that I may lay hold of that for which also I was laid hold of by Christ Jesus. Brethren, I do not regard myself as having laid hold of it yet; but one thing I do: forgetting what lies behind and reaching forward to what lies ahead, I press on toward the goal for the prize of the upward call of God in Christ Jesus" (Phil. 3:11–14).

Nevertheless, a person who is divinely born again is no longer under the pervasive dominion of sin and of Satan. He has a radical new nature and is called and enabled to reflect that new nature in a radically new way of living. By the work of God the Father, we "are in Christ Jesus, who became to us wisdom from God, and righteousness and sanctification, and redemption" (1 Cor. 1:30). The "grace and truth [that] were realized through Jesus Christ" (John 1:17) during His earthly ministry are to be realized and evident in the lives of those who bear His name and His nature. They have "laid aside the old self with its evil practices, and have put on the new self who is being renewed to a true knowledge according to the image of the One who created [them]" (Col. 3:9–10).

Our present earthly life is a time of sanctification, a two-sided process of becoming less and less like our old and sinful self and more and more like our new and Christlike self. "Just as you presented your members as slaves to impurity and to lawlessness, resulting in further lawlessness," Paul explained to believers in Rome, "so now present your members as slaves to righteousness, resulting in sanctification" (Rom. 6:19).

Because sanctification is both negative and positive, separating believers *from* sin and *to* righteousness, so, therefore, is Christ's gracious **instructing** of believers.

Negatively, the Lord instructs **us to deny ungodliness and worldly desires.** Christ's own power, through the work of His indwelling Holy Spirit, not only warns us about but enables us to resist and renounce sin. "Therefore do not let sin reign in your mortal body that you should obey its lusts," Paul admonishes, "and do not go on presenting the members of your body to sin as instruments of unrighteousness; but present yourselves to God as those alive from the dead, and your members as instruments of righteousness to God. For sin shall not be master over you, for you are not under law, but under grace" (Rom. 6:12–14).

To deny carries the idea of a conscious, purposeful action of the will. It means to say no. It is to confess and consciously turn away from that which is sinful and destructive and to move toward that which is good and godly. It includes the commitment a believer makes when he first acknowledges his sin and receives Christ as Savior and Lord as well as the countless other decisions he makes **to deny** and forsake the **ungodliness and worldly desires** that continue to find their way back into his life.

Those who hold the reductionist notion that a person can be delivered from hell without being delivered from sin contradict the clear teaching of Christ and His apostles. Both John the Baptist and Jesus Himself, the Messiah whom John heralded, began their ministries with calls to repentance (Matt. 3:2, 8, 11; 4:17). In the same way, the first work of the Holy Spirit, whom Jesus would send in His name, would be to convict men of sin (John 16:8). After the promised Spirit had descended at Pentecost, those who heard Peter's sermon "were pierced to the heart, and said to Peter and the rest of the apostles, 'Brethren, what shall we do?' And Peter said to them, 'Repent, and let each of you be baptized in the name of Jesus Christ for the forgiveness of your sins'" (Acts 2:37–38).

Christians do not habitually and continually practice sin, because when a person genuinely believes in Jesus Christ, there is a divinely-empowered separation from **ungodliness and worldly desires. Ungodliness** translates *asebeia,* which here refers to lack of true reverence for and devotion to God. It is "against all ungodliness and unrighteousness of men" that "the wrath of God is revealed from heaven" (Rom. 1:18). A person whose life is characterized by **ungodliness** cannot be truly saved, no matter how vocal and orthodox his profession of Christ may be.

The apostle John warns: "Little children, let no one deceive you; the one who practices righteousness is righteous, just as He [Christ] is righteous; the one who practices sin is of the devil; for the devil has sinned from the beginning. The Son of God appeared for this purpose, that He might destroy the works of the devil. No one who is born of God practices sin, because His seed abides in him; and he cannot sin, because he is born of God. By this the children of God and the children of the devil are obvious: anyone who does not practice righteousness is not of God" (1 John 3:7–10).

After giving a long list of "the deeds of the flesh . . . which are: immorality, impurity, sensuality, idolatry, sorcery, enmities, strife, jealousy, outbursts of anger, disputes, dissensions, factions, envying, drunkenness, carousing, and things like these," Paul declares "that those who practice such things shall not inherit the kingdom of God . . . Those who belong to Christ Jesus have crucified the flesh with its passions and desires" (Gal. 5:19–21, 24).

Worldly desires refers to sins that, although we may not actually have committed, we nevertheless long to commit. These **desires** include all of the countless sinful lusts and cravings that characterize the natural man. They include "youthful lusts" (2 Tim. 2:22), "fleshly lusts" (1 Pet. 2:11), and all other "foolish and harmful desires which plunge men into ruin and destruction" (1 Tim. 6:9). When we "walk by the Spirit, [we] will not carry out" the **worldly desires** "of the flesh" (Gal. 5:16).

On the positive side, Christ graciously instructs us to live **sensibly, righteously and godly in the present age.** Having been *declared* and *made* righteous by our justification through Christ, and made capable of righteous behavior by our confession and God's forgiveness of sin, we therefore are to *practice* righteousness in our sanctification. God has ordained our lives in Christ to be lives of ever-increasing righteousness, holiness, and goodness. "As sin reigned in death, even so grace might reign through righteousness to eternal life through Jesus Christ our Lord" (Rom. 5:21).

Sensibly translates the adverb *sōphronōs,* which carries the basic idea of having a sound mind. Paul has used other forms of that word four previous times in this letter in referring to a quality that should characterize elders/overseers (1:8), older men (2:2), young women (2:5), and young men (2:6). The Christian who lives **sensibly** has control over the issues of life. As noted in chapter 3 of this commentary under the discussion of 1:8, the sensible believer does not allow circumstances or the irresponsible influence of others to distract him or affect his own judgment. He not only is careful not to become involved in things that are immoral or unspiritual, but also avoids things that are simply trivial and unproductive. By the enablement and power of the Holy Spirit in his redeemed inner person, he brings the unredeemed flesh under control.

Christ also graciously instructs us to live **righteously,** faithfully obeying the Word of God, the divine standard of what is right, without reservation. And Christ graciously instructs us to live **godly,** which has the obvious meaning of close fellowship with our heavenly Father.

Our gracious instruction could be seen as three-dimensional. The first, living **sensibly,** could relate to the divine and continuing change within us. The second, living **righteously,** connects with our changed relationship toward others, both saved and unsaved. The third, living **godly,** may refer to our changed relationship to God Himself. We are no longer His enemies but His children. We no longer ignore Him, blaspheme

Him, or use His name in vain but instead honor Him in reverent adoration, praise, and worship.

All three of those changes, individually and collectively, give distinct evidence **in the present age** of our spiritual rebirth. They are living and powerful testimony, within the church and before the world, of the saving and transforming power of Jesus Christ.

For many people, the only inducement to listen to the gospel is seeing its transforming power producing holiness, love, peace, and the other fruit of the Spirit (Gal. 5:22–23) in the lives of believers. As Paul declares a few verses later in this letter to Titus, divinely transformed lives are genuinely "zealous for good deeds" (2:14). Faithful believers are therefore to be "careful to engage in good deeds," because "these things are good and profitable for men" (3:8). We are saved in order that God might demonstrate His glorious grace, which produces in us the desire to do what is right and good—thereby giving glory to our Lord and righteously impacting the lives of the unsaved in His name. "For this reason," Paul explained to Timothy, "I found mercy [salvation], in order that in me as the foremost [of sinners, v. 15], Jesus Christ might demonstrate His perfect patience, as an example for those who would believe in Him for eternal life" (1 Tim. 1:16). As our Lord commands, we are to "let [our] light shine before men in such a way that they may see [our] good works, and glorify [our] Father who is in heaven" (Matt. 5:16).

Contrary to the contention of the Pharisees and of most man-made religions, no amount of good works can produce a right relationship with God. It is rather the opposite: only a right relationship with God (secured through personal trust in His Son, Jesus Christ) can produce truly good works. "For by grace you have been saved through faith," Paul explains in his letter to the church at Ephesus, "and that not of yourselves, it is the gift of God; not as a result of works, that no one should boast. We are His workmanship, created in Christ Jesus *for* good works, which God prepared beforehand, that we should walk in them" (Eph. 2:8–10, emphasis added). The transformed living that the apostle describes in Titus 2:1–10 can only become reality through the divine and gracious work of salvation described in verses 11–14.

SALVATION FROM THE PRESENCE OF SIN

looking for the blessed hope and the appearing of the glory of our great God and Savior, Christ Jesus; (2:13)

One of the marvelous truths implied in this promise is that one day, when our salvation is perfected, we will be glorified, made fully like our Lord in purity and righteousness. "Beloved, now we are children of God," John assures us, "and it has not appeared as yet what we shall be. [But] we know that, when He appears, we shall be like Him, because we shall see Him just as He is" (1 John 3:2).

That future blessed encounter with our Lord will bring total and permanent removal of sin from our lives. Not even a trace will remain. Paul could therefore say to believers in Philippi, "For to me, to live is Christ, and to die is gain," because he had the overwhelming "desire to depart and be with Christ" (Phil. 1:21, 23). The apostle could also say to believers in Rome "that the whole creation groans and suffers the pains of childbirth together until now. And not only this, but also we ourselves, having the first fruits of the Spirit, even we ourselves groan within ourselves, waiting eagerly for our adoption as sons, the redemption of our body" (Rom. 8:22–23).

Looking for translates a participle form of *prosdechomai,* which carries the meanings not only of longing and waiting but also of eager and certain expectation. **Hope** translates *elpis,* which, like *prosdechomai,* includes the connotation of confident certainty. It is an especially **blessed,** or happy, **hope** of believers because Paul is not speaking about a fond human wish but about a divinely promised certitude. That certitude is **the appearing of the glory of our great God and Savior, Christ Jesus.** It is for that reason that the apostle calls it, and that Christians throughout the centuries have called it, *the* **blessed hope,** the **hope** that is above all other hopes.

Appearing is from *epiphaneia,* which has the root ideas of uncovering, unveiling, and disclosing. Paul uses the term both of Jesus' first and second comings. At the first "appearing of our Savior Christ Jesus," He "abolished death, and brought life and immortality to light through the gospel" (2 Tim. 1:10). At His second appearing, He will "judge the living and the dead" and establish His earthly kingdom (2 Tim. 4:1). In the meanwhile, His people are to "keep the commandment without stain or reproach until [that second] *appearing* of our Lord Jesus Christ" (1 Tim. 6:14, emphasis added) and are to rejoice that "in the future there is laid up for [them] the crown of righteousness, which the Lord, the righteous Judge, will award . . . to all who have loved His *appearing*" (2 Tim. 4:8, emphasis added).

I do not think Paul is speaking specifically of the Rapture—the time when, just before the seven-year Tribulation, Christ will appear and receive all believers, both living and dead, to Himself (1 Thess. 4:13–17) —as distinguished from His coming in judgment at the end of the Tribulation to establish His millennial kingdom, when "the Son of Man is going to come in the glory of His Father with His angels; and will then recompense every man according to his deeds" (Matt. 16:27). It seems rather that the apostle is here referring to Christ's second coming in general, when He will appear in **glory** and power rather than in humility and submission as in His first coming.

Paul is focusing on the culmination of our salvation, which will be perfected and completed when our Lord calls us up to the place He has prepared (cf. John 14:1–3), when "we shall all be changed, in a moment, in the twinkling of an eye, at the last trumpet; for the trumpet will sound, and the dead will be raised imperishable, and we shall be changed. For this perishable must put on the imperishable, and this mortal must put on immortality" (1 Cor. 15:51–53; cf. Matt. 24:30–31; 25:31). Paul therefore could assure us that "now salvation is nearer to us than when we believed" (Rom. 13:11). Even while we remain on earth, "our citizenship is in heaven, from which also we eagerly wait for a Savior, the Lord Jesus Christ; who will transform the body of our humble state into conformity with the body of His glory, by the exertion of the power that He has even to subject all things to Himself" (Phil. 3:20–21). Even when we come back to earth to reign with Him, we will be untemptable and untouchable by sin. In the New Jerusalem, "there shall no longer be any curse; and the throne of God and of the Lamb shall be in it, and His bond-servants shall serve Him; and they shall see His face, and His name shall be on their foreheads. And there shall no longer be any night; and they shall not have need of the light of a lamp nor the light of the sun, because the Lord God shall illumine them; and they shall reign forever and ever" (Rev. 22:3–5).

The rendering of the NASB (**the appearing of the glory**) is a more accurate rendering than that of the KJV ("the glorious appearing"). In this context, **glory,** like "grace" (2:11), "kindness," and "love" (3:4) is not simply a description of Christ but also a personification. In his incarnation, His first appearing, Christ was grace personified. In His second **appearing,** He will be **glory** personified. He will be the blazing Shekinah glory that Peter, James, and John saw partially revealed at Jesus' transfiguration (Matt. 17:1–8).

Our great God and Savior is one of the many plain declarations in Scripture of the deity of Jesus Christ (see, e.g., John 1:1–18; Rom. 9:5; Heb. 1:1–3). Some interpreters hold that in this passage **God** and **Savior** refer to different beings, the first (**great God**) to the divine Father and the second (**Savior**) to the human Son, **Christ Jesus.** But that explanation has several insurmountable problems. Besides the other clear affirmations of the divinity of Christ in Scripture are several grammatical reasons found in this passage itself. First, there is but one definite article (**the,** *tou*), which indicates the singularity and identity of **God** and **Savior.** Second, both of the singular pronouns in the following verse ("who," *hos*; and "Himself," *heauton*) refer back to a single person. And, although the Old Testament makes countless references to God the Father as **great,** in the New Testament that description is used only of God the Son (see, e.g., Matt. 5:35; Luke 1:32; 7:16; Heb. 10:21; 13:20). Perhaps most importantly, the New Testament nowhere speaks of **the appearing** or Second Coming of God the Father but only of the Son.

SALVATION FROM POSSESSION BY SIN

who gave Himself for us, that He might redeem us from every lawless deed and purify for Himself a people for His own possession, zealous for good deeds. (2:14)

Fourth, and finally, salvation delivers us permanently from sin's possession.

The unregenerate person is in total bondage to sin. Paul asked believers in Rome, "Do you not know that when you present yourselves to someone as slaves for obedience, you are slaves of the one whom you obey, either of sin resulting in death, or of obedience resulting in righteousness?" (Rom. 6:16). Because "we have become united with [Christ] in the likeness of His death," he explains earlier in this chapter, "certainly we shall be also in the likeness of His resurrection, knowing this, that our old self was crucified with Him, that our body of sin might be done away with, that we should no longer be slaves to sin; for he who has died is freed from sin" (6:5–7).

Our gracious Lord **gave Himself for us, that He might redeem us from** our bondage to sin, delivering us from **every lawless deed. Redeem** is from *lutroō*, which refers to the releasing of someone held captive, such as a prisoner or a slave, on receipt of a ransom payment.

Paul reminded the elders from Ephesus of their obligation to "be on guard for yourselves and for all the flock, among which the Holy Spirit has made you overseers, to shepherd the church of God which He purchased with His own blood" (Acts 20:28). Peter reminded his readers, "You were not redeemed with perishable things like silver or gold from your futile way of life inherited from your forefathers, but with precious blood, as of a lamb unblemished and spotless, the blood of Christ" (1 Pet. 1:18–19).

The purpose of the Son of God coming to earth in His incarnation was "to give His life a ransom for many" (Mark 10:45). As a divine sacrifice, He "gave Himself for our sins, that He might deliver us out of this present evil age, according to the will of our God and Father" (Gal. 1:4). Like Paul, every believer can say with full assurance: "I have been crucified with Christ; and it is no longer I who live, but Christ lives in me; and the life which I now live in the flesh I live by faith in the Son of

God, who loved me, and delivered Himself up for me" (Gal. 2:20). He graciously "gave Himself up for us, an offering and a sacrifice to God as a fragrant aroma" (Eph. 5:2; cf. v. 25; 1 Tim. 2:6).

Paul first speaks negatively, focusing on Christ's redeeming **us from every lawless deed,** from the "fleshly lusts, which," as Peter declares, "wage war against the soul" (1 Pet. 2:11).

Positively, Christ also redeems His people in order to **purify for Himself a people for His own possession.** Paul explains that marvelous truth more fully in his letter to the church at Rome. "Thanks be to God," he exults,

> that though you were slaves of sin, you became obedient from the heart to that form of teaching to which you were committed, and having been freed from sin, you became slaves of righteousness. I am speaking in human terms because of the weakness of your flesh. For just as you presented your members as slaves to impurity and to lawlessness, resulting in further lawlessness, so now present your members as slaves to righteousness, resulting in sanctification. For when you were slaves of sin, you were free in regard to righteousness. Therefore what benefit were you then deriving from the things of which you are now ashamed? For the outcome of those things is death. But now having been freed from sin and enslaved to God, you derive your benefit, resulting in sanctification, and the outcome, eternal life. (Rom. 6:17–22)

In order to **purify for Himself a people for His own possession,** "Christ also loved the church and gave Himself up for her; that He might sanctify her, having cleansed her by the washing of water with the word" (Eph. 5:25–26). The Lord's **people** "are a chosen race, a royal priesthood, a holy nation, a people for God's own possession, that you may proclaim the excellencies of Him who has called you out of darkness into His marvelous light" (1 Pet. 2:9; cf. 1 Cor. 6:19–20).

Just as we formerly were possessed and enslaved by sin, now we are possessed by and enslaved to Jesus Christ. His **possession** of His **people** is not temporary but permanent. The Lord Himself made that truth abundantly clear. As already noted, Jesus repeatedly emphasized that a person who believes in Him will be saved with divine security. "All that the Father gives Me shall come to Me," He said, "and the one who comes to Me I will certainly not cast out. . . . And this is the will of Him who sent Me, that of all that He has given Me I lose nothing, but raise it up on the last day. For this is the will of My Father, that everyone who beholds the Son and believes in Him, may have eternal life; and I Myself will raise him up on the last day" (John 6:37, 39–40). On a later occasion Jesus repeated the promise of eternal security: "My sheep hear My voice, and I know them, and they follow Me; and I give eternal life to them, and they shall never perish; and no one shall snatch them out of My hand. My Father, who has given them to Me, is greater than all; and no one is able to snatch them out of the Father's hand" (John 10:27–29). If salvation were temporary, subject to being lost, then, by definition, it could not guarantee eternal life. But even Satan himself cannot rob a believer of salvation. To be able to do so, he would have to be more powerful than the God who made him and who, as Jesus made clear, is "greater than all."

As God's redeemed people, we give still further evidence of our salvation by being **zealous for good deeds,** because "we are [God's] workmanship, created in Christ Jesus for good works, which God prepared beforehand, that we should walk in them" (Eph. 2:10; cf. Titus 3:8). **Good deeds** are not to be an adjunct to our Christian lives, something that we do at our convenience, but are to be a natural, integral, and **zealous** part of our daily living. "How much more will the blood of Christ, who through the eternal Spirit offered Himself without blemish to God, cleanse your conscience from dead works to serve the living God?" (Heb. 9:14). The same Spirit who cleanses us from "dead works" desires to replace them with living works.

It has always been God's purpose for His people to be righteous and holy as a testimony to His own righteousness and holiness before the unbelieving world. "The Lord has today declared you to be His people, a treasured possession, as He promised you," Moses proclaimed to ancient Israel, "and that you should keep all His commandments; and that He shall set you high above all nations which He has made, for praise, fame, and honor; and that you shall be a consecrated people to the Lord your God, as He has spoken" (Deut. 26:18–19). Early in His ministry, in the Sermon on the Mount, Jesus told those who believed in Him, "Let your light shine before men in such a way that they may see your good works, and glorify your Father who is in heaven" (Matt. 5:16). Emphasizing that same truth, Peter wrote, "Keep your behavior excellent among the Gentiles, so that in the thing in which they slander you as evildoers, they may on account of your good deeds, as they observe them, glorify God in the day of visitation" (1 Pet. 2:12). Again from the Lord's own lips, we have no less a standard than being "perfect, as [our] heavenly Father is perfect" (Matt. 5:48).

The Preacher's Authority

8

These things speak and exhort and reprove with all authority. Let no one disregard you. (2:15)

This single verse is one of the clearest and strongest statements in Scripture about the spiritual authority of men whom God calls to minister His Word and shepherd His people. Because the phrase **with all authority** is the foundational truth both for what precedes and what follows it in this verse, its meaning should be considered first.

Authority translates *epitagē*, which refers to something that is in its proper order or place. The term came to be used figuratively of an official command, directive, or injunction. The verb form (*epitassō*) is used of Jesus' power over both the supernatural forces of demons (Mark 1:27; cf. 9:25; Luke 4:36) and the natural forces of "the winds and the water" (Luke 8:25). It also was used of King Herod's authority to order to the executioner to bring him the head of John the Baptist (Mark 6:27) and of the high priest Ananias's command to "those standing beside him to strike [Paul] on the mouth" as the apostle stood before the Sanhedrin in Jerusalem (Acts 23:2). In his appeal on behalf of the slave Onesimus, Paul referred Philemon (the slave owner) to his apostolic authority, saying, "I have enough confidence in Christ to order you (*epi-*

tassō) to do that which is proper, yet for love's sake I rather appeal to you" (Philem. 8–9).

Jews of Jesus' day were used to their religious leaders speaking and acting as if what they said and did carried great weight. But even the common people sensed the difference between religious ostentation and genuine spiritual authority. After listening to the Sermon on the Mount, "the multitudes were amazed at [Jesus'] teaching; for He was teaching them as one having authority, and not as their scribes" (Matt. 7:28–29).

Scribes had rigid religious views and standards, based largely on interpretations handed down by noted rabbis over the previous four or five centuries. Those interpretations, or traditions, eventually became dogma and often were given more honor than Scripture. On one occasion a group of scribes and Pharisees from Jerusalem chided Jesus for allowing His disciples to "transgress the tradition of the elders" by not washing their hands before they ate. Jesus countered by asking, "And why do you yourselves transgress the commandment of God for the sake of your tradition? For God said, 'Honor your father and mother,' and, 'He who speaks evil of father or mother, let him be put to death.' But you say, 'Whoever shall say to his father or mother, "Anything of mine you might have been helped by has been given to God," he is not to honor his father or his mother.' And thus you invalidated the word of God for the sake of your tradition" (Matt. 15:1–6; cf. Mark 7:8). Paul testified that, before his conversion, "I was advancing in Judaism beyond many of my contemporaries among my countrymen, being more extremely zealous for my ancestral traditions" (Gal. 1:14).

After Jesus' first cleansing of the temple, "the chief priests, and scribes, and elders came to Him, and began saying to Him, 'By what authority are You doing these things, or who gave You this authority to do these things?'" (Mark 11:27–28). "These things" referred not only to His driving out the moneychangers from the temple (vv. 15–16) but also to His authoritative teaching (vv. 17–18). Those leaders knew that Jesus had not been educated in a scribal school or personally tutored by a leading rabbi. Nor did He ever credit venerated scribes or rabbis as the source of His teaching. When the men declined to answer Jesus' question about whether John the Baptist's ministry was from heaven or from men, He refused to answer their question about the source of His authority (vv. 29–33).

Jesus' authority did not come from an ecclesiastical title, scribal training, or sacerdotal position, none of which He possessed. Nor did it come from the popular Jewish beliefs of His time, many of which were based on myths, legends, and religious and racial prejudice (cf. Titus 1:14). It clearly did not come from rabbinical tradition. In the Sermon on the Mount, Jesus specifically exposed many of those traditions as being far short of God's standards. One such tradition asserted, "You shall love your neighbor, and hate your enemy" (Matt. 5:43). The first part, loving one's neighbor, was biblical (Lev. 19:18), but the second part, hating one's enemies, was not. Like many other traditions in rabbinical teaching, that tradition was a half-truth, making it all the more deceptive.

On one occasion in the temple, Jesus *did* choose to tell the Jewish leaders the source of His authority. "My teaching is not Mine," He said, "but His who sent Me. If any man is willing to do His will, he shall know of the teaching, whether it is of God, or whether I speak from Myself" (John 7:16–17). In other words, if a Jew, or any other person, sincerely seeks and obeys God the Father, he will recognize the divine authority of the Son. "When you lift up the Son of Man," He said a few days later, "then you will know that I am He, and I do nothing on My own initiative, but I speak these things as the Father taught Me" (John 8:28; cf. vv. 38, 40; 12: 49).

If Jesus, the sinless and perfect Son of God, limited Himself to speaking nothing during His incarnation except the truth He received from His Father, how much more should those who have been called into His ministry speak only on the authority of divine Scripture. That principle is consistent with what Paul wrote in Titus 1:9 and 2:1, as well as with his command to Timothy to "preach the word" (2 Tim. 4:2).

The preacher is called to accurately interpret and proclaim Scripture with sympathy, compassion, and humility. But he also has the divine charge to present biblical truth with strong **authority,** commanding God's people to hear, believe, and obey God's Word.

It is equally important, however, to understand that no pastor has authority of any sort *outside* of God's Word. In a journal article titled "The Preacher and Preaching," theologian J. I. Packer writes,

> Preaching that does not display divine authority, both in its content and in its manner, is not the substance but only the shadow of the real thing. . . .
> [Yet] the Bible is the real preacher, and the role of the man in the pulpit or the counseling conversation is simply to let the passages say their piece through him. . . . For the preacher to reach the point where he no longer hinders or obstructs his text from speaking is harder work than is sometimes realized. However, there can be no disputing that this is the task. (*Presbyterian and Reformed Journal,* Fall 1986, pp. 11, 18)

As long as he is faithful to God's Word, a pastor has the awesome privilege of ministering with God-given **authority.** He is not called to share personal insights or opinions, to philosophize or even theologize, and certainly not to entertain with words that appeal to the whims and prejudices of those to whom he ministers (cf. 2 Tim. 4:3).

The preacher must put himself out of the way and let God's Word speak through him unhindered. No matter what his training, experience, or personal abilities, he has spiritual **authority** only to the extent that what he says conforms to God's Word. But as with Jesus' own teaching, when a minister of God *does* faithfully proclaim that Word, those who reject his teaching reject God's truth and are as much accountable for their rejection as if the Lord had spoken the truth with His own lips. It is in that way, and only in that way, that a pastor is *able* to speak with spiritual authority. It is also in that way that he is *commanded* to speak with spiritual authority.

A brief digression from the text will help to emphasize the importance of the biblical line of pastoral authority. As in the past, the church today is plagued by many false kinds of authority. The first might be called personal. Some pastors assume authority over people's lives in matters of temporal choices and issues, wielding dictatorial control. That is false authority. Others contend that God is obliged to give a positive response to every demand they make on Him "in Jesus' name." But a request that is not made in a spirit of meekness and obedience and that is in any way contrary to Scripture and to the purposes of God cannot rightly be made in Jesus' name. Anything that is truly asked or done in His name (cf. John 14:13–14) is asked and done in accordance with God's revealed Word and in the spirit of humility and total submission to the will of the Father. Pastors have no personal spiritual authority at all. They speak authoritatively only when they speak the Word of God accurately. They may have insight into earthly matters, have an unusual measure of common sense, and be smart and wise—but none of those attributes make what they say spiritually authoritative. They cannot command as representatives of God except when they speak Scripture.

Others who have official positions in the church arrogate to themselves authority that not only is not granted in God's Word but that, in many cases, clearly contradicts that Word. They may, for example, claim to have apostolic-like power over disease, demons, and even Satan. They sometimes invoke power over angels, presuming to command those holy servants of God to do their own human bidding. But they command in areas where they have not the slightest jurisdiction.

While Paul was ministering in Ephesus, "some of the Jewish exorcists, who went from place to place, attempted to name over those who had the evil spirits the name of the Lord Jesus, saying, 'I adjure you by Jesus whom Paul preaches.' And seven sons of one Sceva, a Jewish chief priest, were doing this. And the evil spirit answered and said to them, 'I recognize Jesus, and I know about Paul, but who are you?'" (Acts 19:13–15). The consequence of those men's presumption was immediate, painful, and embarrassing. "The man, in whom was the evil spirit, leaped on them and subdued all of them and overpowered them, so that they fled out of that house naked and wounded. And this became known to all, both Jews and Greeks, who lived in Ephesus; and fear fell upon them all and the name of the Lord Jesus was being magnified" (vv. 16–17).

A second area of presumed authority is ecclesiastical. Certain cults and church organizations claim to wield it. For example, for over fifteen hundred years, the Roman Catholic Church has claimed to be the only true church of Jesus Christ and often has claimed authority over human governments and society, indeed over the very souls of men. Although that church affirms that Scripture is the Word of God, it maintains that, because it was given through the church, the church therefore stands above Scripture rather than under it. Because it believes itself to be the only true church, the Catholic Church also claims that it is the sole reliable interpreter of the Bible and the channel through which divine revelation has been, and continues to be, given. According to Catholic dogma, when the pope speaks ex cathedra (literally, "from the chair," that is, from the papal chair, or throne), he speaks with divine authority. It is also asserted that traditions composing the magisterium, the accumulated pronouncements of church councils and papal decrees, hold the same authority as the Bible. The Catholic Church presumes to grant its priests the authority to forgive sins, not only when prescribed confession is made but also through last rites (extreme unction), even if a person is completely unconscious at the time. All such authority is man-made and false.

A third kind of mistaken authority is intellectualism, the notion that one's own ideas carry authority. The Renaissance and Enlightenment periods brought unqualified trust in man's ability to solve his own problems and determine his own destiny apart from God or any other supernatural power. For many people, reason was elevated virtually to the status of deity.

Man's intellectual power is a gracious gift from God to the creatures He made in His own image. But that divinely bestowed gift is not sufficient to lead men to God. Like all other aspects of his being, man's intellect was corrupted by the Fall. Paul makes clear in his letter to the church in Rome that "that which is known about God is evident within" even unrighteous and rebellious men; "for God made it evident to them. For since the creation of the world His invisible attributes, His eternal power and divine nature, have been clearly seen, being understood through what has been made, so that they are without excuse" (Rom. 1:19–20). The overwhelming evidence not only of God's existence but also of His power and glory is inescapable. But despite that evidence, sinful mankind does not honor God or give Him thanks. Because men trust in their own intellect and are determined to have their own way, they become futile in their speculations, and their foolish hearts are darkened (v. 21). The best of human ideas are impotent to transform the soul, to bring spiritual life, to make a new creation, or to break the power of sin.

In our own day, many theologians and biblical scholars think they have authority over the Bible. They presume that their education and erudition qualifies them to decide if and when Scripture is true and binding. On a less scholarly but equally disastrous level, many pastors suppose that, with their own skills and insights, they can help people solve their problems and surmount whatever moral, spiritual, or emotional shortcomings they may have. But Paul would say to such people what he said almost two thousand years ago to believers in the worldly-wise city of Corinth: "When I came to you, brethren, I did not come with superiority of speech or of wisdom, proclaiming to you the testimony of God. For I determined to know nothing among you except Jesus Christ, and Him crucified" (1 Cor. 2:1–2).

A fourth kind of mistaken authority, perhaps the dominant one in our day, is experiential. Such statements as "I know this is right (or true) because I feel it is" are tragically common, even among Christians. But intuition is not knowing. Feeling and emotion cannot discern truth and have no necessary relation to the truth. There is no reliability or authority in mere experience.

Yet it is common for people to believe something is true simply because they feel it is true or because they experience something that leads them to conclude that it is true. With utter disregard for careful biblical study and interpretation, they whimsically mishandle the truth and thereby forfeit true spiritual authority.

The challenge for the preacher is to keep his own intuition and experience out of the text and to keep himself out of the sermon so that the voice of God alone is heard. Again J. I. Packer offers helpful insight:

> Self-projection . . . undermines and erodes authority. If by his words and manner the preacher focuses attention on himself, thus modeling some mode of self-absorption or self-satisfaction rather than humble response to the word that he proclaims, he precludes all possibility of his channeling any sense of divine authority: what he does not feel himself he cannot mediate to others. James Denney said somewhere that you cannot convey the impression both that you are a great preacher and that Jesus Christ is a great Savior; he might have added: or that the Lord is a great God. God-projection and Christ-projection rather than self-projection is the way to communicate and engender in one's hearers a sense of divine authority in one's preaching. Self-reliance in the act of preaching is a further hindrance to true authority in preaching, just

as self-projection is. It too has the effect of inducing the hearers to attend to the messenger rather than the message—in other words, to man rather than to God—and authentic authority is eliminated when that happens. ("From the Scripture to the Sermon," *Ashland Theological Journal,* vol. xxi [1990], p. 50)

Congregations who for decades have heard only a preacher's insights and learned the most recent psychological and social theories are shocked and offended when they hear "Thus says the Lord." To them the truth and the standards of Scripture seem unloving, inhibiting, and outdated. And the man of God who preaches that truth and holds believers to those divine standards is himself considered insensitive, judgmental, unloving, and perhaps even irrelevant.

Many churchgoers simply do not want to hear authoritative and demanding preaching about an authoritative and demanding God. Like those about whom Paul warned Timothy, they are not inclined to "endure sound doctrine; but wanting to have their ears tickled, they . . . accumulate for themselves teachers in accordance to their own desires" (2 Tim. 4:3). In our own day, there is no shortage of preachers who are willing to oblige such self-centered hearers. By and large, the most popular preaching is broad-minded, anecdotal, entertaining, ego-building, and, above all, never confrontational or dogmatic. It offends no pride, disturbs no conscience, and is a clear reflection of the humanistic spirit of the age, in which tolerance and unity at any cost are the supreme virtues.

It is essential to preach the Word with authority in order to counteract the prideful rejection of God's truth and authority that is the root of all sin. Satan rebelled against God in heaven and later lured man into rebelling against God on earth. Consequently, fallen man has no regard for God's law, God's will, God's holiness, or God's sovereignty. And when God and His Word are rejected, it is inevitable that spiritual and moral absolutes are rejected. All beliefs and all standards become relative and optional, a matter of personal choice. Only an authoritative Word from God that is heard, believed, and obeyed can rescue sinners from their rebellion.

A generation of parents who have failed to discipline their children has added to the anti-authority mentality, and they have produced a generation of young people who fail to respect their parents, their teachers, the police, or the government—not to mention God. That general rebellion against and resistance to authority is, of course, exacerbated when both parents work and have little time for their children. Even more destructive is divorce, especially when accompanied by the sexual infidelity, physical and mental abuse, or alcohol and drug addiction of parents. Preaching authoritatively to such a generation is a challenge.

For over half a century, educational philosophies have accommodated natural resentment of authority by exalting personal rights, personal choice, personal independence, self-expression, and self-sufficiency. During this time, the secular media has waged an ever-increasing campaign against social authority—parental, religious, police, and political. Personal vengeance and civil disobedience are glorified as legitimate answers to injustice, real or perceived.

Even many church leaders are far from being models of virtue and integrity. Moral and ethical scandals involving preachers and leaders of Christian organizations have become almost commonplace and do devastating damage to an already weakened church that has been infected by those who reject authority.

The message that Titus was to proclaim with authority is summarized in the phrase with which the verse begins—**these things,** which refers back to what Paul has mentioned so far in this chapter regarding holy living and the precious gospel, summed up in the phrase "the things which are fitting for sound doctrine" (2:1). It was these divine truths that Titus was, in turn, to **speak and exhort and reprove** as he ministered in the churches on Crete.

Speak (from *laleō*) points to the pastor's responsibility to preach, announce, reveal, and disclose, with the intent of making clear God's truth so that those who hear may understand. Careful and faithful biblical preaching gives them knowledge of that truth.

Exhort is from *parakaleō*, which carries the ideas of beseeching, entreating, and pleading. It involves more than simply stating and explaining truth. The preacher who exhorts seeks by every means at his disposal to persuade and encourage his hearers not simply to understand but to believe God's truth.

Whereas **exhort** is a positive command to do what is right, **reprove** (*elenchō*) is a negative command meaning "to convince and correct one who does not yet recognize or admit that he must turn away from what is wrong." William Barclay writes, "The eyes of the sinner must be opened to his sin. The mind of the misguided must be led to realize its mistake. The heart of the heedless must be stabbed broad awake. The Christian message is no opiate to send men to sleep; it is no comfortable assurance that everything will be all right. It is rather the blinding light which shows men themselves as they are and God as He is" (*The Letters to Timothy, Titus and Philemon* [Philadelphia: Westminster, 1960], p. 296).

Summing up, the preacher must strive to bring his hearers to understand, believe, and obey God's truth.

Paul's closing admonition in this chapter, **Let no one disregard you,** adds muscle to the command to speak with authority. The phrase **let no one** clearly allows for no exception. No believer should be allowed to reject or disregard God's truth. In effect, Paul is giving a call to church discipline as outlined in Matthew 18:15–17, 1 Corinthians 5:1–2, and Titus 3:10–11.

Disregard is from *periphroneō,* which has the literal meaning of "thinking around something, usually for the purpose of evasion." Eventually, the word came to be used almost exclusively in the negative sense of strongly disagreeing with an idea and of treating it with disrespect or disregard. God's truth is to be proclaimed with authority, and obedience to it demanded in the church. No disobedience can be tolerated or overlooked.

The Christian's Responsibility in a Pagan Society

9

Remind them to be subject to rulers, to authorities, to be obedient, to be ready for every good deed, to malign no one, to be uncontentious, gentle, showing every consideration for all men.
For we also once were foolish ourselves, disobedient, deceived,
enslaved to various lusts and pleasures, spending our life in
malice and envy, hateful, hating one another. But when the kindness of God our Savior and His love for mankind appeared, He
saved us, not on the basis of deeds which we have done in righteousness, but according to His mercy, by the washing of regeneration and renewing by the Holy Spirit, whom He poured out
upon us richly through Jesus Christ our Savior, that being justified by His grace we might be made heirs according to the hope
of eternal life. This is a trustworthy statement; and concerning
these things I want you to speak confidently, so that those who
have believed God may be careful to engage in good deeds.
These things are good and profitable for men. (3:1–8)

Here Paul moves from how believers are to live in the church
(chapter 2) to how they are to live in society. This is a crucial section of
instruction for today. The United States essentially is now a pagan na-

tion. After being blessed with some 150 years of strong Christian, biblical influence, our country has been rapidly declining, especially during the last half of the twentieth century. Millions of Americans still attend church regularly, and many more consider themselves to be Christians. According to polls, most Americans claim to believe in God. But practical atheism and moral relativism have dominated our society for many decades. For the most part, the few vestiges of Christianity still reflected in our culture are weak and compromising. A growing number of those vestiges have become apostate or cultic.

Many observers have referred to this period in the United States, and in Western society in general, as post-Christian. By any measure, it is certainly sub-Christian. Although many parts of our culture still wear some sort of religious mask, in reality it is largely pagan. Through its leaders, its legislative bodies, and its courts it has adopted not simply a non-Christian but a distinctively anti-Christian stance and agenda. Anything and everything that is explicitly Christian and biblical has been swept away under such guises as separation of church and state, equal rights, and religious and moral tolerance.

The many biblical tenets and standards that once were part of the fabric of our country, and that provided the undeniable cultural benefits of morality, are now gone. Whatever its form or practical benefits may have been, cultural Christianity is dead. Self-expression, moral freedom, materialism, and hedonism are the prevailing gods. Those gods, as clearly pagan as any in the ancient Greek or Roman pantheons, have inevitably spawned the epidemic breakdown of families, illegitimate births, sexual evils of every sort, unequaled growth of drug addiction and crime, and the wanton destruction of unborn babies. In the name of intellectual and scientific progress, godless philosophies have long dominated secular as well as much private education.

Not surprisingly, most of those who have grown up in this standardless society strongly resist any sort of controlled behavior. Consequently, we do not have enough laws to cover the rapidly increasing and more sophisticated forms of crime. Nor do we have enough police to arrest lawbreakers, enough courts to try them, or enough prisons to incarcerate them.

The spiritual revival of the 1970s swept across the campuses of many colleges and universities. Despite the excesses and distortions that Satan inevitably uses to try to frustrate the work of the Holy Spirit, many students received Christ as Savior and Lord. Mass baptisms were conducted in rivers, lakes, and even oceans. That same period of time witnessed the release of several new versions of the English Bible. Christian publishing and broadcasting had remarkable growth, and an undeniable wind of the Spirit was blowing. In many ways, those days caused evangelical Christians to rejoice. Understandably, many believers expected that movement to usher in a new day of blessing.

But the revival of the seventies soon turned into the debauchery of the eighties and nineties. Many government leaders, educators, celebrities, college students, and much of society in general became openly disparaging of biblical standards of morality and of Christianity as a whole. Laws were written, court decisions were made, and school standards—from kindergarten through graduate level—were adopted that were avowedly contemptuous of religion in general and of biblical Christianity in particular.

Evangelicals became as resentful of this secular trend as they had been encouraged by the spiritual revival that preceded it. Believers became alarmed that legislatures, courts, and administrations began to openly sanction deviant sexual behavior, especially homosexuality. They became sickened that in many, if not most, public-school sex education courses the only real dangers for teens who are sexually active are held to be sexually transmitted disease or unwanted pregnancy. They are repulsed that criminals are being exonerated and innocent victims disregarded. They are appalled that biblical standards of ethics are blatantly rejected and that vulgarity, profanity, and blasphemy not only have become condoned but admired.

In reaction to the rapid and pervasive escalation of immorality and ungodliness, believers have become both saddened and angered. Hostility among some of them has been intensified still further when they learn that their taxes are being used to fund ideas and practices that only a few generations ago were condemned even by most secularists. They fear for their children and even more for their grandchildren because of the kind of world into which they will be born, educated, and have to live.

Many well-meaning Christian leaders have founded organizations to counteract anti-Christian influences and assaults. Attempting to fight fire with fire, as it were, Christian organizations, publishers, and broadcasters have sought to counter anti-Christian ideas and programs by using non-Christian tactics. They have decided it is time to stand up for their "rights" and have declared war on the prevailing non-Christian culture, especially the liberal national media. They have become hostile to unbelievers, the very ones God has called them to love and reach with the gospel.

But neither the New Testament nor the example of the early church justifies such a mentality. The cause of Christ cannot be protected or expanded by social intimidation any more than by government decree or military conquest. Ours is a spiritual warfare against human ideologies and beliefs that are set up against God and that can only be successfully conquered with the weapon of the Word (see 2 Cor. 10:3–5). In his book *The Evangelical Pulpit,* John Seel writes,

> A politicized faith not only blurs our priorities, but weakens our loyalties. Our primary citizenship is not on earth but in heaven. . . . Though few evangelicals would deny this truth in theory, the language of our spiritual citizenship frequently gets wrapped in the red, white and blue. Rather than acting as resident aliens of a heavenly kingdom, too often we sound [and act] like resident apologists for a Christian America. . . . Unless we reject the false reliance on the illusion of Christian America, evangelicalism will continue to distort the gospel and thwart a genuine biblical identity. . . .
> American evangelicalism is now covered by layers and layers of historically shaped attitudes that obscure our original biblical core. ([Grand Rapids: Baker, 1993], pp. 106–7)

We must repudiate our confused loyalties and concerns for the passing world and put aside our misguided efforts to change culture externally. To allow our thoughts, plans, time, money, and energy to be spent trying to make a superficially Christian America, or to put a veneer of morality over the world, is to distort the gospel, misconstrue our divine calling, and squander our God-given resources. We must not weaken our spiritual mission, obscure our priority of proclaiming the gospel of salvation, or become confused about our spiritual citizenship, loyalties, and obligations. We are to change society, but by faithfully proclaiming the gospel, which changes lives on the inside.

As this passage in Titus and many others in the New Testament make clear, we must not become so engulfed in trying to force social behavior to conform to our standards that we become enemies of those our Lord has called us to win to Himself. We must reject sin and never compromise God's standards of righteousness. But we also must never engage in defamation and denigration of the lost sinners who make up our corrupt culture. When Christians become political, sinners become the enemy instead of the mission field.

Paul obviously was consumed with the divine mandate to evangelize when he wrote this letter to Titus. It was not his desire for Christians living in the pagan culture of Crete to turn on the unbelievers and try to force changes in cultural standards and personal behavior in order to be less offended by their society.

No Christian can help wishing that the moral standards of society were better. We do grieve over the rampant lewdness, indecency, deceitfulness, vulgarity, unchastity, extreme self-indulgence, and every other form of depravity that is corroding our society. But, as noble as the desire to reform culture may be, God does not call the church to impact society by promoting laws and judicial decisions that support biblical standards of behavior.

The single divine calling of the church is to bring sinful people to salvation through Christ. Like ancient Israel, we are to be "a spiritual house for a holy priesthood, to offer up spiritual sacrifices acceptable to God through Jesus Christ, . . . a chosen race, a royal priesthood, a holy nation, a people for God's own possession, that you may proclaim the excellencies of Him who has called you out of darkness into His marvelous light" (1 Pet. 2:5, 9; cf. Ex. 19:6).

The purpose of a priest is to bring God to people and people to God. If we do not lead the lost to salvation, nothing else we do for them, no matter how beneficial at the time, is of any eternal consequence. Whether a person is an atheist or a theist, a hooligan or a model citizen, a criminal or a policeman, a sexual pervert or a paragon of virtue, a brutal tyrant or a gracious benefactor—if he does not have a saving relationship to Jesus Christ, his destiny is hell. Whether he is a militant proabortionist or a militant antiabortionist, if he is not saved, he will spend eternity apart from God. It makes no difference whether a person goes to hell as a policeman, a junkie, or a judge. The end is the same.

When the church adopts a moralizing approach, its energy and resources are diverted and evangelization suffers. When Christians become hostile to government and to society in general, they almost inevitably become hostile to the unsaved leaders of that government and the unsaved citizens who live in that society.

We cannot afford to weaken our spiritual mission or our priority of gospel proclamation and kingdom consciousness by getting involved in efforts to change cultural behavior. Even more important, we cannot become enemies of the very ones we seek to win to Christ, our potential brothers and sisters in the Lord. When people come to Christ, He changes them and they change the sphere that they influence.

Really changing society starts when a Christian's moral and spiritual concern is for his own virtue and godliness. It is our righteous attitude and conduct that make us not only more pleasing to the Lord but more pleasing to the unsaved. It is righteous living that makes the saving message of the gospel believable to the lost. If we claim to be saved from sin but still live sinful lives, our preaching and teaching, no matter how orthodox, is likely to fall on deaf ears.

In Paul's day, of course, there was no cultural Christianity to confront and denounce, only blatant paganism—with all the malevolent trappings that Satan could generate within it—and weak, superficial, and hypocritical Judaism.

Because of his wide-ranging education before his conversion, Paul was particularly familiar with both superficial Judaism and established paganism. He knew what it was like to live in a world of murderous tyrants, gross inequality and injustice, and sexual looseness and perversion. The Roman Empire, which in that day comprised all of the known Western world and some of the eastern, was engulfed by idolatry, ritual prostitution, slavery, extortion, and exorbitant taxation. Only Roman citizens had reasonable protection under the law, and even that privileged status could easily be forfeited. There was plenty to make believers angry at their society.

Yet Paul, like Jesus, did not spend his time condemning pagan beliefs and practices. He did not admonish believers to impact pagan culture by trying to reform its idolatry, immorality, and corruption. Nor did he call for nonviolent, much less violent, resistance against unjust laws or inhuman punishments. He called rather for believers to preach, teach, and witness to the transforming power of salvation through the Lord Jesus Christ and to live lives that gave clear evidence of that power. And particularly he did not want believers to resent unbelievers, but rather to show them love and compassion. To excite such love toward the wicked who corrupt the world, Paul urges Titus to help believers remember several essential realities.

In the first eight verses of chapter 3, Paul admonishes Titus to remind Christians on Crete of realities they had heard many times before. The four major areas of remembrance pertain to our duties as Christians (vv. 1b–2), to our former condition of unbelief and sin (v. 3), to our salvation through Jesus Christ (vv. 4–7), and to our mission to an unbelieving, lost world (v. 8).

Remind is from *hupomimnēskō* and is here an imperative of command that applies to all of the admonitions in this passage. The present tense gives this verb the additional connotations of continuity and persistence. Reminding Christians of these truths should keep them from feeling hostile toward and superior to the unconverted.

REMEMBER YOUR DUTIES

to be subject to rulers, to authorities, to be obedient, to be ready for every good deed, to malign no one, to be uncontentious, gentle, showing every consideration for all men. (3:1b–2)

These seven Christian duties apply to all believers at all times. They are the attitudes and dispositions that should always characterize our lives among those who do not belong to God. The Holy Spirit here defines our obligation to pagan culture.

Willing obedience to human authority demonstrates to the world that the ways and workings of this world are not to be major concerns for believers. Our work is in this world but not of it, because our true citizenship is in heaven (Phil. 3:20). Our focus is to be on holy living and on winning the lost to Jesus Christ, who Himself came "to seek and to save that which was lost" (Luke 19:10). In obedience to the Lord and as a testimony to the world, we are not to "be conformed to this world, but be transformed by the renewing of [our minds], that [we] may prove what the will of God is, that which is good and acceptable and perfect" (Rom. 12:2).

As Christians, we "are a chosen race, a royal priesthood, a holy nation, a people for God's own possession, that [we] may proclaim the excellencies of Him who has called [us] out of darkness into His marvelous light" (1 Pet. 2:9). It is for that reason that we are to keep our "behavior excellent among the Gentiles, so that in the thing in which they slander [us] as evildoers, they may on account of [our] good deeds, as they observe them, glorify God in the day of visitation" (2:12). Continuing the lesson in earthly citizenship, Peter mentions several duties that Paul cites in Romans 13. "Submit yourselves for the Lord's sake to every human institution," he commands, "whether to a king as the one in authority, or to governors as sent by him for the punishment of evildoers and the praise of those who do right. For such is the will of God that by doing right you may silence the ignorance of foolish men. . . . Honor all men; love the brotherhood, fear God, honor the king" (vv. 13–15, 17).

First, we are to **be subject to rulers, to authorities.** This duty pertains to our attitude and conduct in regard to secular government. It is important to note that Paul specifies no particular kind or level of government or any particular kind or level of government official. He allows for no exceptions or qualifications.

On one of the many occasions when Jewish leaders tried to maneuver Jesus into heresy or treason, the Pharisees and Herodians "sent their disciples to Him, . . . saying, 'Teacher, we know that You are truthful and teach the way of God in truth, and defer to no one; for You are not partial to any. Tell us therefore, what do You think? Is it lawful to give a poll-tax to Caesar, or not?'" (Matt. 22:16–17). They knew that if Jesus said "Yes," He would be discredited with the Jewish populace, who hated and chafed under excessive Roman taxes. If He said "No," He would have been arrested for treason against Rome. Perceiving their malice, Jesus replied, "'Why are you testing Me, you hypocrites? Show Me the coin used for the poll-tax.' And they brought Him a denarius. And He said to them, 'Whose likeness and inscription is this?' They said to Him, 'Caesar's.' Then He said to them, 'Then render to Caesar the things that are Caesar's; and to God the things that are God's'" (Matt. 22:15–21).

Jesus did not suggest that the tax was fair or that it would be used for good purposes. He was fully aware that Caesar claimed to be a god and that Jews therefore considered his likeness on the coin to be a form of idolatry. Yet He declared unambiguously that the tax should be paid. On an earlier occasion, He made clear that, even as God's incarnate Son, He did not exempt Himself from payment of taxes (Matt. 17:24–27).

In Romans 13, Paul mentions seven reasons why all people, including believers, are under divine obligation to respect and obey human government. First, "the governing authorities. . . . which exist are established by God" (v. 1). Second, the person "who resists authority has opposed the ordinance of God" (v. 2a). Third, those who oppose such authority "will receive condemnation upon themselves" (v. 2b). Fourth, government is designed to restrain evil and is therefore "not a cause of fear for good behavior, but for evil" (v. 3). Fifth, it is divinely designed to promote the good of individuals and of society, "a minister of God to you for good" (v. 4a). Sixth, and conversely, it also is divinely empowered to punish wrongdoers, if necessary, by capital punishment ("the sword"), as "an avenger who brings wrath upon the one who practices evil" (v. 4b). Seventh, for believers "it is necessary to be in subjection [to government] not only because of wrath, but also for conscience' sake" (v. 5). "For because of this you also pay taxes," the apostle continues, "for rulers are servants of God, devoting themselves to this very thing. Render to all what is due them: tax to whom tax is due; custom to whom custom; fear to whom fear; honor to whom honor" (vv. 6–7).

The Roman government under which the early church lived not only was thoroughly pagan and morally debauched but also was despotic, oppressive, unjust, and brutal. Nevertheless, Paul makes clear that the Christian's obligation to respect and obey human government does not rest on its being democratic or just but solely on its being the God-ordained means by which human society is regulated. Therefore, as Paul makes clear in the passage just cited, the person who resists and opposes human government, resists and opposes God.

Second, we are **to be obedient** to human authorities. The only exception regards their commanding us to do something that is against the command of God. Such an exception is found in the account of Acts 4. When the Sanhedrin, the Jewish high council in Jerusalem, ordered Peter and John "not to speak or teach at all in the name of Jesus," the apostles replied, "Whether it is right in the sight of God to give heed to you rather than to God, you be the judge; for we cannot stop speaking what we have seen and heard" (Acts 4:18–20; cf. 5:40–42).

Third, we are **to be ready for every good deed.** Paul is not speaking of reluctantly doing what we know we should do in society but of willingly and sincerely being **ready** and prepared to perform **every good deed** toward the people around us that we have opportunity to do. He is referring to a sincere, loving eagerness to serve others. No matter how hostile the society around us may be, we are to be good to the people in it whose lives intersect with ours. "While we have opportunity, [we are to] do good to all men, and especially to those who are of the household of the faith" (Gal. 6:10). We are to be known for what might be described as consistent aggressive goodness, done not simply out of duty but out of love for our Lord and for other people.

That attitude is in direct contrast to that of false teachers. As Paul mentions earlier in this letter, such men "profess to know God, but by their deeds they deny Him, being detestable and disobedient, and worthless for any good deed" (Titus 1:16).

The lives of believers should continually demonstrate the spiritual transformation they have received through faith in Jesus Christ.

Fourth, we are **to malign no one,** not even those who contribute most to the assault on biblical standards. Even while contending against the worst of sins committed by the worst of sinners, we must never stoop to maligning those whose sin we detest. **Malign** is from *blasphēmeō,* from which we get the English *blasphemy.* It is to slander, curse, and treat with contempt, and it can never be done from a righteous motive. It is tragic that many Christians speak contemptuously of politicians and other public figures, not realizing that in doing so they hinder the work of redemption. "I urge that entreaties and prayers, petitions and thanksgivings, be made on behalf of all men," Paul admonishes, "for kings and all who are in authority, in order that we may lead a tranquil and quiet life in all godliness and dignity. This is good and acceptable in the sight of God our Savior, who desires all men to be saved and to come to the knowledge of the truth" (1 Tim. 2:1–4).

Fifth, we are **to be uncontentious,** meaning friendly and peaceful toward the lost rather than quarrelsome and belligerent. In an ungodly, immoral society it is easy to become angry with those who corrupt it, condemning them and writing them off as hopeless and beyond the pale of God's grace. But we have no right to become hostile when unbelievers act like unbelievers. "If possible," Paul admonished believers in Rome, "so far as it depends on you, be at peace with all men" (Rom. 12:18). If God so limitlessly and unconditionally loved the world that He sent His sinless Son to redeem it, how can we, as sinful recipients of His redeeming grace, be callous and loveless toward those who have not yet received it?

Sixth, we are to be **gentle.** *Epieikēs* (**gentle**) carries the basic idea of that which is moderate, fair, and forbearing in regard to treatment of others. It has been referred to as "sweet reasonableness," an attitude that does not hold grudges but always gives others the benefit of any doubt.

Seventh, and finally, we are to be **showing every consideration for all men,** a characteristic closely related to the previous two. In

Greek literature *prautēs* (**consideration**) was sometimes used of a feigned, hypocritical concern for others that is motivated by self-interest. But in the New Testament it is always used of genuine **consideration** for others and is sometimes translated in this verse as "meekness" (KJV), or "humility" (NIV).

In his *Synonyms of the New Testament,* Richard Trench comments that *prautēs* refers to "an inwrought grace of the soul; and the exercises of it are first and chiefly towards God. It is that temper of Spirit in which we accept His dealing with us as good, and therefore without disputing or resisting. . . . It is only the humble heart which is also the meek, and which, as such, does not fight against God and more or less struggle and contend with Him. This meekness, however, being first of all a meekness before God, is also such in the face of men, even of evil men, out of a sense that these, with the insults and injuries which they may inflict, are permitted and employed by Him for the chastening and purifying of His elect" (in W. E. Vine, *An Expository Dictionary of New Testament Words* [Westwood, N.J.: Revell, 1940], 3:55–56). "Described negatively," Vine goes on to comment, "[*prautēs*] is the opposite of self-assertiveness and self-interest; it is equanimity of spirit that is neither elated nor cast down, simply because it is not occupied with self at all" (Vine, 3:56).

Our Lord Himself is the supreme example of genuine **consideration** [*prautēs*] **for all men** that should characterize His followers. In his second letter to believers in Corinth, Paul speaks of "the meekness [*prautēs*] and gentleness of Christ" (2 Cor. 10:1). Quoting from the Septuagint (Greek Old Testament) rendering of Zechariah 9:9, which predicts the Lord's triumphal entry into Jerusalem, Matthew uses the adjective form (*praus*) to describe Jesus as "gentle, and mounted on a donkey, even on a colt, the foal of a beast of burden" (Matt. 21:5). In a gracious appeal to His followers, Jesus used the same adjective of Himself, saying, "Take My yoke upon you, and learn from Me, for I am gentle [*praus*] and humble in heart; and you shall find rest for your souls" (Matt. 11:29).

Our attitude toward unbelievers should always reflect a spirit of **consideration,** of meekness and gentleness. "Sanctify Christ as Lord in your hearts," Peter tells us, "always being ready to make a defense to everyone who asks you to give an account for the hope that is in you, yet with gentleness and reverence" (1 Pet. 3:15). We also are to deal with sinful and disobedient fellow believers "in a spirit of gentleness" (Gal. 6:1), "with gentleness correcting those who are in opposition, if perhaps God may grant them repentance leading to the knowledge of the truth" (2 Tim. 2:25).

As I have commented on that verse from 2 Timothy:

Although He [Jesus] was God incarnate, and at any moment could have destroyed His enemies with a word or had at His "disposal more than twelve legions of angels" (Matt. 26:53), He chose rather to submit to every indignity, because that was His Father's will for Him in His incarnation.

In the same way, though to a much more limited degree, the faithful bond-servant of Jesus Christ who has great strength of conviction, and who may have leadership authority in the church, willingly expresses and defends his convictions and exercises his authority in a spirit of gentleness [*prautēs*]. The truly meek person is submissive as a matter of choice, because he *wants* to obey his Master and to be like Him. (*2 Timothy*, MacArthur New Testament Commentary [Chicago: Moody, 1995], p. 100)

It is not surprising, therefore, that *prautēs* is a fruit of the Spirit ("meekness," Gal. 5:23) and that the adjective (*praus*) is a beatitude ("meek," Matt. 5:5 KJV). Paul admonishes "those who have been chosen of God, holy and beloved, [to] put on a heart of compassion, kindness, humility, gentleness [*prautēs*] and patience" (Col. 3:12).

The phrase **all men** is not hyperbole or exaggeration. Paul is speaking of every human being, particularly the unsaved. Three times in his first letter to Timothy, the apostle urges "that entreaties and prayers, petitions and thanksgivings, be made on behalf of all men" (2:1). He reminds us that God "desires all men to be saved and to come to the knowledge of the truth" (2:4) and "is the Savior of all men, especially of believers" (4:10; cf. 2:6). Earlier in this letter to Titus he rejoices that "the grace of God has appeared, bringing salvation to all men" (2:11).

Genuine, heartfelt **consideration** for **all men** is one of the most foundational spiritual virtues. As followers and imitators of Jesus Christ, our calling is not to fight for our rights or privileges against the ungodly. Rather, as we live in this corrupt world in subjection and obedience to human authority, doing good deeds, maligning no one, and being uncontentious, gentle, and meek, we will thereby demonstrate the gracious power of God to transform sinners and make them like Himself.

REMEMBER YOUR FORMER CONDITION

For we also once were foolish ourselves, disobedient, deceived, enslaved to various lusts and pleasures, spending our life in malice and envy, hateful, hating one another. (3:3)

Rather than resent and slander unbelieving leaders, educators, the media, and people in the entertainment industry, and rather than becoming incensed and venomous in our attacks on the immoral agendas of various organizations and movements, we should remember that **we also once were** like those whom we now are inclined to defame and condemn. We were once just like them and would still be like them if it were not for the saving grace of God, which alone delivered us.

Paul frequently gives lists of sins that typify unbelievers. Speaking of those "who suppress the truth in unrighteousness, . . . [who] knew God, [but] did not honor Him as God, or give thanks," he points out that "they became futile in their speculations, and their foolish heart was darkened. . . . They did not see fit to acknowledge God any longer, God gave them over to a depraved mind, to do those things which are not proper, being filled with all unrighteousness, wickedness, greed, evil; full of envy, murder, strife, deceit, malice; they are gossips, slanderers, haters of God, insolent, arrogant, boastful, inventors of evil, disobedient to parents, without understanding, untrustworthy, unloving, unmerciful; and, although they know the ordinance of God, that those who practice such things are worthy of death, they not only do the same, but also give hearty approval to those who practice them" (Rom. 1:18, 21, 28–32).

The apostle gives similar lists in his letters to the church at Corinth (1 Cor. 6:9–11), the churches of Galatia (Gal. 5:19–21), and the church at Ephesus (Eph. 4:17–19; cf. 2:1–3). He does not exempt himself, confessing that before his conversion he "was formerly a blasphemer and a persecutor and a violent aggressor" (1 Tim. 1:13; cf. Acts 8:3; Phil. 3:6).

It is not that every believer once lived in or advocated the most extreme sin. If we were converted as a child, we perhaps had not even heard of some of the sins that Paul mentions. Even if we became a believer as an older adult, we may have lived a relatively moral and socially responsible life. But as unsaved human beings, we *all* were depraved in our very nature and were at enmity with God (Rom. 5:10; Eph. 2:3; Col. 1:21), no matter how outwardly moral, respectable, and religious we may have been.

As we grow in the things of the Lord, it is difficult not to be enraged at the unbelievably rapid growth and acceptance of such things as homosexuality, pornography, gratuitous sex, New Age philosophy, abortion on demand, and school sex education that promotes almost everything but chastity. Those and many other such beliefs and practices are unquestionably evil, corrupt, destructive, and ungodly. They ravage individual lives and society as a whole and they dishonor our holy God.

But that has always been true and will continue to be true until the Lord returns. As his lists of sins indicate, Paul was well acquainted with the most extreme evils. The very name of Corinth, a Greek city where the apostle ministered for some eighteen months (Acts 18:1–17; 1 Cor. 2:3), was a byword for gross sexual immorality even in the pagan world of that day.

In order for us as believers to give a godly testimony in a pagan culture, we must remember that such is to be expected from the ungodly. In our former condition, **we also once were foolish ourselves,** just like the unbelievers among whom we now live and witness and by whom we are so agitated. To reinforce his point, Paul lists seven vices that characterize the unsaved, vices in which we ourselves were once engaged.

First, Paul reminds us, **we also once were foolish ourselves,** ignorant and uninformed. *Anoētos* (**foolish**) denotes complete lack of understanding, total ignorance in regard to a particular area of knowledge. Paul's point here is that, no matter how advanced a person's education and intellectual accomplishments may be, if he does not recognize God and trust in Him for deliverance from sin, he is **foolish** concerning the most important truth regarding himself. With God, even the wisdom of men is foolishness (cf. 1 Cor. 1:20, 25).

In his fascinating book *The Intellectuals,* Paul Johnson, one of the foremost contemporary historians of Western civilization, documents the morass of unspeakable moral filth and ungodliness that has characterized most of the leading intellectual architects of modern Western culture. Their astounding mental capacities and their profound impact on modern society are incontestable. Yet they are precisely those whom Paul described nearly two thousand years ago, whom, because "they did not see fit to acknowledge God any longer, God gave . . . over to a depraved mind" (Rom. 1:28). Their biographies are studies in wretchedness. A brilliant mind not only is capable of gross evil, but, because of that very brilliance, is capable of the most heinous evils. The appalling atrocities of the Nazis, for example, were conceived and perpetrated by brilliant men in arguably the most intellectually, scientifically, and culturally advanced nation of modern times.

That should not surprise us. It was Lucifer, after all, the most brilliant of archangels, the "star of the morning, son of the dawn," who opposed God and was cast out of heaven with his fellow rebellious angels (Isa. 14:12; cf. Rev. 12:9) and who became Satan, the prince of demons.

Second, we should be patient and gracious to the unsaved of our society because, as unbelievers, we too were once by nature **disobedient** to all authority instituted by God. Through Jeremiah the Lord revealed that "the heart is more deceitful than all else and is desperately sick; who can understand it?" (Jer. 17:9). Jesus declared that "out of the heart come evil thoughts, murders, adulteries, fornications, thefts, false witness, slanders," and everything else that defiles a man (Matt. 15:19–20).

It is for that reason that, although human laws and powers are ordained by God to help restrain and punish evil behavior and maintain a certain amount of social order and safety, they have no power to change the human heart, from which every evil, every sin, every defilement, every debauchery emanates.

Third, as unbelievers we were once, by our very nature, **deceived**. *Planaō* (**deceived**) has the basic idea of being purposely led astray. Satan's objective is to lead sinners into ever greater sin and ungodliness. John refers to him as "the great dragon [who] was thrown down, the serpent of old who is called the devil and Satan, who deceives the whole world" (Rev. 12:9). Whether they acknowledge it or not—and the vast majority do not—all unbelievers are children of their "father the devil, and . . . want to do the desires of [their] father, . . . [who] was a murderer from the beginning, and does not stand in the truth, because there is no truth in him. Whenever he speaks a lie, he speaks from his own nature; for he is a liar, and the father of lies" (John 8:44). Reflecting the nature and following the example of their spiritual father, "evil men and impostors will proceed from bad to worse, deceiving and being deceived" (2 Tim. 3:13). In the end times, "false Christs and false prophets will arise and will show great signs and wonders, so as to mislead, *if possible*, even the elect" (Matt. 24:24, emphasis added).

Fourth, as unbelievers we were once, by our very nature, **enslaved to various lusts and pleasures.** Although the unsaved, natural man willfully chooses to sin, he does so because his very constitution is sinful, and he has neither the desire nor the ability to be anything but sinful. He is therefore both willingly and inevitably **enslaved** to sin in its many and **various** forms.

In Romans 3:10–18, Paul graphically depicts the sad state of sinners:

> As it is written, "There is none righteous, not even one; there is none who understands, there is none who seeks for God; all have turned aside, together they have become useless; there is none who does good, there is not even one. Their throat is an open grave, with their tongues they keep deceiving, the poison of asps is under their lips; whose mouth is full of cursing and bitterness; their feet are swift to shed blood, destruction and misery are in their paths, and the path of peace have they not known. There is no fear of God before their eyes."

Therefore, although we cannot help being dismayed when we see evil flourishing, we should not be surprised. Apart from saving trust in Jesus Christ, a person has no alternative to sin. Paul reminded believers in Rome that before salvation, "you presented your members as slaves to impurity and to lawlessness . . . resulting in further lawlessness" (Rom. 6:19).

Lusts refers to sinful desires and **pleasures** to sinful satisfactions. The apostle is speaking of the full gamut of things that fallen men naturally pursue and enjoy. **Pleasures** is from *hēdonē*, from which we derive *hedonism*, the insatiable pursuit of self-satisfaction that so characterizes modern society. Whether the particular **lusts and pleasures** involve misuse of good things that the Lord provides or are intrinsically evil, the natural man desires and enjoys them for purely selfish and sinful reasons.

Fifth, as unbelievers we were once, by our very nature, **spending our life in malice**. **Spending** translates a form of *diagō*, which has the basic meaning simply of living. But this present active participle carries the further idea of a normal, typical manner of life and is therefore here rendered as **spending our life**. **Malice** translates *kakia*, meaning "evil" or, as one Greek scholar refers to it, "the vicious character generally." To varying degrees, but inevitably, the unsaved person spends his life maliciously.

Sixth, as unbelievers we were once, by our very by nature, living in **envy**. **Envy** is a sin that carries its own reward: it guarantees its own frustration and disappointment. By definition, the envious person cannot be satisfied with what he has and will always crave for more. His evil desires and pleasures are insatiable, and he cannot abide any other person's having something that he himself does not have or having more of something than he himself has.

Seventh, as unbelievers we were once, by our very nature, **hateful**. Hate is a natural fruit of envy, but it is also produced by many other things. It often has no rational base and simply is expressed for its own sake. It does not need a reason. **Hateful** persons despise anyone or anything that stands in their way or displeases them. They find themselves **hating one another** and eventually hating everyone, including those who are most like them. Hatred is not an appealing sin, even to the **hateful.**

Husbands and wives divorce because their egos clash, each wanting his or her own way, even at the cost of their marriage and the welfare of their children. Children raised by hateful parents will themselves likely become hateful, of each other, of their parents, of their teachers, of any person who threatens their freedom and self-will, and eventually of their friends. Hatred is perhaps the loneliest of sins.

Blind to God's truth, God's standards, God's will, and all spiritual reality, unbelievers generate exactly the kind of world that is ours today. They can do nothing else. But although we despise the sins that characterize, motivate, and drive them, we must constantly keep in mind Paul's point in this verse: All of us, without exception, were ourselves once characterized, motivated, and driven by the same sins that are repulsive to us now. That awareness should humble us and be a guard against hating those who are sinful and who need salvation through Jesus Christ, just as we did.

We must look at the unsaved as our Lord looked at them during His incarnation and still looks at them now—with grief and tears over their lostness and a compassionate desire to see them repent, believe in Jesus Christ, and be saved.

REMEMBER YOUR SALVATION

But when the kindness of God our Savior and His love for mankind appeared, He saved us, not on the basis of deeds which we have done in righteousness, but according to His mercy, by the washing of regeneration and renewing by the Holy Spirit, whom He poured out upon us richly through Jesus Christ our Savior, that being justified by His grace we might be made heirs according to the hope of eternal life. (3:4–7)

As the apostle moves to his third reminder, the transitional conjunction **But** turns the emphasis from remembering our former condition of lostness to the equally important need to remember our present condition of salvation. Again, Paul lists seven categories (as in both previous points), this time the seven aspects of salvation that are revealed in the single sentence that comprises verses 4–7.

In this short passage Paul sweeps across the glorious truths of salvation, every facet of which is sovereignly initiated and empowered by God alone. There are doctrines here that could be studied and pondered for months without mining all their truth.

We are now radically different from the way we once were, and from the way the unsaved still are, solely because of God's **kindness, His love, His mercy,** His **washing of regeneration,** His **renewing by the Holy Spirit,** His Son **Jesus Christ our Savior,** and **His grace.**

Among other things, remembering our salvation should motivate us to keep in mind that the only reason we are different now is that **He saved us.** When we are bombarded by our ungodly culture—by ungodly media, ungodly educators, ungodly politicians, ungodly entertainers and sports figures, ungodly books and magazines, ungodly neighbors and co-workers, and even by ungodly friends and relatives—we should focus above all else on the sovereign grace of God, who delivered each one of us from that life purely by His own will and for His own glory and not because of anything desirable or worthy that was in us. It is God "who desires all men to be saved and to come to the knowledge of the truth" (1 Tim. 2:4), who does not wish "for any to perish but for all to come to repentance" (2 Pet. 3:9), and who "so loved the world, that He gave His only begotten Son, that whoever believes in Him should not perish, but have eternal life, . . . that the world should be saved through Him" (John 3:16–17).

Every aspect of salvation is from God and from God alone. First, we should remember that we were saved by **the kindness of God our Savior.** *Chrēstotēs* (**kindness**) connotes genuine goodness and generosity of heart. Our salvation from sin and lostness and death issued wholly from God's **kindness,** His loving, benevolent, and entirely gracious concern to draw us to Himself and redeem us from sin forever.

It is God's nature to be kind to the lost. "Love your enemies, and do good, and lend, expecting nothing in return," Jesus commanded; "and your reward will be great, and you will be sons of the Most High; for *He Himself is kind to ungrateful and evil men*" (Luke 6:35, emphasis added). God is kinder still to His children, those who are saved. In his letter to the church at Ephesus, Paul declared, "God, being rich in mercy, because of His great love with which He loved us, even when we were dead in our transgressions, made us alive together with Christ (by grace you have been saved), and raised us up with Him, and seated us with Him in the heavenly places, in Christ Jesus, in order that in the ages to come *He might show the surpassing riches of His grace in kindness toward us in Christ Jesus*" (Eph. 2:4–7, emphasis added).

Paul again refers to **God** as **Savior,** the central title for both God the Father and for Christ the Son and the theme of this letter (see also 1:3, 4; 2:10, 11, 13; 3:6). Near the beginning of his letter to believers in Rome, the apostle asked rhetorically, "Do you think lightly of the riches of His [God's] kindness and forbearance and patience, not knowing that the kindness of God leads you to repentance?" (Rom. 2:4; cf. 11:22). It is the sovereign **kindness of God** that initiates repentance, the first step in salvation.

Second, we should remember that we were saved by God's uninfluenced and unearned **love for mankind,** a phrase that translates the compound Greek noun *philanthrōpia,* from which the English *philanthropy* is derived. It is composed of *phileō* ("to have affection for") and *anthrōpos* ("man," or **mankind**) and refers to compassion, especially the eagerness to deliver someone from pain, trouble, or danger. It involves more than mere emotion and always finds a way to express itself in some form of helpfulness.

In the last two chapters of Acts, Luke records two instances of unsaved Gentiles showing *philanthrōpia*. Before Paul boarded ship to be taken as a prisoner to Rome, the centurion "Julius treated Paul with consideration [*philanthrōpia*] and allowed him to go to his friends and receive care" (Acts 27:3). After the shipwreck off the coast of Malta, Paul and all the others on board managed to safely reach shore, just as God had promised (27:22–26). Luke then reports that "the natives showed us extraordinary kindness [philanthrōpia]; for because of the rain that had set in and because of the cold, they kindled a fire and received us all" (28:2).

The Old Testament speaks often of the Lord's lovingkindness, which never ceases or fails (Lam. 3:22). David declared, "Thou, O Lord, art a God merciful and gracious, slow to anger and abundant in loving-kindness and truth" (Ps. 86:15; cf. 145:8). Another psalmist proclaimed, "He has made His wonders to be remembered; the Lord is gracious and compassionate" (Ps. 111:4).

In the present passage, **kindness** and **love for mankind** are virtually synonymous. The two words together, especially in the context of these four verses, reflect the even deeper *agapē* love that God has for fallen **mankind**. The best-known and most beloved passage that expresses God's *agapē* love is "For God so loved the world, that He gave His only begotten Son, that whoever believes in Him should not perish, but have eternal life" (John 3:16). Because of God's great and compassionate **love for mankind,** He delivers sinners from the oppression and fatal danger of their iniquity.

It was through the incarnation of Jesus Christ that God's sovereign **kindness** and **love for mankind appeared,** at which time His grace also appeared (Titus 2:11). "God, being rich in mercy, because of His great love with which He loved us, even when we were dead in our transgressions, made us alive together with Christ (by grace you have been saved), and raised us up with Him, and seated us with Him in the heavenly places, in Christ Jesus" (Eph. 2:4–6). All believers can exult with Paul: "I have been crucified with Christ; and it is no longer I who live, but Christ lives in me; and the life which I now live in the flesh I live by faith in the Son of God, who loved me, and delivered Himself up for me" (Gal. 2:20; cf. Rev. 1:5).

John Calvin wrote that, although God

> testifies his goodness and love to all, yet we know it by faith only, when he declares himself to be our Father in Christ. Before Paul was called to the faith of Christ, he enjoyed innumerable gifts of God, which might have given him a taste of God's fatherly kindness; he had been educated, from his infancy, in the doctrine of the law; yet he wanders in darkness, so as not to perceive the goodness of God, till the Spirit enlightened his mind, and till Christ came forth as the witness and pledge of the grace of God the Father, from which, but for him, we are all excluded. Thus he means that the kindness of God is not revealed and known but by the light of faith.

Third, we should remember that we did not save ourselves by self-effort or any other means, but that God **saved us, not on the basis of deeds which we have done in righteousness, but according to His mercy.**

Saved is from *sōzō,* which, although it is sometimes used in the New Testament of physical, temporal deliverance (see, e.g., Matt. 8:25; John 12:27), is most often used of spiritual salvation. Those words have always been cherished by those who *have been* **saved.** Our salvation is the most important and precious thing about us, to which nothing else can begin to compare. Biblical Christianity is a saving religion, and salvation has always been the central theme of Christian songs and hymns.

In the negative sense, salvation relates to our deliverance from the penalty of sin, that is, from divine wrath, spiritual death, and hell. Still again, we are pointed to that beloved text in the gospel of John. "For God so loved the world, that He gave His only begotten Son," the Son Himself declared, "that whoever believes in Him should not perish, but have eternal life. For God did not send the Son into the world to judge the world, but that the world should be saved [*sōzō*] through Him" (John 3:16–17).

In the positive sense, salvation grants us the privilege "to come to the knowledge of the truth" (1 Tim. 2:4), to be made "alive together with Christ" (Eph. 2:5), to be delivered "from the domain of darkness, and transferred . . . to the kingdom of His beloved Son" (Col. 1:13), and to have "the hope of eternal life" (Titus 1:2).

After Pentecost, "the Lord was adding to their number day by day those who were being saved" (Acts 2:47). In words that may have been part of an early church creed, Paul wrote, "It is a trustworthy statement, deserving full acceptance, that Christ Jesus came into the world to save sinners" (1 Tim. 1:15). The purpose of the incarnation was to accomplish the sacrifice that would save lost sinners, among whom we all were once numbered (Eph. 2:5).

The Savior did not redeem us because of anything that we were, or could ever be, in ourselves. Ephesians 2:8–9 makes it clear: "For by grace you have been saved through faith; and that not of yourselves, it is the gift of God; not as a result of works, that no one should boast" (Eph. 2:8–9). No **deeds,** even those **done in** relative **righteousness,** could have earned or merited our salvation. We made no contribution to God's sovereign and gracious work of salvation. We did not deserve deliverance from sin and death. We did not deserve to be born again, recreated in the very image of our Lord. We did not deserve to become God's children and joint heirs with His only begotten Son, Jesus Christ. We did not deserve the promise of everlasting life, which we will spend in heaven in the continual presence of God.

We were rather saved **according to His mercy. Mercy** is from *eleos*, which refers to the outward manifestation of pity and assumes need on the part of those who receive it and sufficient resources to meet the need on the part of those who show it. In some ways, **mercy** is similar to grace, which Paul mentions in verse 7. But whereas grace relates to guilt, **mercy** relates to affliction. Whereas grace relates to the state of the sinner before God the judge, **mercy** relates to the condition of the sinner in his sin. Whereas grace judicially forgives the offender for his wrongdoing, **mercy** compassionately helps him recover.

Fourth, we should remember that we were saved by God's mercifully deciding to grant the **washing of regeneration.** When we were saved, we were cleansed of our sin, the decay and filth that is produced by spiritual deadness. Speaking of that truth in his letter to the church at Ephesus, Paul explains that we were cleansed "by the washing of water with the word" (Eph. 5:26). James declares that, "In the exercise of His will He [God] brought us forth by the word of truth, so that we might be, as it were, the first fruits among His creatures" (James 1:18). Peter reminds us that we "have been born again not of seed which is perishable but imperishable, that is, through the living and abiding word of God" (1 Pet. 1:23).

Palingenesia (**regeneration**) carries the idea of receiving new life, of being born again, or born from above. Jesus told the enquiring Nicodemus, "Truly, truly, I say to you, unless one is born of water and the Spirit, he cannot enter into the kingdom of God" (John 3:5; cf. Eph. 5:26). In his first letter, the apostle John repeatedly speaks of the marvelous truth of the new birth. We are assured that, "If [we] know that He [Christ] is righteous, [we also] know that everyone also who practices righteousness is born of Him" (1 John 2:29). Conversely, we also are assured that "No one who is born of God practices sin, because His seed abides in him; and he cannot sin, because he is born of God" (3:9; cf. 5:18). We are assured that "everyone who loves is born of God and knows God" (4:7) and that "Whoever believes that Jesus is the Christ is born of God" (5:1).

Fifth, we should remember that our salvation came through our **renewing by the Holy Spirit.** This phrase moves to the next logical step: the effect, or result, of regeneration—namely, the new life that emerges from the new birth. In Romans 8:2, Paul reveals that "the law of the Spirit of life in Christ Jesus has set you free from the law of sin and of death." **The Holy Spirit,** working through the Word, empowers our new life in Christ. "If any man is in Christ," the apostle explains in his second letter to the church in Corinth, "he is a new creature; the old things passed away; behold, new things have come" (2 Cor. 5:17). That is the Spirit's work of sanctification (cf. 1 Pet. 1:2). He begins moving the believer up the ladder of glory from one level to the next (cf. 2 Cor. 3:18).

The Father not only saved us through His **Holy Spirit,** but **He poured out** His Spirit **upon us richly** and without measure when we were born again (cf. Acts 2:38–39; 1 Cor. 12:7, 11, 13). The Lord "is able to do exceeding abundantly beyond all that we ask or think, according to the power [of His **Holy Spirit**] that works within us" (Eph. 3:20). Because of that available power in us, we are commanded to "be filled with the Spirit" (Eph. 5:18). **The Holy Spirit** gives us spiritual life, sustains our spiritual life, empowers our spiritual life, and guarantees that our spiritual life will become eternal life, because He is the seal, or guarantee, of eternal life (Eph. 1:13–14).

Sixth, in order to prevent feelings of hostility toward the corrupters of our society, we should remember that we were saved only by the substitutionary and atoning sacrifice of God's Son, **Jesus Christ our Savior,** which God, by His eternal decree, made efficacious for us before we were even born. His death in our place and for us is the means, and the only means, of our salvation. In his sermon at Pentecost, Peter declared to the assembled Jews that, although Jesus was put to death by their own ungodly leaders, He nevertheless was sovereignly "delivered up by the predetermined plan and foreknowledge of God" (Acts 2:23). And the death that He died in God's plan was a death in which He bore all the sins of all who would ever believe.

The seventh aspect of sovereign salvation is equally from God alone. We should remember that we were saved by God's **grace,** as Paul has already alluded to in verse 5. In his second letter to Timothy, the apostle explains in more detail that God "has saved us, and called us with a holy calling, not according to our works, but according to His own purpose and grace which was granted us in Christ Jesus from all eternity" (2 Tim. 1:9; cf. Rom. 4:2–8; 9:11; Eph. 2:8–9).

Paul is not here using **justified** in its narrow, forensic sense of God's declaring believers righteous based on the merits of Jesus Christ that are applied on their behalf (see, e.g., Rom. 4:6–8; cf. 3:24, 26; Gal. 2:7). He is rather using **justified** in its broad, more general sense as a synonym for salvation. Even John Calvin, a stickler for the narrow, precise definition of justification, recognized that in this passage it refers to salvation in general. He says, "What does he mean by the word justified? The context seems to demand that its meaning shall be extended further than to the imputation of righteousness."

Paul used his own life as proof that salvation is based entirely on the gracious merit and work of Christ. "If anyone else has a mind to put confidence in the flesh, I far more," he testifies:

[I was] circumcised the eighth day, of the nation of Israel, of the tribe of Benjamin, a Hebrew of Hebrews; as to the Law, a Pharisee; as to zeal, a persecutor of the church; as to the righteousness which is in the Law, found blameless. But whatever things were gain to me, those things I have counted as loss for the sake of Christ. More than that, I count all things to be loss in view of the surpassing value of knowing Christ Jesus my Lord, for whom I have suffered the loss of all things, and count them but rubbish in order that I may gain Christ, and may be found in Him, not having a righteousness of my own derived from the Law, but that which is through faith in Christ, the righteousness which comes from God on the basis of faith. (Phil. 3:4–9)

Because Jesus paid the price for our sins, they are graciously removed; justice is fully satisfied; and God's kindness, love, mercy, regeneration, renewing, and grace are therefore enabled to act. Grace gives us what we do not and cannot deserve. We do not deserve to be forgiven, to have our sins removed, to have Christ's own righteousness imputed to us, to be given heavenly citizenship, to be justified, sanctified, and one day glorified in the very presence of our gracious Savior and Lord. The bottom line is stated in the three words: **He saved us!**

That divine saving grace provides another amazing benefit to undeserving sinners: By faith they are **made heirs according to the hope of eternal life.** As Paul declares more fully in his Roman letter, "The Spirit Himself bears witness with our spirit that we are children of God, and if children, heirs also, heirs of God and fellow heirs with Christ, if indeed we suffer with Him in order that we may also be glorified with Him" (Rom. 8:16–17). Peter exults: "Blessed be the God and Father of our Lord Jesus Christ, who according to His great mercy has caused us to be born again to a living hope through the resurrection of Jesus Christ from the dead, to obtain an inheritance which is imperishable and undefiled and will not fade away, reserved in heaven" (1 Pet. 1:3–4).

Remember Your Mission

This is a trustworthy statement; and concerning these things I want you to speak confidently, so that those who have believed God may be careful to engage in good deeds. These things are good and profitable for men. (3:8)

Fourth, and finally, if we want to live the way God wants us to live in a pagan society, not resenting the very people we are to reach, we must remember our divinely ordained mission to that society. We must live as we have been instructed in chapter 2.

These things refer to everything Paul has emphasized in that chapter and in the first seven verses of chapter three: namely, the way believers should live and act in regard to one another within the church (2:1–15) and the way they should live and act before the unbelieving world (3:1–7).

Titus was **to speak confidently** about those truths to the churches, in order that, as Paul already has mentioned (3:1), **those who have believed God may be careful to engage in good deeds.** This young elder was not to be hesitant, indecisive, or vacillating but rather bold and intense, speaking and acting with the firm conviction that he was obediently fulfilling his divinely appointed ministry.

Those who have believed God does not refer to theists as opposed to atheists but to genuine Christians, those who have been saved by God's grace and who take **God** at His word. Biblically grounded and faithful believers remember their duty to submit to human authority, even that which is unjust, ungodly, and pagan. They remember their former condition as unbelievers, knowing that, but for the grace of God, they would still be lost and condemned. They remember the marvelous gift of salvation, which they have received because of God's kindness, His love, His mercy, His washing of regeneration, His renewing by the Holy Spirit, by His Son—all by His sovereign grace. And they remember that the Lord has called them to be His witnesses before the lost and condemned world in which they now live. They therefore recognize that it is not their calling to change culture, to reform outward behavior, to try to redeem society superficially.

They are **careful to engage in good deeds,** genuine acts of virtue that benefit the unsaved and are produced by a loving heart that is empowered to be fruitful by God's Holy Spirit. Among those **good deeds** are our sincere prayers for those who are lost, **deeds** that the lost may not even know about but which will work to their blessing and hopefully to their salvation.

When Christians exalt the Word of God and demonstrate God's power to transform lives, **these things are good and profitable for men**—for the believers themselves and, even more significantly as far as the emphasis of this passage is concerned, for the unsaved sinners around them who are drawn to Christ by the exemplary lives of those He has graciously transformed.

The Last Word on Relationships

10

But shun foolish controversies and genealogies and strife and disputes about the Law; for they are unprofitable and worthless. Reject a factious man after a first and second warning, knowing that such a man is perverted and is sinning, being self-condemned.

When I send Artemas or Tychicus to you, make every effort to come to me at Nicopolis, for I have decided to spend the winter there. Diligently help Zenas the lawyer and Apollos on their way so that nothing is lacking for them. And let our people also learn to engage in good deeds to meet pressing needs, that they may not be unfruitful. All who are with me greet you. Greet those who love us in the faith. Grace be with you all. (3:9–15)

God's plan of salvation calls for strong churches that proclaim and live the reality of the transforming gospel so that it is attractive to the lost. Such testimony is built on sanctified relationships.

As noted in the Introduction, chapter 1 of Titus deals with the relationship of believers in the church with the Lord of the church, as exemplified by its leadership. Chapter 2 deals with believers' relationships with each other, and the first half of chapter 3 deals with the relationship of believers with the unregenerate society in which they live. In the last half of chapter 3, the end of the letter, Paul gives what might be called "The last word on relationships," which emphasizes the relationship of church leaders with each other.

When a person has an important conversation or correspondence with a friend or counselor, the most personal, and sometimes the most urgent, concerns are mentioned last. That seems to be true in this epistle. In his closing words, Paul mentions four distinct and important categories of personal relationships within the church that are of special importance: relationships with false teachers, with factious people, with fellow servants, and with faithful friends.

FALSE TEACHERS

But shun foolish controversies and genealogies and strife and disputes about the Law; for they are unprofitable and worthless. (3:9)

Believers on the island of Crete had been overexposed to a large number of men who claimed to represent the Lord, to be His servants, and to teach His Word. In reality, however, they were spiritually corrupt and were enemies of the Lord, His Word, and His church. Those men had generated so much confusion that Paul had admonished Titus to "set in order what remains, and appoint elders in every city . . . [who would hold] fast the faithful word which is in accordance with the teaching, that [they] may be able both to exhort in sound doctrine and to refute those who contradict," namely, the "many rebellious men, empty talkers and deceivers, especially those of the circumcision, who must be silenced because they are upsetting whole families, teaching things they should not teach, for the sake of sordid gain" (1:5, 9–11).

Titus faced a large ("many," 1:10) and formidable group of leaders in the Cretan churches who were deluding believers about central truths of the gospel. The most influential and dangerous were Jewish legalists, "those of the circumcision" (v. 10), who promoted "Jewish myths and commandments of men" (v. 14). They were not even honest false teachers, because their primary motive was not to instruct, even in falsehood, but rather to earn "sordid gain." Nevertheless, they were causing great damage to the cause of Christ and were to be refuted (v. 9), silenced (v. 11), and reproved (v. 13). They professed "to know God," Paul explained, "but by their deeds they deny Him, being detestable and disobedient, and worthless for any good deed" (v. 16).

Like those about whom the apostle warned Timothy, these false teachers held "to a form of godliness, although they [had] denied its power" (2 Tim. 3:5). They were not disobedient believers; they were not believers at all, as evidenced by the fact that they espoused ungodly doctrines and lived ungodly lives. They were to be ejected from the churches immediately.

Paul himself had been dogged by judaizing false teachers and leaders throughout his ministry and was well aware both of their danger and their persistence. One of his encounters with them had involved Titus. Some years earlier, accompanied by Barnabas and Titus, Paul had gone to Jerusalem to explain his Gentile ministry to Jewish Christian leaders there. In his letter to the churches of Galatia, he explains that, contrary to the demands of the Judaizers, "not even Titus who was with me, though he was a Greek, was compelled to be circumcised" (Gal. 2:3). "It was because of the false brethren who had sneaked in to spy out our liberty which we have in Christ Jesus, in order to bring us into bondage," he goes on to say. "But we did not yield in subjection to them for even an hour, so that the truth of the gospel might remain with you" (vv. 4–5). At the end of that epistle he comments further about "those who desire to make a good showing in the flesh [and] try to compel you to be circumcised, simply that they may not be persecuted for the cross of Christ" (6:12).

Shun translates a form of the verb *periistēmi,* which in the middle voice, as here, means "to turn oneself around, to purposely turn away from something or someone." Titus, the other elders, and the congregations on Crete were to turn the other way from morally and spiritually destructive false teachers, who not only corrupted the churches but, by their sinful and sordid lifestyles, were a great hindrance to the credibility of the gospel. The effect of false teaching is explained in several New Testament passages. It unsettles the soul (Acts 15:24), shipwrecks faith (1 Tim. 1:19), leads to blasphemy (v. 20) and to the ruin of the hearers (2 Tim. 2:14), produces ungodliness (v. 16), and spreads "like gangrene" (v. 17).

In this single verse Paul mentions four specific categories of errors these false teachers were espousing: **foolish controversies and genealogies and strife and disputes about the Law.**

Foolish is from *mōros,* from which comes *moron*, and **controversies** is from *zētēsis,* which has the basic sense of searching or investigating but came to be used for discussion or debate, especially that which was controversial and contentious.

In Paul's letters *zētēsis* always has a negative connotation and is used in warnings—similar to the one given here—about Christians becoming involved in futile arguments about matters of philosophy, or even theology, that are based on human reason and imagination rather than God's Word. Paul uses it three times in his words to Timothy. At the beginning of his first letter, the apostle admonishes that other young elder to "instruct certain men not to teach strange doctrines, nor to pay attention to myths and endless genealogies, which give rise to mere *speculation* rather than furthering the administration of God" and which inevitably result in "fruitless discussion" (1 Tim. 1:3–6, emphasis added). Near the end of that letter he repeats the warning: "If anyone advocates a different doctrine, and does not agree with sound words, those of our Lord Jesus Christ, and with the doctrine conforming to godliness, he is conceited and understands nothing; but he has a morbid interest in *controversial questions* and disputes about words, out of which arise envy, strife, abusive language, evil suspicions, and constant friction between men of depraved mind and deprived of the truth, who suppose that godliness is a means of gain" (1 Tim. 6:3–5, emphasis added). In his second letter, Paul further exhorts Timothy: "But refuse foolish and ignorant *speculations,* knowing that they produce quarrels" (2 Tim. 2:23, emphasis added).

False teachers in the church invariably distort and contradict Scripture, replacing it with novel insights, ideas, and notions that confuse and mislead God's people and undercut their trust in God's revealed truth. The danger of false doctrine is made all the worse because, appealing to the natural man, it finds ready acceptance among unbelievers and even among worldly, self-centered Christians who are poorly grounded in the Word. It is for that reason that Paul instructs Timothy to "be diligent to present yourself approved to God as a workman who does not need to be ashamed, handling accurately the word of truth. But avoid worldly and empty chatter, for it will lead to further ungodliness, . . . [and will] spread like gangrene" (2 Tim. 2:15–17). Once a false teacher is exposed, he is to be rejected by the church and given no platform to spread his spiritually cancerous and destructive falsehoods. He is not to be debated but denounced and expelled (cf. 2 Cor. 6:14–18).

One wonders how many hours and years and lifetimes of Christians have been lost to genuine teaching of God's Word and to effective evangelism and discipling because of time wasted with **foolish controversies.** Although false doctrines themselves certainly are foolish, Paul's point here is that wasting time discussing them is a seriously foolish **behavior** for God's people to be involved in.

Equally worthless for believers is becoming involved in interpretations of **genealogies.** Paul was not, of course, belittling the many **genealogies** that are found in both the New and Old Testaments. Those **genealogies** were critical for determining the God-given lineage of the priesthood, the kings of Judah and Israel, and even the Messiah. Matthew's gospel opens with "the genealogy of Jesus Christ, the son of David, the son of Abraham. . . ." (Matt. 1:1; cf. 2–17). Paul's warning to Titus concerned rather the many fanciful and allegorical interpretations of such **genealogies** that had fascinated many Jews for centuries.

The fourth-century church historian Eusebius reported that when the apostles died, a conspiracy of godless error arose through deceptive false teachers, who arrogantly propagated their insidious lies in opposition to God's Word. It is obvious from Paul's counsel to Timothy and Titus that those godless errors were a serious threat to the church even before all of the apostles were gone.

A third kind of error that Christians on Crete faced is simply referred to as **strife,** a general term that carries the ideas of all kinds of self-centered rivalry and contentiousness about the truth.

Because the early church included so many converted Jews, a fourth common error involved **disputes about the** Mosaic **Law.** Paul refers to that problem in his letter to the Galatian churches. "Those who desire to make a good showing in the flesh try to compel you to be circumcised," he warned, "simply that they may not be persecuted for the cross of Christ. For those who are circumcised do not even keep the Law themselves, but they desire to have you circumcised, that they may boast in your flesh" (Gal. 6:12–13; cf. 1 Tim. 1:6–7).

The Council of Jerusalem was called for the specific purpose of dealing with Judaizers, including "certain ones of the sect of the Pharisees who had believed, [and who said], 'It is necessary to circumcise them [Gentiles], and to direct them to observe the Law of Moses'" (Acts 15:5). The first speaker at the council was Peter, who ended his comments with the question, "Now therefore why do you put God to the test by placing upon the neck of the disciples a yoke which neither our fathers nor we have been able to bear? But we believe that we [Jews] are saved through the grace of the Lord Jesus, in the same way as they [Gentiles] also are" (vv. 10–11). After Paul, Barnabas, and others had spoken, James, the moderator of the council and probably the half-brother of Jesus (see Acts 12:17; 21:18), closed the meeting with the words, "It is my judgment that we do not trouble [with circumcision and observance of the Mosaic Law] those who are turning to God from among the Gentiles" (v. 19). For believers who recognize the authority of the apostles and of God's Word, **disputes about the Law** of Moses and its relation to Christians were permanently settled at that time.

Things such as Paul mentions in this verse are to be shunned because they **are unprofitable and worthless.** Arguing theology, doctrine, or morality with those who distort or disregard God's Word is unavoidably fruitless. Unlike believers, who accept the authority of Scripture and discuss its meaning, Paul is here referring to discussion with false teachers, who have no desire to accept divine truth.

False teachers are themselves taken in by "deceitful spirits and doctrines of demons" (1 Tim. 4:1). Unfortunately, however, they seem never to lack for disciples. Peter said of them: "Many will follow their sensuality, and because of them the way of the truth will be maligned"

(2 Pet. 2:2). Throughout church history, those who "will not endure sound doctrine" have been plentiful. "Wanting to have their ears tickled, they . . . accumulate for themselves teachers in accordance to their own desires; and . . . turn away their ears from the truth, and . . . turn aside to myths" (2 Tim. 4:3–4).

FACTIOUS PEOPLE

Reject a factious man after a first and second warning, knowing that such a man is perverted and is sinning, being self-condemned. (3:10–11)

Just as we are to shun the ungodly, fruitless, and corrupting endeavors mentioned in verse 9, we are to **reject a factious man.**

Reject is from *paraiteomi,* which is also translated, "have nothing to do with" (1 Tim. 4:7) and "refuse" (2 Tim. 2:23). In the first case Paul is referring to "worldly fables fit only for old women" and in the second to "foolish and ignorant speculations that . . . produce quarrels." **Factious** is from *hairetikos,* from which *heretic* is derived. The original word simply meant "to choose," but eventually the term came to signify the placing of self-willed opinions above the truth, refusing even to consider views contrary to one's own. In its noun form, it is associated with such serious "deeds of the flesh" as "immorality, impurity, sensuality, idolatry, sorcery, enmities, strife, jealousy, outbursts of anger, disputes, dissensions, *factions,* envying, drunkenness, carousing" (Gal. 5:19–21, emphasis added). The **factious** person will not submit to the Word or to godly leaders in the church. He is a law to himself and has no concern for spiritual truth or unity.

Although false teachers certainly are the most devastatingly **factious,** Paul is here casting a broader net, which includes *anyone* in the church who is divisive and disruptive. Because the consequences of insubordination, nonsubmission, and bickering can be so destructive of unity among the Lord's people, the apostle commands that a **factious man,** or woman, as the case may be, should be rejected by the church if they do not heed **a first and second warning.** The issues themselves may be trivial, but arguing about them is not.

The apostle's harsh words apply not only to heretics and apostates but to anyone who is **factious.** "I urge you, brethren," Paul warned believers in Rome, "keep your eye on those who cause dissensions and hindrances contrary to the teaching which you learned, and turn away from them. For such men are slaves, not of our Lord Christ but of their own appetites; and by their smooth and flattering speech they deceive the hearts of the unsuspecting" (Rom. 16:17–18).

Speaking of false teachers and others who were **factious,** Paul commanded the church at Thessalonica: "If anyone does not obey our instruction in this letter"—which, even at that early time in the life of the church, carried the weight of Scripture—"take special note of that man and do not associate with him, so that he may be put to shame. And yet do not regard him as an enemy, but admonish him as a brother" (2 Thess. 3:14–15). Church discipline should always be given in a way that is loving, nonjudgmental, remedial, restorative, and redemptive. It should be administered in humility, "with gentleness correcting those who are in opposition, if perhaps God may grant them repentance leading to the knowledge of the truth" (2 Tim. 2:25).

Unity in divine truth and in spiritual fellowship is imperative for effective evangelism. It is testimony to the world, Jesus said, that "Thou [the Father] didst send Me . . . [and] didst love Me." Shortly before that prayer, in what is often called the Upper Room Discourse (John 13:1–16:33), the Lord told the Twelve, "By this all men will know that you are My disciples, if you have love for one another" (13:35).

Genuine, godly love is the binding force of genuine spiritual unity and is an integral, divinely ordained part of our testimony before the world. "We, who are many," Paul declares, "are one body in Christ, and individually members one of another" (Rom. 12:5). In his letter to believers in Ephesus, the apostle sets forth the same basic truth in different words: "There is one body and one Spirit, just as also you were called in one hope of your calling; one Lord, one faith, one baptism, one God and Father of all who is over all and through all and in all" (Eph. 4:4–6). Paul goes on to explain that God's plan for apostles, prophets, evangelists, pastors, and teachers is "for the equipping of the saints for the work of service, to the building up of the body of Christ; until we all attain to *the unity of the faith,* and of the knowledge of the Son of God, to a mature man, to the measure of the stature which belongs to the fulness of Christ" (vv. 11–13, emphasis added).

Perhaps Paul's most comprehensive teaching about the nature and importance of genuine unity in the church is found in his first letter to the church in Corinth, which was confused and fractured by false doctrine, personal animosities, and factionalism. "I exhort you, brethren," he said,

> by the name of our Lord Jesus Christ, that you all agree, and there be no divisions among you, but you be made complete in the same mind and in the same judgment. For I have been informed concerning you, my brethren, by Chloe's people, that there are quarrels among you. Now I mean this, that each one of you is saying, "I am of Paul," and "I of Apollos," and "I of Cephas," and "I of Christ." Has Christ been divided? Paul was not crucified for you, was he? Or were you baptized in the

name of Paul? . . . . Is not the cup of blessing which we bless a sharing in the blood of Christ? Is not the bread which we break a sharing in the body of Christ? Since there is one bread, we who are many are one body; for we all partake of the one bread. . . . For even as the body is one and yet has many members, and all the members of the body, though they are many, are one body, so also is Christ. (1 Cor. 1:10–13; 10:16–17; 12:12)

Paul's last words to that quarrelsome, problem-ridden church were, "Finally, brethren, rejoice, be made complete, be comforted, be like-minded, live in peace; and the God of love and peace shall be with you" (2 Cor. 13:11).

To a believer who is well grounded in the Word, the errors and sinfulness of factious and divisive people in the church should be obvious, **knowing that** a person who persists in quarreling over foolish ideas **is perverted and is sinning, being self-condemned. Perverted** translates *ekstrephō,* which has the meaning of "turning inside out, or twisting." The factious person, who is twisted by his constant **sinning**, will manifest his wicked condition by his own words and actions, thereby becoming **self-condemned.**

It is sad that men and women in evangelical churches who teach ideas that are utterly foreign to Scripture often are not only not disciplined but are instead praised and given opportunity for promulgating their aberrations.

FELLOW SERVANTS

When I send Artemas or Tychicus to you, make every effort to come to me at Nicopolis, for I have decided to spend the winter there. Diligently help Zenas the lawyer and Apollos on their way so that nothing is lacking for them. (3:12–13)

Turning to the positive side, Paul moves from condemning false teachers to commending church leaders who were genuinely being used by the Lord and who blessed his own life. In an especially personal word, Paul asked two favors of Titus—first, to visit him and second, to care for two fellow servants.

Paul did not know **when** he would **send** a replacement for Titus or whether it would be **Artemas or Tychicus.** We know nothing at all about **Artemas** and can only surmise that, because Paul obviously had confidence in his godliness and leadership ability, he was a faithful pastor and teacher who was well qualified to assume direction over the Cretan churches.

Tychicus is mentioned a number of times in the New Testament. He accompanied Paul on the missionary journey from Corinth to Asia Minor (Acts 20:4), delivered Paul's letter to the church in Colossae (Col. 4:7) and probably the one to Ephesus (Eph. 6:21). In the first of those two references **Tychicus** is called "our beloved brother and faithful servant and fellow bond-servant in the Lord" and in the second "the beloved brother and faithful minister in the Lord." That remarkable man of God had earlier been sent by Paul to replace Timothy in Ephesus (2 Tim. 4:12). That he must have done a commendable job in Ephesus is clear from Paul's confidence in him to take over the much larger task of administering and dealing with the problems in the numerous churches on Crete.

There were perhaps as many as nine cities in New Testament times that were called **Nicopolis,** which means "city of victory," so named by various military conquerors to commemorate a decisive victory. The **Nicopolis** where Paul planned **to spend the winter** was probably on the west coast of Achaia, the southern province of Greece, and founded by Octavian (the first Roman Emperor, later named Augustus) after his great victory over Marc Antony and Cleopatra at the battle of Atrium in 31 B.C.

Paul probably wrote this letter to Titus from somewhere in Macedonia (northern Greece), perhaps from Philippi. The apostle obviously was still free at this time, but it is likely that he was arrested in **Nicopolis** and taken to Rome for his last imprisonment. It also was from that city that Titus later traveled to Dalmatia (2 Tim. 4:10), in the general area of modern Croatia and Serbia.

Before Titus left Crete to join Paul, he was asked to **diligently help Zenas the lawyer and Apollos on their way so that nothing is lacking for them.** As with Artemas, we know nothing about **Zenas** apart from this brief mention, which identifies him as a **lawyer.** Whether he was a Roman litigator or a Jewish expert on the Mosaic Law we cannot tell. The fact that he had a Roman name means little in this regard, because many Jews of that day, including Paul, were given or had adopted Roman names. Also as with Artemas, we can safely assume that **Zenas** was a godly believer in whom the apostle had great confidence and for whom he had great love.

Apollos, on the other hand, is mentioned numerous times in the New Testament, always favorably. He was an eloquent Jewish preacher of the gospel from Alexandria, Egypt, who "was mighty in the Scriptures" and who "had been instructed in the way of the Lord," was "fervent in spirit, . . . speaking and teaching accurately the things concerning Jesus, [but was] acquainted only with the baptism of John" (Acts 18:24–25). When he came to Ephesus and "began to speak out boldly in the synagogue, . . . Priscilla and Aquila heard him . . . [and] took him aside and explained to him the way of God more accurately. And when he wanted to go across to Achaia, the brethren encouraged him and wrote to the disciples to welcome him; and when he had arrived, he helped greatly those who had believed through grace" (vv. 26–27).

Although **Apollos** had not yet visited Corinth by the time Paul wrote his first letter to the church there (see 1 Cor. 16:12), apparently some of his converts had come to that city and formed one of the factions about which Paul lamented. "For I have been informed concerning you, my brethren," he wrote, "that there are quarrels among you. Now I mean this, that each one of you is saying, 'I am of Paul,' and 'I of Apollos,' and 'I of Cephas,' and 'I of Christ'" (1 Cor. 1:11–12).

Whenever **Zenas** and **Apollos** were to arrive on Crete and wherever they may have been headed as they passed through, Titus was urged to help them **on their way so that nothing is lacking for them.** They were cherished partners of Paul and faithful co-laborers in the work of the kingdom. Paul doubtless sensed that his time of freedom would soon end and that, if he lived to carry on the Lord's work at all, it would be from a prison cell. It was therefore all the more imperative that the men he had trained and left behind be encouraged and supported.

That spirit of mutual support and care should always characterize Christ's church, especially its spiritual leadership. Under the sovereign Lord, leaders are interdependent, called and commissioned to trust and assist one another as fellow servants of our Lord Jesus Christ.

FAITHFUL FRIENDS

And let our people also learn to engage in good deeds to meet pressing needs, that they may not be unfruitful. All who are with me greet you. Greet those who love us in the faith. Grace be with you all. (3:14–15)

In closing, Paul gives a last word on faithful friends. Like Titus and the other elders on Crete, the **people** among whom they ministered were **also [to] learn to engage in good deeds to meet pressing needs.**

It is not possible for a pastor, or even a team of pastors in a large church, to meet all of the many **pressing needs** of a congregation. Not only is there not enough time for one man to do it all, but other believers in the church invariably have spiritual gifts and abilities that the pastor does not have, by which certain **good deeds** can be accomplished and certain **pressing needs** of fellow believers can be met.

Beyond that, a harmonious, loving, and serving church also will be a beacon to the world, attracting unbelievers to the light of salvation through trust in Christ.

Paul's final word *for* faithful friends is **love** for others **in the faith.** His final word *to* faithful friends is **Grace be with you all.**

Bibliography

Barclay, William. *The Letters to Timothy, Titus and Philemon.* Philadelphia: Westminster, 1960.

Harvey, H. *Commentary on the Pastoral Epistles, I & II Timothy and Titus, and the Epistle to Philemon.* Philadelphia: American Baptist Pub. Soc., 1890.

Hiebert, D. Edmond. *Titus and Philemon.* Chicago: Moody, 1957.

Hendriksen, William. *New Testament Commentary: Expositions of the Pastoral Epistles.* Grand Rapids: Baker, 1965.

Kent, Homer A., Jr. *The Pastoral Epistles: Studies in I & II Timothy and Titus.* Chicago: Moody, 1958.

Spurgeon, Charles Haddon. *Lectures to My Students.* Grand Rapids: Zondervan, 1955.

Trench, Richard C. *Synonyms of the New Testament.* Grand Rapids: Eerdmans, 1960.

Vincent, Marvin R. *Word Studies in the New Testament.* Vols. 3, 4. New York: Scribner's, 1904.

Westcott, B. F., and F. J. A. Hort. *The New Testament in the Original Greek.* New York: MacMillan, 1929.

Wuest, Kenneth S. *Word Studies from the Greek New Testament.* Vol. 2, *Philippians, Hebrews, the Pastoral Epistles, First Peter.* Grand Rapids: Eerdmans, 1966.

Indexes

Index of Greek Words

Index of Hebrew Words

Index of Scripture

Index of Subjects

Titles in the
MacArthur New Testament Commentary Series

MOODY
PUBLISHERS
THE NAME YOU CAN TRUST

1-800-678-6928 www.MoodyPublishers.org

SINCE 1894, Moody Publishers has been dedicated to equip and motivate people to advance the cause of Christ by publishing evangelical Christian literature and other media for all ages, around the world. Because we are a ministry of the Moody Bible Institute of Chicago, a portion of the proceeds from the sale of this book go to train the next generation of Christian leaders.

If we may serve you in any way in your spiritual journey toward understanding Christ and the Christian life, please contact us at www.moodypublishers.com.

"All Scripture is God-breathed and is useful for teaching, rebuking, correcting and training in righteousness, so that the man of God may be thoroughly equipped for every good work."
—2 TIMOTHY 3:16, 17

MOODY
PUBLISHERS

THE NAME YOU CAN TRUST®

TITUS (MNTC) TEAM

ACQUIRING EDITOR
Greg Thornton

COPY EDITOR
Anne Scherich

COVER DESIGN
Ragont Design

PRINTING AND BINDING
Quebecor World Book Services

The typeface for the text of this book is
Cheltenham